THE
POWER
OF US

BOOKS BY DAVID PRICE

OPEN: How We'll Work, Live and Learn in the Future
Education Forward: Moving Schools into the Future

THE
POWER
OF US

DAVID PRICE

Thread

Published by Thread in 2020

An imprint of Storyfire Ltd.
Carmelite House
50 Victoria Embankment
London EC4Y 0DZ

www.thread-books.com

Illustrations by John Biggs. www.johnbiggs.art

David Price has asserted his right to be identified
as the author of this work.

ISBN: 978-1-80019-119-8
eBook ISBN: 978-1-80019-118-1

For Clare, who taught me to believe in the power of us.

CONTENTS

INTRODUCTION

At the end of February 2020, Ryan Jun-seo Hong, a 19-year-old computer science student from Seoul, South Korea, was suffering from a bad case of sleep deprivation. He'd been up for three straight nights, writing code for a new app, coronamap.live. The pressure he'd been feeling had recently intensified because of the actions of a religious cult group, the Shincheonji Church of Jesus. Their leader, Lee Man-hee, downplayed the sudden spike of a mystery respiratory illness within his congregation, claiming it was the incarnation of 'evil'. He also insisted that illness was no excuse to miss their weekly service. Attending Mass in a church in Daegu, one of Shincheonji's followers – a woman in her 60s who became known as 'patient 31' – turned out to be a 'super-spreader' of Covid-19, infecting many hundreds of people in Daegu. From being hailed as an early exemplar in controlling the spread of the virus, Korea's health service was in danger of becoming overwhelmed by an exponential rise in cases – most of which could be traced back to patient 31.

That Korea was able to regain control of the virus was due, in no small part, to the ingenuity of Ryan Jun-seo Hong. Thanks to the efforts of a large number of volunteers and a huge government-released haul of CCTV footage, credit-card data and geo-tagging information, coronamap.live was able to track the movements of people who'd either tested positive for the virus, or who were displaying symptoms. The app used a red-yellow-green designation, based upon the recent location of those infected, and included a special feature called 'see whether I'm safe'. As a result, people had access to an incredibly detailed trace of the spread of the virus and were able to move about South Korea with some confidence. Within a month, the app had 300,000 hits daily, significantly contributing to the subsequent 30-fold reduction in reported new cases in South Korea. The global strategy, pioneered in South Korea, of 'test, track and trace' was seen as the best route out of the house arrest of national lockdowns. South Korea invited anyone to come up with human-tracing software, and Ryan was far from alone in rising to the challenge. The success of coronamap.live, and other tracing apps, can be attributed to a powerful combination of open data – with minimal restrictions upon use – and the ingenuity of its citizens.

The contrast between East and West could not have been more stark. On 3 March 2020, South Korea reported 5,000 confirmed cumulative cases of Covid-19. The UK, on the same day, reported that there'd been just 51 cases, and the USA declared 126. By 30 May, those numbers had been dramatically reversed. South Korea's cases had increased to 11,000 (including 270 deaths). But the UK reported *274,000 cases, with 38,000 deaths, while the USA confirmed 1.8 million cases and over 106,000 deaths.* Saturday, 30 May was also the day that the UK launched its Track and Trace programme, while in the USA – the most technologically advanced nation in the world – the administration's Center for Disease Control inexplicably still dithered over how to develop an app. At that time, most countries built their mobile solutions by using the combined power of Google and Apple's collaborative application programme interface (API). The UK, however, chose a different path and its National Health Service's (NHS) Covid-19 app was beset by problems from the outset. Concerned by privacy issues, both Google and Apple had insisted upon data anonymity, but the NHS argued that retaining patient data could save lives in the future and so developed their own API. It was found to be incompatible with 96% of the iPhones that half of its population owned. By mid-June, the UK government bowed to the inevitable, announcing that they had abandoned their centralised Covid-tracker app and were going to use the Apple-Google API which, despite it being open-source, would apparently not be ready until the end of 2020.

The announcement came four months after a 19-year-old student, living with his parents, on the other side of the world, created one in three days.

Communities outperform bureaucracies

Ryan's innovation, though inspiring, was far from unique. All over the world, groups of geeks, nerds and makers came together – virtually – to collaboratively problem-solve what by now had become the biggest planetary crisis in a century. In response to the enormity of the challenge, the traditional divisions between producer and consumer disappeared. It didn't matter if you led a multinational corporation or wrote code in your bedroom – everyone's ideas counted.

The pandemic arrived just as I was writing this book. And then I had to rewrite it. Not because I needed to rethink my thesis, but because, firstly, the novel coronavirus of 2020 provided the most emphatic confirmation of the conclusions I'd reached. And secondly, well, how could you *not* incorporate the biggest global event since 1945?

The response to the coronavirus merely shone a very bright light on what was already becoming apparent. A wave of self-determined, self-organised activism – the power of us – is sweeping over all aspects of our lives. Users of products and services are no longer passively consuming. They are rewriting the rules that shape our lives – not least the rules that determine how we are governed. The smart organisations, and smart countries, are becoming 'people-powered' – they accept that they can no longer do things on their own. They're co-designing, co-producing, co-campaigning. It may have taken a global pandemic to get us to recognise it, but the torrent of improvised solutions to the shortage of protective medical equipment, ventilators, treatments and vaccines during Covid-19 illustrates something that was there all along. It merely needed a lightning rod, and the pandemic provided it.

What we routinely call the 'wisdom of crowds' was initially coined to denote a collaborative approach to decision-making by groups. We're now, however, so much further along that path – we're harvesting the *ingenuity* of crowds, as people-powered innovation reshapes our world. This book attempts to describe the actions, products and services that are to be found wherever people come together. It represents an approach to problem-solving, to engineering solutions, in all aspects of society, that's at once unconventional, occasionally rebellious and rooted in a communal desire to make the world a better place. We're a remarkably creative species, uniquely capable of abstract thought, complex communication systems and laterally combining ideas from myriad knowledge domains in order to figure things out.

One day, we will have defeated the pandemic, and we will not be consumed by horrific death tolls, mass testing and relentlessly grim news footage. The power of us will get us to that point, and we must ensure that, once alert to it, we fully realise our potential in a post-Covid world.

This book is the result of a bet. In 2017 I was invited to speak at the South by Southwest* (SXSW) festival, in Austin, Texas. If SXSW is new to you, all you need to know is that it's where the latest ideas and products in music, technology, education, film and media are showcased and discussed. And it's huge – like the Edinburgh Festival for hipsters. So, it's impossibly cool.

Because its focus is on emerging trends, I decided to pitch some ideas that I'd found myself researching in the months leading up to the festival. But because it's impossibly cool, I was sure that no one would want to attend a session by a completely unknown British senior citizen. I was *definitely* not their demographic. In fact, I was so sure that no one would turn up that I did two stupid things: I didn't prepare my talk to anything like ready-state (my normal condition is to be anally over-prepped). The second stupid thing I did was to bet my wife that if more than 10 people showed up, I'd turn those nascent ideas into a book.

In the event, the organisers were turning people away and I asked the 500 or so who crammed into the hall to let me know if they thought there was something in the ideas I was sharing. A large number stayed to talk. So, that was it. During the intervening two years, I researched and tried to make sense of the patterns that I thought were starting to emerge.

I fully accept that, to some, the argument I'm making here is antithetical to the times we're living in. A strong case could be made that we're far from the sharing, caring communities I've experienced, and that we've never been so polarised. The rise of populism has felt damagingly divisive. Many Western nations have witnessed stark, and seemingly unbreachable, fissures emerge: the USA is portrayed as 'two nations' (pro/anti-Trump); similarly, the UK is divided over Brexit (Leave/Remain). These tensions can be seen being played out daily in angry, binary exchanges on social media. Even pandemics become politicised. Such polarities demand winners and losers, victors and vanquished ('You lost, get over it').

And yet…

Something is happening. I'm calling it 'people-powered innovation', because there is now a human calling, across all spheres of human endeavour to do things differently. It's not always easy to hear, among the shock-jock dog-whistles and the white noise of twenty-first-century life. But it's there all the same.

We are witnessing the emergence of bottom-up, self-empowering and self-managed movements presenting challenges to business-as-usual in education, government, healthcare, finance, travel, hospitality: you name it, there are groups of ordinary people working together to create new solutions. And you don't need to look very far for challenges to fix. Fortunately, we have new ways of working together and new mindsets to see things differently.

Why should it matter to leaders?

The underlying message, therefore, for all those who lead organisations is this: you need to understand what's happening here because the future – *your* future – depends upon how you respond to people-powered innovation. If you work with it – understanding how to foster it within the people working *with* you (not for you), which now includes the end users of your products or services – I'd argue that your organisation will thrive. If you treat it like a fad, you should enjoy the success your superior financial resources and power might bring in the short-term. But eventually you'll either have to work with it or you'll be left behind. And if you try to ignore it, well, you're doomed, sooner rather than later.

How to use this book

After that initial pitch at SXSW, I spent 24 months visiting organisations: large corporations, non-governmental organisations, artisanal start-ups, even small K–12 schools. I was consciously looking for organisations that shared a number of characteristics:

- They were highly successful.
- They were demonstrably innovative.
- They enjoyed strong employee and user engagement.
- They had built powerful learning environments.

All of them, therefore, were hotbeds of what I call 'mass ingenuity'. I've shared their experiences as case studies and interviews, with a focus upon three elements:

1. How they're structured.
2. How they lead innovation.

3. How they learn to innovate (with a particular focus on the
   innovators of tomorrow).

Full disclosure: let me make it clear that this book is not meant to be a dispassionate, evidence-driven, academic analysis. I have consciously sought out organisations and people that exemplify open innovation, great employee engagement, self-determined learners and the rest, because I believe that maximising the power of us is good for business, good for society and good for the planet. And because I'm looking for behaviours, values and strategies that we can all learn from, I've focused upon their commonalities rather than their differences – and believe me, they have plenty of differences. I also believe there are clear connections in the leadership styles employed by the innovation pioneers featured in the case studies, and I hope you'll be inspired by them. I know I was.

After I returned from my research trips, we moved house. I'm a keen gardener but I've reached the point in my life where I'm looking for as close to a maintenance-free garden as possible. So this time I decided to go for raised-bed gardening. And that's a useful analogy – not just for organising this book but also for building an organisation that is sustainable and low-maintenance. It also gives me an opportunity to introduce you to the German concept of *Hügelkultur*. Hugel-what?

Hügelkultur is a design system that provides a base for long-term growth. You lay a base with organic matter: logs, twigs, any kind of bulky material. This organic matter releases heat as it begins to break down, ensuring that the growing medium (top soil, compost, manure) above it receives nutrients for a very long time. This is how it is with people-powered innovation.

So, the structure of the book follows the *Hügelkultur* design of people-powered innovation:

- Section One reminds us that **context** is everything. So the book is topped and tailed with the recent historical context and ends with a discussion about the future context. Societies are, essentially, just very large organisations. How we relate to each other – governments and governed – shapes how functional, or dysfunctional, our organisations become.

- Section Two explains that understanding the **mindset** that determines how communities connect, innovate and take action together is, in many ways, the key to understanding its power. Organisations need to think differently, precisely because such communities do.

- Section Three explores the **operating system** of innovative organisations: how they're structured, how they learn, how they manage themselves and their external relationships. There's a particular emphasis here upon how they turn users into peer innovators.

- Section Four looks at the new **leadership** models that are needed to maintain a healthy environment, so that innovation is sustainable and self-renewing.

- Section Five presents a practical **toolkit**, detailing the strategies adopted by the organisations I've studied. They've achieved remarkable success in fostering cultures of mass ingenuity. We need to learn how they've done it.

- Section Six brings us back to context and the power of us in a post-Covid world. It also has a focus upon new forms of activism – already emerging Before Corona – that will define how we live after it. For obvious reasons, there is a particular focus here on the young people we'll come to rely upon.

The headings above can be seen in many books on organisational management. This book, however, looks beyond organisational boundaries, through the lens of users: the hackers and hobbyists, campaign groups and advocates, citizen scientists and lead patients. Until the appearance of the coronavirus, such people were hidden in the margins. Now that the pandemic has moved them centre stage, they'll ensure that things will never be the same again. They, after all, are all of us, and we've rediscovered a power we'd forgotten we had.

Is that the time?

It's become a cliché that the pace of innovation is relentlessly accelerating. Being a cliché doesn't stop it from being true. As far back as 1810, Jonathan Swift wrote that 'Falsehood flies and the truth comes limping after it'. What would he make of today's news cycle? If change is now a constant, we have to find new ways of thinking, new ways of working and new ways of making sense of our lives. A decade ago, the sharing economy was in its infancy (Uber and Airbnb launched in 2008); Facebook had a mere 58 million users (now over 2 billion); DNA testing was just becoming available through organisations like 23andme; Netflix and Amazon announced they were about to start streaming movies; people assumed the 'gig economy' was what musicians did; the #MeToo, #BlackLivesMatter, #Occupy, #Time'sUp and a host of other hashtag social movements didn't exist (not least because the hashtag wasn't used on Twitter until 2008). All of these – and many more – happened because of how we now routinely access knowledge. But we've barely started.

The next 10 years will transform how that knowledge is put to use – in finding solutions to social, political, cultural, health and environmental problems – through the simple power of people working together on collaborative, creative projects. I am not being naïve about this utopian combination of people, knowledge and power. Will the forces that exist to preserve the commercial, political and cultural status quo willingly share the space (and the spoils) with we the people, we the users or we the customers? Undoubtedly not. Some will fight tooth and claw to keep things just the way they are. But there are already plenty of organisations pointing the way to co-producing with users, advocates and customers to give credence to the idea that this is an irreversible trend. In time, others will be convinced to follow.

The power of us will transform the corporate and public domains. We're already seeing the old established institutional models creaking under the strain. In education, Covid-19 isolation accelerated the already sophisticated homeschooling alternatives, forcing us to ask 'What *is* school, anyway?' In manufacturing, 'user-led innovations' (a term first coined by Eric von Hippel, to whom I owe an enormous debt in shaping my thinking) are forcing companies to rewrite their research and development strategies. New tech start-ups impatiently urge that their philosophy of 'fail fast and rapidly iterate' be applied to the fields of health and social policy. I can think of no sector, public or private, that will not – nor indeed, *should not* – be touched by the power of us.

By the same token, this book isn't predicting the imminent collapse of free-market capitalism. It is, however, urging organisations to recognise that our natural propensity to solve problems creatively and collaboratively has been suppressed for a very long time – perhaps during the whole of the industrial era. Too many generations have experienced the crushing numbness of an education system designed to quash individual talents and passions, followed by a working lifetime of repetitive routine – all in pursuit of conformity and compliance. Now, with the coming of the creative and artisanal economy, and with artificial intelligence (AI) and robotics offering the potential removal of routine drudgery, we have the opportunity to reshape our world.

Before we can appreciate the changes still to come, however, we have to acknowledge the axis-tilt that has occurred in recent years.

PART ONE

Context

*Understanding how societal shifts and global pandemics
are challenging our beliefs and values is crucial
to realising the power of us*

CHAPTER ONE

A World Turned Upside Down

If ever you needed evidence that change is happening faster than ever, and is therefore more difficult to predict, the current decade leaves you spoiled for choice.

Following the economic ravages of the 2008 global financial crisis, things, surely, could only get better? The five-year period from 2010 to 2015 saw the fleeing of dictators in Tunisia, Libya, Yemen and Egypt as the Arab Spring swept through the Middle East and North Africa. The clamour for democracy was intense, and not just in faraway places. Neoliberalism – the belief in the power of free markets to regulate all aspects of public and private life – had not only become a dirty word, it was facing extinction. Social media, in bringing these protests to a global audience, was seen, almost unquestionably, as a force for good. Disintermediation and knowledge process outsourcing (the cheap farming out of high-level knowledge-based work to developing countries) became highly disruptive forces in the way that we work, live and do business with each other. And short-term contract work was about to threaten the very concept of 'the job'.

Other drivers starting to emerge during this period were rising geo-political tensions and a dissatisfaction with globalisation. There was a growing feeling in the USA that countries like China were 'eating the lunch' off the tables of patriotic, if sleepwalking, Americans. The era of austerity, following the global financial crisis of 2007–8, seemed to punish the victims, and not the perpetrators. 'Disaster Capitalism' (a term made popular by author and activist Naomi Klein) went from conspiracy theory to plausible policy. Overall, however, there were considerable grounds for optimism: the possibilities of a coming 'age of abundance', where energy becomes too cheap to monitor; the potential of a hyper-connected world; a public insistence upon transparency in government – all good reasons to be cheerful. And Barack Obama found an economic tide to lift all other countries' boats, skilfully steering the US economy out of recession. By 2015 the Arab Spring was about to morph into a democratic summer, and the end of austerity was imminent.

A succession of shocks

In the second half of the decade, the world turned upside down. And the most mystifying part? *Almost no one saw it coming.* In fairness, it wasn't just the futurologists, academics or journalists that failed to anticipate Brexit, Trump and the return of the demagogues – precious few politicians predicted it either. When, for instance, British Prime Minister David Cameron pledged to hold an in/out referendum on Europe, he did so largely because all opinion polls suggested that it was an easy argument to win. He could then finally end decades of internal squabbling and scepticism within the Conservative Party. Sounded like a plan.

At around the same time, the US Democratic Party was confident that, with the obvious experience that Hillary Clinton had, and with the domestic economy becoming stronger by the day, it was inevitable that she would see off all threats – whether internal or from the Republican Party.

It's almost impossible to overstate the sense of shock and disbelief felt in 2016, when Trump and Brexit happened – especially as only four months separated them. The impact went far beyond national boundaries, both politically and personally. I attended a family wedding in Poland the day after the Brexit vote came in – that was awkward. Similarly, I had to give a talk to a conference of librarians in Aarhus, Denmark, the morning Donald Trump became the USA's 45th president (the audience was even quieter than you'd expect).

Before discussing the implications of these two political upheavals, let's look at some of the broader context. And a warning to those of an emotionally delicate disposition: there's quite a lot of Shawshank before we get to the Redemption…

A hysteria of isms

The backlash to the hegemony of the liberal left has seen the unwelcome return of some ideologies we thought we'd seen the back of. Whether the decisions to exit Europe and elect a business TV celebrity fit within a conclusive ideological pattern is not entirely clear, but there has been no shortage of attempts to link them (not least because Trump himself did so) and to fathom a rationale. In the immediate aftermath of Brexit, psephologists (those who study opinion polls and election results) scrambled to explain why the British had voted to leave the European Union (EU). Frustratingly, no simple explanation held up. The reasons couldn't be found purely in geography, gender, political allegiance, class, ethnicity or age. The polling analytics simply threw up too many contradictions. A correlation between voting Leave and income levels appeared to give credence to the theory that people voted to leave because they felt economically 'left behind'. But this didn't explain why so many baby boomers – now with a solid pension – were also leavers.

The only correlation, made by Lord Ashcroft, a Conservative peer/psephologist, that makes sense to me *and* seems to have echoes in the subsequent US voting patterns is voter response to a range of social and cultural movements over the past couple of decades: the 'isms' that define the shifting shape of cultural politics. A clear majority – more than 70% – of leavers thought multiculturalism, social liberalism, feminism, globalism, environmentalism, same-sex marriage had been forces for ill, while a clear majority of remainers (more than 60%) thought they'd all been forces for good. In other words, it was those feeling *culturally,* not economically, left behind who wanted to give those seen as 'the elites' a good kicking. During the Blair/Clinton/Obama years, the bemoaning of single-sex marriage, the abolition of capital punishment, feminism and multiculturalism had become socially unacceptable (excepting 'locker room' talk), which may help to explain why pre-Brexit opinion polls got it spectacularly wrong in predicting a clear victory for remainers – people simply didn't want to declare their dissatisfaction for fear of being labelled 'politically incorrect'.

There's always a place for an angry old man

It was as if Donald Trump had looked at those isms and decided to make it his campaign playlist. The self-declared billionaire, without a shred of irony, attacked the elites at every opportunity. Similarly, Brexit's cheerleader, Michael Gove, a former Secretary of State for Education, who would fit any definition of an intellectual, shamelessly said: 'I think that the people of this country have had enough of experts.' We'll come to the question of post-truth politics in a moment. For now, let's see if we can understand the behavioural and ideological shifts which seem to have taken place recently.

Whilst the anger that drove the Arab Spring – and the post-crash mass unemployment seen in Southern Europe – stemmed from a sense of indignity, what we saw following BrexiTrump was altogether more sinister – and uglier. Both campaigns, fuelled by right-wing media, stoked up fear of, and anger towards, people who were different from us, leading to a new word: 'othering'. Headlines like 'A vote for Remain is a vote for mass immigration from Turkey' (*Daily Telegraph*) and '1 in 5 Brit Muslims have sympathy for Jihadis' (*The Sun*) became commonplace in the run-up to the EU referendum. They were not only factually incorrect – Turkey isn't even a member of the EU – they triggered a predictably depressing result: the legitimation of hatred and abuse towards migrants in the UK. In the year following the Brexit referendum, racially and religiously aggravated hate crimes rose by an average of 23%, to over 50,000. And they are just the reported cases.

President Trump – who had now become the disintermediator-in-chief – deployed Twitter as the vehicle to get his views directly to his followers. And truth appeared to be inconsequential, to either the sender or the recipient.

'Alternative facts'

There were two points in BrexiTrump where it felt like the Rubicon had been crossed, and we'd not be able to go back.

The first was when the Leave campaign bus had the following slogan painted on it: 'We send the EU £350 million a week. Let's fund our NHS instead.' When fact-checked, it was clear that this was a knowing lie. Firstly, the net contribution to the EU was a weekly £199 million. And even this figure didn't take into account the money returned from the EU to universities and research organisations. When retractions were sought from the Leave campaign leaders, Boris Johnson and Michael Gove, they insisted the slogan was true.

Meanwhile, back in Trumpland, the tone for the new administration was set relatively early, when White House adviser Kellyanne Conway was a guest on Chuck Todd's *Meet The Press* programme shortly after Trump's inauguration. Challenging the statement of then White House Press Secretary Sean Spicer that the inauguration was the 'largest audience to ever witness an inauguration, period', Todd suggested that the facts showed that Spicer's claim was a falsehood. The exchange between Todd and Conway topped the Yale Law School's list for the most notable quote of 2017:

> Conway: 'You're saying it's a falsehood and Sean Spicer, our press secretary, gave alternative facts to that.'
>
> Todd: 'Alternative facts are not facts. They are falsehoods.'
>
> Conway: 'If we're going to keep referring to the press secretary in those types of terms, I think we're going to have to rethink our relationship here.'

Conway's comeback was an ominous foretaste of the administration's approach: essentially anyone who criticised the President could not expect to be called upon to ask questions in conferences and, by the summer of 2018, an emboldened Trump intimated that critics could expect to lose their security clearance. Similarly, the UK election of 2019 saw a Boris Johnson-led Conservative landslide despite a slew of fake videos, media intimidation and an apparent disregard for anything resembling an objective truth.

'You can't just make stuff up'

We are at a critical juncture in the battle for truth and democracy. A mere five years ago, the battle to keep knowledge open was primarily seen in terms of corporate values (Apple versus Google) or the fight for net neutrality. And yet here we are, having to make the case that truth matters, that democracy matters, that holding political leaders to account matters. Few expected that to be the state of things, but BrexiTrump shows us that the very essence of knowledge has to be fought for all over again, and if learning means anything, it means we have to respect one another's opinions, but based upon facts, not emotions. Giving a major speech in South Africa, to commemorate what would have been Nelson Mandela's 100th birthday, Barack Obama reflected upon the so-called 'post-truth' era. I've quoted him at length, but that's partly because we need to remind ourselves what world leaders engaging in logic, reason and oratory used to sound like:

> Unfortunately, too much of politics today seems to reject the very concept of objective truth. People just make stuff up. They just make stuff up. You have to believe in facts. Without facts, there is no basis for cooperation. I can find common ground for those who oppose the Paris Accords because, for example, they might say 'well, it's not going to work – you can't get everybody to cooperate', or they might say 'it's more important for us to provide cheap energy for the poor, even if it means in

the short term that there's more pollution'. At least I can have a debate with them about that and I can show them why I think clean energy is the better path. I can't find common ground if somebody says climate change is just not happening, when almost all of the world's scientists tell us it is. I don't know where to start talking to you about this. If you start saying it's an elaborate hoax... where do we start?

Indeed. Where *do* we start? He went on to summarise the global anxiety that has surprised us all:

A politics of fear and resentment and retrenchment began to appear, and that kind of politics is now on the move. It's on the move at a pace that would have seemed unimaginable just a few years ago [...] In the West, you've got far-right parties that oftentimes are based not just on platforms of protectionism and closed borders, but also on barely hidden racial nationalism. Many developing countries now are looking at China's model of authoritarian control combined with mercantilist capitalism as preferable to the messiness of democracy. Who needs free speech as long as the economy is going good? The free press is under attack. Censorship and state control of media is on the rise. Social media – once seen as a mechanism to promote knowledge and understanding and solidarity – has proved to be just as effective promoting hatred and paranoia and propaganda and conspiracy theories.

Obama seemed to instinctively know that career politicians would not be able to restore our faith in democracy and confidence in each other. Seeking the same cause for optimism as this book, he has focused his post-presidential career upon supporting grassroots activism among young people.

The erosion of trust

The retreat of truth prompted a retreat of trust. Each year, Richard Edelman's PR company releases its 'Barometer of Trust'. The year 2018 was something of a watershed moment, on a number of fronts. During 2013–17, there were some steady, consistent, observable patterns of trust in the public realm:

- Trust in the traditional media we consume remained positive.
- Trust in business plummeted after the global financial crash.
- Trust in governments generally stayed high.
- There was a steady rise in 'horizontal trust' – we believed what we heard from colleagues and friends.

All of that changed in 2018. Governments and the media are now vying for the title of 'least trusted institution in public life'.[1] And if you're a political leader seeking to govern through fear and distrust, what better strategy than to stoke up hatred for *both* government and media? And it has worked: horizontal trust has evaporated and we have turned against one another. A 'mass class divide' has widened and hardened: our views have become polarised and rigid. As Richard Edelman observed, you will never convince a Trump loyalist that the President ever referred to some African countries as 'shitholes'. Given the Facebook scandals, it was to be expected that there'd be a loss of trust in search engines and social media. But losing trust in our peers? That is deeply concerning.

Aside from a brief upsurge in the period immediately following the coronavirus outbreak, governments have seen the most dramatic decline in trust – only 1 in 3 people believe governments

1 Edelman Trust Barometer, 2020. All of the numbers quoted in this section are from Edelman's Barometers, from either 2019 or 2020.

are 'honest and fair', while half of us believe they lack a vision we can believe in. At the start of 2020, the percentage of people who trusted the US government was a mere 39%. In the UK (perhaps due to a succession of general elections), trust fell even further, down to 36%. The seriousness of this erosion was captured by Steve Schmidt, then Vice Chair of Public Affairs at Edelman:

> We're at the end of the lifespans of the men and women who stormed the beaches of Normandy, who saved the world and built the U.S. liberal-led world order. Now that order seems to be unravelling in many directions. And we haven't yet seen leadership in any area that promises to put us back onto a trajectory of trust.

Capitalism under siege

Edelman also reported that, globally, only 18% of people felt that capitalism was still working for them. There was also a clear divide in economic optimism: the half of the world whose economies are developing (Africa, South America, most of Asia) have a majority of people who feel they'll be better off in 2025. In the more established economies (Western Europe, Australia, Japan) pessimism abounds: in Japan and France fewer than 1 in 5 think they'll be better off. The 2020 Edelman Trust Barometer revealed that 83% of people were fearful of losing their jobs to either the gig economy, automation, a looming recession, mass migration or companies relocating.

A world turned upside down – again

To recap: the aftermath of the global financial crash led to a fearfulness about the future, a widespread rise of authoritarianism with a concomitant support for nationalism, and a loss of trust in, well, just about everything. For good measure, you can throw in the 2019 apocalyptic scenes (that I witnessed first-hand) of the hottest, worst bushfires ever seen in Australia as a presage of the climate emergency.

But as my mother used to say: 'So long as you have your health, everything else is gravy.'[2] When Covid-19 appeared at the end of 2019, we were about to lose even that.

It's too early to speculate on the long-term public health impact of the virus. The coordinated, Herculean efforts to 'flatten the curve' of infection, however, suggests that the suppression of the disease could be a long-term project. We will see hotspots shift as lockdowns are lifted and outbreaks recur. The likelihood is that Covid-19 will never be fully eliminated. It will take its place alongside other strains of the flu and (please God) our annual flu vaccines will put it back in its malevolent box. Until then, it's reckless to predict how many of our most vulnerable citizens will perish, just as no one could have predicted the final death toll at the start of World War Two.

The pandemic has been frequently compared to the Spanish Flu of 1918 and has also been described as the world war the baby boomers thought they'd dodged. Both comparisons have validity, but they differ in one crucial aspect: during those two defining events in the twentieth century, the general populace were unable to learn about actions taken on their behalf. With Covid-19, data is everywhere, and the power of us has come to the fore. Take the challenge of personal hygiene, and the policing of a concept we never knew we needed: social distancing.

Governments urged us to wash our hands and keep two metres from each other. But the reason why most of us became Howard Hughes overnight, sacrificing our personal and social freedoms, was

---

2 Maybe they weren't her exact words, but you get my drift.

a welcome return to a sense of collectivism. We knew we were 'all in this together' – even allowing for the fact that people of colour and/or facing social disadvantage were disproportionately picked on by the virus. We shared data on other countries' measures and the correlation to infection rates. We applauded health and care workers. And if selfish, irresponsible idiots chose to put their personal freedoms ahead of the common good, by congregating in public spaces, they were shamed on social media, as #Covidiots. But informed citizens knew more about the coronavirus than almost anyone did during the Spanish Flu.

Tell us the truth

When he first noticed a number of his patients presenting with SARS-like[3] symptoms, Dr Li Wenliang posted a warning to his colleagues on social media, urging them to wear protective clothing. It was the penultimate day of 2019 and, perhaps keen to make a positive start to the new decade, the Chinese authorities told him to stop spreading false rumours. They claimed that people could only become infected if they had close contact with animals being sold at the Wuhan market.

We'll never know how the pandemic might have developed had the state not tried to initially conceal the truth, but we know that Dr Li paid a tragic price by becoming one of the first medics to die of coronavirus, in early February 2020. A traumatised state reversed its position and the dwindling respect of its citizens by releasing the genetic code of the virus for the world to begin a frantic search for a vaccine. China released daily updates as the virus spread and, if there's any comfort to be gained from the Covid-19 pandemic, it's found in the commitment to global data transparency and to scientific collaboration beyond borders. Future historians will look

---

3 SARS was a previous deadly virus which first appeared in 2003.

back with astonishment at the superhuman, transnational effort to develop testing kits, treatments and vaccines. The global hostility to the (unsubstantiated) rumours that the US government was trying to buy the exclusive rights to a promising vaccine, being developed by German biotech lab CureVac, should serve as a warning to exceptionalism in times of crises. Globalisation may have played a part in the virus spreading exponentially around the world, but it's *only* through globalised mass ingenuity that we'll see an end to the pandemic.

'When China sneezes...'

If it is too soon to assess the health impact of Covid-19, it will be no easier to predict the economic fallout. The line about China sneezing and the rest of the world catching a cold had become a literal truth. By March 2020, governments were desperately trying to strike a balance between keeping economies afloat and preventing hospitals from being overwhelmed. The UK's initial response appeared to favour the economy, at the expense of the elderly. Boris Johnson mused that pursuing a 'herd immunity' policy (allowing 40–60% of the population to catch the virus, so that immunity is reached sooner rather than later) might lessen the impact upon the economy. That strategy was soon exposed when fatality projections of over a quarter of a million deaths among the elderly emerged. The noise of grinding gears into reverse was palpable – within days, the UK government took the unprecedented step of offering to pay 80% of every employee's salary, for as long as it took, so long as everyone kept their distance, and washed their hands for *at least* 20 seconds, to the tune of 'Happy Birthday to You' – twice.

Other countries wrote similar blank cheques. A global recession, if not depression, was, by and large, accepted as a price worth paying in order to save lives. And there will be no swift economic recovery. Indeed, some economists have speculated that the already fractured model of capitalism might shatter under the strain of successive economic lockdowns.

The coronavirus devastation has been traumatic – it cares not for national borders, rich or poor, race or religion. There have, however, been many positives, even at this early stage. One unexpected beneficiary has been the environment. National lockdowns triggered swift improvements in water quality (who knew there were fish in Venetian canals?) and carbon emissions. This prompted the lunatic fringe to claim that Covid-19 was the 'planet's plague', sent by Gaia to teach us all a lesson. A more realistic assertion is that, when this is all over, carbon commitments and pledges will count for little as the focus switches to creating jobs and stimulating an economic recovery. Or perhaps there will be a planetary realisation of what really matters in times of peril. What are we actually living (and dying) *for*?

We, the people

Even though we're going to be dealing with the aftermath of Covid-19 for a very long time, there's already been a large helping of soul-searching on social media. For a brief moment in time, Twitter reverted to being a source of compassion, not conflict, before normal service and rancour resumed. News bulletins alternated gruesome intensive care unit (ICU) footage with tales of generosity and good humour. We continue to debate – and will do so for a very long time – the world we want to make after this is all over.

I'm writing this barely three months into the crisis. Thomas L. Friedman, writing in the *New York Times* in March 2020, gave authors like me some sound advice (which I'm about to ignore):

'Whatever nonfiction book you're working on now, put it down. There is the world B.C. — Before Corona — and the world A.C. — After Corona. We have not even begun to fully grasp what the A.C. world will look like.'

He's right, of course, but all things must pass – even pandemics. My fervent hope (and why I've written this book) is that the pandemic of 2020–21 will lead to an outpouring of innovation as we reclaim our desire for self-determination, through a rejection of individualism and an embracing of the common good.

And I seriously doubt that we'll describe YouTube videos as 'going viral' *ever* again.

Redemption songs

Given the dramatic events highlighted in this chapter, let's try to agree on one thing: these are remarkable, turbulent times that we're living through, where all of the accepted norms are being questioned. The main players in BrexiTrump are often labelled as proponents of 'creative destruction' – a concept first defined by the Austrian economist Joseph Schumpeter that adheres to the radical destruction of old systems as a necessary step towards improved economic systems. What seems to have changed is that polarisation has swept around much of the world, but the usual polarities have shifted. It's no longer possible to say that the world is divided between left and right, or between rigid class divisions. Former British Prime Minister Tony Blair argued that the divide we're seeing now is between open and closed. What is Brexit but an attempt to close off the UK from the rest of Europe? Globalists believe in frictionless trade, while Trump chants 'America First' and imposes economic sanctions on all and sundry. The choice between open and closed is still at play and, for the moment, it feels like supporters of open are in retreat. I have to believe, however, that we discover our better selves through being open, so the pendulum will reverse direction, sooner rather than eventually.

Too often the retreat back into national insularity has been portrayed as a return to some kind of 'natural' order. In fact, nothing could be further from the truth. In 2014, Deborah MacKenzie wrote a sobering article for the *New Scientist* magazine. In 'End of nations: Is there an alternative to countries?' she reminds us that the concept of a nation state is a relatively recent one. Until the late eighteenth century, travellers in Europe would identify themselves by the town or village they hailed from but couldn't name the country they lived in. There were no passports, no border checks. MacKenzie further argues that nationalism is a poor apparatus for tackling complex, global problems (which perhaps explains why many 'closed' advocates are also in denial over climate change). Instead, she favours a form of 'neo-Mediaevalism' because:

> We must manage vital matters like food supply and climate on a global scale, yet national agendas repeatedly trump the global good. At a smaller scale, city and regional administrations often seem to serve people better than national governments. There is empirical evidence that […] social and ecological systems can be better governed when their users self-organise than when they are run by outside leaders.

George Monbiot, environmental activist and author of *Out of the Wreckage: A New Politics for an Age of Crisis*, is enthusiastic about our potential to self-organise on a local basis, whether that is solutions to everyday problems or maintaining our survival as a species:

> We are extraordinary creatures, whose capacity for altruism and reciprocity is unmatched in the animal kingdom […] When

we emerge from the age of loneliness and alienation, from an obsession with competition and extreme individualism […] we will find a person waiting for us. It is a person better than we might have imagined, whose real character has been suppressed. It is the one who lives inside us, who has been there all along.

Monbiot is eloquently describing the power of us. We'll return to the matter of how we harness it to chart our way out of the current predicament in the final chapter. First, let's see how these turbulent events have impacted upon our ways of living and our ways of seeing.

CHAPTER TWO

'How Are You Feeling?'

Our capacity to envisage, let alone exercise, the power of us, is critically dependent upon the impact that external political, societal and cultural events have upon us, in our lives and in our work. Sometimes the scale of change is relatively minor, and we barely notice the difference in our day-to-day existence. At other times, the reach and severity of change triggers either a spate of despair or a surge of resistance. And what is beyond dispute is the slew of dramatic changes during the period 2016–20. That we are conditioned by events can be clearly seen through the effects upon our mindset and our culture. Brexit momentarily turned a previously tolerant UK into a place where migrants were afraid to travel on public transport, for fear of abuse. The exodus of European waiters, labourers and fruit-pickers came back to haunt the government during the attempts to kick-start the economy during the Covid-19 pandemic. On 25 May 2020, George Floyd was callously murdered under the knee of a white policeman in Minneapolis. The Trump administration's perceived heavy-handed response to the subsequent street protests was widely seen as an attempt to sow division between white and black people of America. It could be argued that the military response actually precipitated an unprecedented reaction from white citizens: to challenge the complacency of other whites witnessing police brutality.

Authoritarian regimes are capable of turning mild-mannered communities into seething mobs (as we witnessed in Nazi Germany), so what effect have recent events had upon our personal and national psyche? In other words, how are we feeling?

The answer to this question could be a whole book in itself. But, given our focus, I want to highlight six emergent trends – some positive, others less so – that are critical to understanding how we become more innovative, adaptive and resilient going forward:

- **a crisis of identity;**
- **a sense of learned helplessness;**
- **the return of the artisan;**
- **the opening of knowledge;**
- **the dawn of scalable learning;**
- **the quest for self-determination.**

A crisis of identity

To help me understand how these phenomena help determine organisational mindset and culture, I interviewed speaker, writer, consultant and just about the smartest tack in the box, Heather E.

McGowan. Heather spends her time helping organisations make sense of the shifting external environmental factors, and how they respond to the challenges and opportunities they present. If you're looking for the big picture, Heather's the one with the paint brush. I met her as she was finishing her book, *The Adaptation Advantage*, on a beautiful spring day in New York, in 2018. Heather divides her time between Boston and New York and, like many Eastern Seaboard liberals, she was still trying to make sense of the Trump election victory. As we chatted in one of those out-of-a-movie New York coffee shops, we discussed how the double-whammy of a radical change of political direction, coupled with the loss of traditional blue- and white-collar jobs would affect our sense of self. For Heather, it's extremely concerning.

> We have to think differently about identity. The whole Trump phenomenon was about a loss of identity, it was about social norms, and it was about professionals no longer feeling valued. Studies have shown that loss of your job can take two times as long to recover from as loss of your primary relationship.

We still equate people's identities with their jobs, so how did she think we would define ourselves in the future?

> We ask kids 'What are you going to be when you grow up?' We ask undergraduates 'What's your major?' and we ask each other 'What do you do?' So, we have to think differently about how we form identity. Indeed. But what does identity mean at a time when even highly educated graduates will be unable to find work due to artificial intelligence and increasing automation?

It may seem harsh on Mr Trump to blame him for identity uncertainty. And perhaps it's too easy, too glib, to blame Trumpism or

Brexit for the recent appearance of a slew of social phenomena we never knew existed: ***identity politics*** (affixing political affiliations exclusively around the cultural, religious or sexual identity of a group of people), ***virtue signalling*** (the conspicuous showing of 'goodness' by your disgust of others), ***othering*** (treating individuals or groups as being intrinsically different to the norm) or ***ad hominem*** attacks (abusing the person rather than offering counter propositions). These labels have all sprung up to describe a deteriorating public discourse and a new-found determination to win an argument, at all costs. It appears that there's a cast-iron requirement now to declare which side you're on: pro/anti-Trump; Leave or Remain; nationalist or globalist. Liberal talk-show host James O'Brien, in his excellent book *How to Be Right in a World Gone Wrong*, exposes the identity angst that people seem to be suffering ('We're being overrun by migrants'; 'Christianity is a minority religion in this country'; 'We're not allowed to be British by the EU').

Somewhere along the line, we seem to have lost our sense of who we really are – our true selves. This is particularly acute for young people, as the epidemic of youth self-harm and low self-esteem confirms. Their current identity crises seem now to revolve around not a set of entitlements but rather what they *don't* expect: a comfortable retirement; a self-earned house; a regular job. Additionally, it's already clear that the post-Covid recession will disproportionately punish young people.

'Generation Uphill' are the most visible face of another malaise we seemed to be witnessing…

A sense of learned helplessness

To some extent we're all experiencing it, but it's particularly acute in our young people. Many of them have had a form of schooling that insists upon compliance, recalling facts and test prep – when the fast-growing knowledge industry hires on rebellious curiosity, problem-solving and critical thinking. We have machines that can now think for themselves and students that can't. And almost every machine can only be replaced, not repaired. Cars where the engine is invisible under the hood, the unfathomable intricacy behind the internet of things… It's hardly surprising that we're losing the ability to figure things out. When prospective leaders declare that 'Only I can fix this', is it any wonder that we find such confidence, however misplaced, reassuring?

As Heather points out, we seem to be losing this resourcefulness, just at the point when we need it most. The gig economy means that increasing numbers of people define themselves as 'slashers' (as in 'I'm an illustrator/DJ/barman/special-needs teaching assistant'). She feels that, as a society, we're just at the start of a problem that can only get worse:

> We've only digitized about 20% of our economy, or less, so you've got a huge workforce that came out of that factory pipeline and nobody's talking about what to do with them. We've been competing with machines – that's been part of the problem. What's the 'Last Mile'? Humans are good at two things: understanding the problem and then making sense of it – the Last Mile. We've been training kids to do the things that the machines can do much better.

This was turning into a depressing conversation, but here, at least, Heather offered hope through the analogy of the 'Last Mile'. This is a reference to a problem that besets a number of services: broadband services have super-fast fibre running across seabed floors, but your internet speed is dependent upon the quality of the connection covering the last mile or so from the nearest node to your home. Similarly, logistics people agonise over the fact that they can ship parcels halfway around the world quickly and efficiently, but once they reach the last leg of the journey, the speed slows down, and costs rack up – up to 30% of the costs of a delivery accrue in the final leg of a parcel's journey. The 'Last Mile' is what humans can do really well, and machines are very bad at (for the moment at least) The plumber/electrician who comes to your home to diagnose the problem is doing something incredibly sophisticated and displaying non-routine thinking skills that robots can only dream about (if they were capable of dreaming). These are the skills that machines won't acquire for a very long time, yet non-routine vocational skills are precisely the ones we've been neglecting– even denigrating – for decades in our educational policies. Kind of dumb, isn't it?

Of course, for every action, there's often an equal and opposite reaction. So it's no surprise that, alongside that sense of learned helplessness, there's been a welcome resurgence in community-curated practical skills.

The return of the artisan

The immediate worldwide response to the Covid lockdown was as unexpected as it was comforting: we baked. Sourdough, banana bread, scones… For a while it was easier to find toilet rolls in the shops than flour or yeast. Although ridiculed as a middle-class fad, the reality is that it was simply the surfacing of a trend that had been around for some time. The phenomenal growth in craft brewing, traditional arts and crafts, maker spacers, FabLabs ('Forget do-it-yourself, FabLabs do-it-together'), even community choirs, gardening, ballroom dancing – all point to our innate desire to produce, not just consume.

It would, therefore, be a mistake to assume that we'll all go back to buying our beer, bread and clothes when the pandemic ends. The renaissance of creative arts and crafts – not seen since perhaps the mid-twentieth century – is much more than a mindless pastime. Now, there are hundreds of online platforms like Etsy, Patreon, eBay, even Amazon – all allowing makers and crafters to reach a global audience and generate income. Mark Carney, the former Governor of the Bank of England has predicted the global growth of this phenomenon, calling it the 'artisanal economy':

> … in an age where anyone can produce anything anywhere through 3D printing, where anyone can broadcast their performance globally or sell to China whatever the size of their business, there is an opportunity for mass employment through mass creativity. Technology platforms such as TaskRabbit, Alibaba, Etsy, and Sama can help give smaller-scale producers and service providers a direct stake in global markets. Smaller-scale firms can bypass big corporates and engage in a form of artisanal globalisation; a revolution that could bring cottage industry full circle.

The return of the artisan is a striking example of user-innovation in action. My visit to the BrewDog craft brewery in Scotland, detailed at the end of this section, demonstrated the potential for this artisanal economy – especially when it retains the loyalty of its community of users (don't call them customers). And this has been made possible by the next phenomenon…

The opening of knowledge

As noted earlier, our ability to freely share knowledge, and to bring about change as a result, is fiercely contested as repressive regimes fight a losing battle in trying to suppress bad, or embarrassing, news. In the B.C. world, the chief contender for the first major international news story of the 2020s was Iran's catastrophic shooting down of the Ukraine Airlines flight 752 on 8 January 2020, killing 176 passengers and crew. The Iranian regime immediately dismissed claims that the plane was brought down by a surface-to-air missile strike, labelling such claims as a US 'psychological operation'. Ten years ago, they may have been successful in covering up the truth. This time, however, social-media outlets were flooded with citizen journalists' videos of the strike, and of the bulldozers brought in to clear the site of incriminating evidence. Within three days, a humiliated Iranian President, Hassan Rouhani, was forced to apologise for the 'unforgivable mistake'. The public reaction was shocking: spontaneous street protests, referring to Supreme Leader Ayatollah Ali Khamenei, were heard chanting 'Death to the dictator'. I'm willing to bet that, during the current decade, we will see more of these 'Chernobyl' moments – where state incompetence and obfuscation are suddenly, brutally, exposed – and more of these domestic conflicts on our TV screens, as the forces of authoritarianism and nationalism falter and stumble.

Short of confiscating all of our mobile phones, or closing down the internet, it's hard to see how authorities can stop the truth from emerging (though that doesn't seem to stop them from trying). But it's not just a demand for political transparency that the opening of knowledge facilitates. Our ability to connect, organise and mobilise is contingent upon it, and it is having a profound effect upon the way we view intellectual property. Aside from the increasing futility in attempting to keep information confidential, technologies like blockchain are demonstrating that, used responsibly, information can actually be *more* secure when it's freely shared. Equally, the coronavirus response was significantly accelerated by successive decisions to make data 'open-source'.

The opening of knowledge has such profound consequences that we'll investigate it more fully in Section Three.

The dawn of scalable learning

Investing in organisational learning has historically been viewed as a kind of 'performance bonus'. When things are going well, learning and development is supported. But when money is tight, we just need to *ship product*. It's always seemed a counter-productive proposition: surely you invest in learning as a result of money being tight? Things, however, are changing quickly. What management consultant John Hagel has called 'The Big Shift' is now in full flow, accelerated by the advent of big data. We'll see this process in action when we visit the culture consultancy sparks & honey, in Section Three. For now, let's celebrate the shift Hagel is observing. It implies that we're moving away from pushing more and more product through ever-cheaper pipelines to learning faster and more efficiently: from scalable efficiencies to scalable learning.

Hagel cites Toyota's new production philosophy as an example of the shift. Toyota urged their production-line workers to actually *slow* the production process down, in order to accelerate learning, saying to them:

> Your real job is to identify problems. Not just identify the problem and file a problem report after your shift is over, but to solve the problem as soon as you identify it. If you cannot solve it, we are going to put a pull cord next to your station, you pull the cord, and the assembly line will come to a halt and we are going to swarm you with a team of people to help you solve that problem you identified. You will be a hero for having pulled the cord.

'You will be a hero.' It's a great example of how to build a culture that promotes mass ingenuity. It demands, however, an equal psychological shift – from an egocentric blindness to failure, to a willingness to admit mistakes and learn collectively from them. Once again, the pandemic ruthlessly exposed some stark differences. Those countries that were willing to acknowledge fallibility and swiftly change policy direction – including New Zealand,

Norway, Sweden – tended to fare better in containing the outbreak than those that were either in denial or refusing to admit mistakes – most notably, the UK, Russia, Brazil and the USA, which were faced with catastrophic death tolls.

The organisations I visited graphically demonstrate Hagel's concept of 'scalable learning'. A learning disposition within organisations, however, doesn't happen by accident – it's a direct consequence of mindset, operating system and culture.

The quest for self-determination

Perhaps the most significant – though least discussed – consequence of the events detailed in the previous chapter is an insistent (often irrational) urge to be more in control of our lives. The UK's 'Vote Leave' campaign succeeded through its relentless message to 'take back control', and demagogues everywhere were claiming that only they could bring order to the chaos that living in a globalised, free-moving, fast-changing world represented. Never mind that the pandemic and the climate emergency provided ample evidence that we can never truly be in control. People seemed willing to buy the snake oil for the illusion of reassurance.

That's the deficit model of self-determinism. There is a more positive side to it, related to the previous two phenomena. We now know more about the world before we've graduated from high school than our ancestors did in their entire lives. We now learn socially, as well as in the formal environments of school, college or the workplace. The constraints upon knowledge have largely disappeared. It's inevitable, therefore, that we want to put that cognitive surplus to good use. Whether it's creating a trivial hack that might help video gamers, or coordinating a campaign to change legislation, we now have more control – over our immediate lifescape at least – and we zealously value it.

Understanding the motivational effect of self-determination is critical to understanding how, and more importantly *why*, organisations and communities become the focus of mass ingenuity. It's also a central thread of this book, so it's worth taking a little time to define it. I apologise if it gets a little technical, but you can't really understand mindset, culture and leadership without an appreciation of what makes us tick and what drives us.

The theory of self-determination (SDT) – better described as a meta-theory, covering lots of smaller theories – is concerned with what motivates us as humans. It has been around for the past couple of decades and, in recent years, has become an industry in itself. A bewildering amount of academic jargon surrounds it, but essentially it argues that people have three psychological needs in order to fulfil their potential – at work and in life – and to feel good about themselves:

1. Competence – the belief that you are in control of your life, or even of a specific task.
2. Relatedness – being connected to other people, to care for other people.
3. Autonomy – to have the freedom to make decisions.

I know this could easily be filed under 'no shit, Sherlock', but despite these apparently obvious conclusions, the theory of self-determination has had hundreds of studies carried out, reinforcing the importance of these three concepts. It's astonishing that the weight of evidence has not had more impact upon the management of organisations, but there it is – an example of the knowing-doing gap.

What concerns us here – and I kid you not – is what is known as the *organismic dialectical perspective* of SDT. This is a very fancy way of saying that people are living, breathing humans and that while the three needs above are innate – we're all born with them – they can all be affected, positively and negatively, by the environments we live and work in. Equally, they all affect the two forms of motivation that are the keys to human performance: *extrinsic* (rewards-driven or avoiding punishment) and *intrinsic* (coming from within: pride in achieving a goal, improving self-worth, establishing a sense of purpose). Put simply, until the two fathers of SDT, Edward Deci and Richard Ryan, came along, the received wisdom was that extrinsic motivation was the only driver that mattered in raising performance. My father's advice to me upon leaving school was typical of a widely held belief: 'Always choose the job that pays the most money – you're never going to enjoy going to work, so you may as well make money doing it.'

Fortunately, I ignored his advice (as all 16-year-olds do) and experienced the penniless hedonism that only professional musicians enjoy, for the next 15 years.

I digress, but not by much.

We are finally seeing organisations recognise that, with better understanding of the science of motivation, we need to invest less in bonus schemes and perks, and rather more in building a culture that fosters greater intrinsic motivation. And they can better do *that* through understanding the motivations and aspirations of groups driven by nothing more than the purity of a desire to help others.

To recap: a number of societal trends have emerged in response to the political, technological and social disruptions of the previous five years. In turn, the extent to which organisations can become centres of people-powered innovation will be calibrated by their responses to:

- a societal *crisis of identity,* accompanied by
- a *learned helplessness,* exacerbated by the rise of automation, but countered by
- the *return of the artisan,* fuelled by
- the *opening of knowledge,* leading to

- the *dawn of scalable learning,* making possible
- the *quest for self-determination.*

Before digging deeper into the history and definitions of people-powered innovation, let's reflect upon perhaps the most powerful example of the power of us, from a pre-internet era when society, technology and politics looked very different.

CASE STUDY: ACT UP

'We were brought in at the end to make
them cry before the hat got passed.'
Michael Callen

In the late 1980s, the USA was the epicentre of a very different kind of pandemic. To this day, a vaccine has still not been found. But, thanks largely to the coordinated efforts of a group of people representing those whose lives were being cut short, a vaccine has not been necessary. Their intervention saved millions of lives, and the lessons we can learn go far beyond the fields of public health and social justice. Their mindset, values and attitudes, coupled with their ability to self-organise and self-educate, were critical to their success.

The AIDS Coalition To Unleash Power (Act Up) campaign group formed in New York in March 1987. At that time, men were dying of AIDS in alarming numbers. Faced with corporate greed, governmental indifference and societal hostility (initially, 51% of Americans favoured putting AIDS patients into quarantine[1]), this group of patients and carers almost single-handedly ensured that the pandemic AIDS/HIV crisis was, if not ended, at least brought under manageable control. At the start of the epidemic, medical

---

1 Balzar, J. (1985) 'The Times poll: Tough New government action on AIDS backed'. *Los Angeles Times*, 19 December. Available at www.latimes.com/archives/la-xpm-1985-12-19-mn-30337-story.html, accessed 19 June 2020.

and political forums almost never involved people with AIDS. In the words of musician Michael Callen:

> Heaven forbid that a [person with AIDS] should express an opinion about etiology, about organizational structure, about service delivery, about the politics of AIDS! No, we were only permitted to participate in forums as performing bears brought in at the end to make them cry before the hat got passed.

Act Up's achievement was not simply to transform the public perception of AIDS patients. It also demanded a sense of governmental urgency which had hitherto been absent. Even after 6,000 men had died from the disease, the then President, Ronald Reagan, had still not spoken publicly about it and only *one* pharmaceutical company was researching drug treatments. Federal spending on AIDS research was a fraction of the amounts spent on far less deadly diseases. It was seen as a 'gay plague' and, for some, a twisted form of divine retribution. By 1987 – the year of Act Up's formation – over 40,000 had died in the USA, 5–10 million worldwide.

Act Up soon realised that unbridled anger was not enough. Their strategy became tri-fold: change public perception; demand regulatory change; become experts in the science of AIDS. In 1988, the first national demonstration, outside the headquarters of the US Food and Drug Administration, forced the regulators to switch the model of clinical trials. Instead of a small number of patients being observed for a long period of time, Act Up demanded that a large cohort of patients be studied for a much shorter period. As one of the Act Up organisers said at the time: 'We are now the experts – we don't give them the power when we go there and say "You're the experts". We're the experts also, and we can talk to them as equals.'

Their creative design of non-violent protests – barricading health and government offices, exposing those discriminating against people with AIDS, staging a 'Day of Desperation', when loved ones in coffins were delivered to state and government offices, and their ashes scattered on the White House lawns – all were created to maximise publicity. Important though the five-year daily barrage of protests was, of equal importance was the knowledge management strategy, carefully planned to educate those living with AIDS and to counter the misinformation spread by a hysterical mainstream media. They designated this as an 'inside-outside' strategy.

The depth of their collaborative knowledge meant that pretty soon people with AIDS turned to Act Up before their medical consultant for treatment advice, thus extending the lives of countless people. Within 10 years, they achieved the status whereby, in the words of organiser Gregg Bordowitz, 'People with AIDS [were] involved at every-level of decision-making concerning research and a cure for our disease.' The major breakthrough came in 1996, when Highly Active Anti-Retroviral Therapy (HAART) became widely available, thanks mainly to Act Up's political and cognitive power. It's worth remembering that up until that point, researchers and pharmaceutical companies alike tended to study drug interventions in isolation, primarily to make it easier to connect cause and effect. Act Up's urgency and collaborative knowledge successfully demanded the trial of multi-drug therapies or cocktails to find drug combinations that could work synergistically.

The pioneering treatments they insisted upon have now become the standard of care around the world. While AIDS-HIV has not been eliminated (and possibly never will be), it is now considered a chronic, though manageable condition, rather than a death sentence. In 2010 alone, an estimated 700,000 lives were saved by the use of HIV-AIDS multi-drug therapies, while there are currently 500,000 men in the USA alone living full and active lives with AIDS.

By the late 1990s, one might have expected Act Up's work to have been largely completed. But their attention now switched to issues of equity, especially since the costs of drug treatments were prohibitive for many. In 1997 they won their fight to make HAART affordable for all people with AIDS.

One wonders why there hasn't been an Act Up movement for cancer. Is it simply too big or complex a problem? Do cancer patients see themselves as passive recipients of treatment programmes, rather than co-authors of innovative and complementary treatments? Certainly, the change in emphasis in modern cancer treatments – from monotherapies (single drugs or procedures) to the cocktails more commonly prescribed now – may not have been possible without Act Up's insistence upon a multi-drug strategy, subsequently adopted by oncologists. Whatever the reason, one can't help feeling that had the Act Up organisation targeted cancer, we wouldn't still be talking about a cure in decades to come. As Anna Blume said in *United in Anger*, the powerful documentary story of Act Up: 'I see it as a remarkable model of what can be done […] when people draw upon their strengths, their different strengths, and do things they don't know they can do.'

Key points:

- Innovation is not solely the creation of new products or services. It's also the insistence upon finding alternative strategies to seemingly intractable problems.
- 'Inside-outside' approaches can enable breakthrough thinking. The input of user perspectives can prevent group-think and habitual thinking.
- 'Inside-outside' also applies to paying heed to external perceptions of campaigns, while negotiating internal innovations.

- Having diverse group membership can help prevent 'solutionitis' (finding the solution before the problem has been fully explored).
- User anger – when appropriately directed – can cut through complacency and stimulate urgency.
- Building an open learning environment is a cornerstone of agile innovation.

CHAPTER THREE

A Brief History of People-Powered Innovation

On a warm summer's evening in 1853 (or so legend has it), a tired businessman walked into the Half-Moon Lake House restaurant in Saratoga Springs, New York state. It had been a long and difficult day, and he was in need of something sustaining. He ordered a side dish, cooked in a style which President Thomas Jefferson had made popular, ever since his chef Honoré Julien prepared 'potatoes served in the French manner'. What later came to be known as 'French Fries' arrived at his table and the customer was not happy. Sending them back, he ordered the potatoes to be less thickly sliced.

Unfortunately, the duty chef that evening was George Crum, half Native American, half African American and all irascible. His legendary volatility was not going to take kindly to criticism, so, in a fit of pique, he sliced some potatoes as thinly as he could manage, threw them in the deep fryer until they were hard and burnt, and then for good measure smothered them in salt. The potatoes were sent back out to the table and chef Crum waited for the explosion.

Except no such thing occurred. The customer loved them, asking for more. What soon became known as the 'Saratoga Chip' ended up being the restaurant's signature dish, with wealthy elites like the Vanderbilts queuing for hours just to eat chips from a newspaper cone. Crum became famous enough to open his own restaurant (no small achievement for a mixed-race young man, raised in near poverty), where each table had an ever-present basket of chips.

The invention of the humble potato chip paved the way for what is now estimated to be a $6 billion industry. Crum never patented his invention – had he done so, he could have opened as many restaurants as he wished.

It's a good story but a hotly disputed one. Some have argued that recipes with something similar to the Saratoga Chip had been published 30 years before that fateful kitchen tantrum. Others maintain that it was actually George's sister, Catherine Wicks, who accidentally dropped a potato shaving into the fryer. Regardless, the Saratoga Chip remained a local delicacy until the 1920s, when salesman Herman Lay began distributing potato chips as he travelled throughout the south of the country, eventually mass-producing Lay's chips in the 1930s.

We'll probably never know for sure who invented the potato chip. I've chosen to highlight it as an early example of people-powered innovation because it typifies a unique aspect: distributed ownership. Who actually 'invented' the chip in this story? Was it the customer/user (who gave instructions on his preference) or the chef/producer (who modified the original design of the French Fry)? Further, the story of Crum's chip is typical of the pattern of a user-innovation becoming appropriated (in this case by Lay's) when mass production takes over.

What is people-powered innovation?

Throughout this book, I'll be describing and analysing organisations and groups that exemplify the power of us through the process of people-powered innovation. It's a process whereby change is driven from the bottom-up, not top-down. To avoid confusion, when I refer to 'organisations', I'm using it as blanket terminology: any time two or more people come together to fulfil a purpose, some form of organised activity is taking place, however spontaneous or informal it appears.

Because we need to rethink the process of figuring things out, I'll only rarely mention 'customers'. I know all of us are sometimes passive consumers, but this book is focusing upon a much more dynamic set of interactions, so I'll use the term 'users' instead:

- **Users** are people who, unsurprisingly, regularly make use of a service or product.
- **User-innovators** are people who adopt one of the three forms of people-powered innovation listed below to fix a problem or improve a product or service.
- **Producers** are organisations that manufacture products, or manage services, at scale.

Most of the examples you'll discover here are attempting to alter the dynamic between user-innovators and producers. Why? Because many organisations have taken the notion of user-innovation for granted and that, to my mind, is a *big* mistake. Not least because we're at a point where self-organised groups increasingly no longer need producers – they're capable of self-sufficiency.

According to a 2019 study,[1] 54% of significant inventions are the result of user-innovation. Think about that: most new products and services owe their existence not to large corporations' research and development (R & D) departments, but to small groups of enthusiasts: us, in other words. The World Wide Web, Braille systems, the game of basketball, mountain bikes, surfboards, skateboards, Facebook, Google, Microsoft, Apple – and pretty much every other piece of software ever written – were all created by user-innovators.

When does people-powered innovation occur?

People-powered innovation occurs when users:

1. **Advocate for new products or services;**
2. **'Hack', or tinker with, existing products or services in order to better suit their needs;**
3. **Create new products and services from scratch.**

It could be argued that the first of these isn't really innovation, and that the third doesn't really exist, since almost every new product or service is built on the back of existing ideas. (One of my favourite definitions of innovation was coined by my friend Mark Stevenson when he said: 'Innovation is just two ideas having sex'). I'm including them both here, however, because the advocacy campaigns that succeed (as we saw with Act Up) usually combine a process of deep learning with ingenious implementation, which subsequently leads to new products or services. In other words, it's as useful to imagine people-powered innovation as a process of persuasion as it is the

---

1 Bradonjic, P., Franke, N. and Lüthje, C. (2019) *Decision-makers' underestimation of user-innovation*. Elsevier.

inventor in a shed. Similarly, while truly new/original creations are comparatively rare, the wheels of any economy turn on the improved versions of existing products and services.

Ingenuity vs Innovation

I'll refer throughout to both people-powered innovation and mass ingenuity. Think of the former as a process of change. The latter is the quality that organised groups need to make change happen. The words 'innovation' and 'ingenuity' are often used interchangeably but they are not the same. Innovation often reflects a process that adds value. But an innovation can occur without a challenge or problem – a new product can be created without there necessarily being a need for it. Ingenuity, on the other hand, is usually the disposition needed to turn a challenge into a solution. *Collins Dictionary* defines it as 'the skill at working out how to achieve things'. So it's solution-focused. Indeed, the Latin root '*ingenium*' (translation: engineering) suggests that solutions are engineered.

For the purposes of this book, it might help to use an ecological analogy: **ingenuity provides the nutrients that feed the process of people-powered innovation.** I consciously refer to 'mass' ingenuity because it's my belief that we have tended to see creative or imaginative individuals as somehow 'special'. Some organisations still persist in having roles defined as 'creatives', thus reinforcing their difference. I hope to persuade you, over the coming sections, that not only *can* anyone exercise ingenuity, organisations *must* foster *mass* ingenuity, such are the challenges we face. If we get the mindset and culture right, it's eminently achievable – and that's where leadership comes in.

That still leaves 'the power of us' part. Now, I'm perfectly happy to accept that, in a world turned upside down, it may be considered naive to be singing the praises of my fellow human beings, precisely at a time when we seem to be at each other's throats. Candidly, I set about my research in the hope of finding reasons to be cheerful. Since everywhere I seemed to go during the latter part of 2016 turned into a voyage of pessimism, I started to intentionally seek out instances where the power of us had made a difference – to people's lives and to their aspirations.

Eventually, it began to dawn on me that, at a time when we are disengaged by our work, the ability we display, in fixing problems that really matter to us in our 'non-work' time, is as impressive as it is underutilised elsewhere. The examples of mass ingenuity that I'm sharing here are the tip of the iceberg. Personally, I find it thrilling, and the fact that so much of the power of us these days is being led by young people gives me great hope.

How did we get here?

It is fundamentally important to understand the milestones along the way to the phenomenon that we're seeing. Not just because it tells us where we might be heading. Nor because it suggests the requisite mindsets of innovators. The main reason to understand the informal, often rebellious, history of people-powered innovation, is to fully grasp how it has become assimilated and is now part of mainstream organisational practice – at least for those organisations that understand its power. That process of assimilation is at once an accolade and a real threat to its unique identity.

Let's take it as read that people have grouped together to make things ever since we discovered fire. And up until the Industrial Revolution, it could be argued that *all* we had were products and services created by users. What I'm concerned with here is the post-internet history – when location, affiliation and age designation were rendered irrelevant, all *kinds* of things became possible.

Put crudely, the sequence, with overlaps, goes roughly like this:

- **collaborative knowledge;**
- **collaborative consumption;**
- **collaborative creation;**
- **cooperative production.**

First, we learned how to share what we know (**collaborative knowledge**). The advent of social technologies and platforms has transformed organisational collaboration, and vastly increased and democratised the store of knowledge available to us. So much so that we now know far more than we can ever apply in our paid employment, so we share and deepen that knowledge when we're not at work. Author Clay Shirky called this our 'cognitive surplus'.

Collaborative knowledge has been, and will continue to be, a transformative force. But the past two decades have been marked by an enthusiasm for sharing much more than information. **Collaborative knowledge** begat **collaborative consumption** (sharing what we own). The aforementioned cognitive surplus hitched up to the age of abundance and, lo, it was good. Just about everything we ever possessed – cars, homes, couches, pets, bits of tat in the attic, the place where we park the car and *especially* our skills – all became shareable assets. In the early days it was driven by a real sense of altruism. It was perhaps inevitable that the astonishing growth of the sharing economy meant it would soon become a victim of 'proprietary assimilation'. We quickly went from 'It seems a shame to waste it' to 'I wonder how much I could get for it?' to 'How much are my Uber shares worth?' But let's not be too hard on ourselves. We'll deal with proprietary assimilation (and why it's good news) in Chapter Four.

Besides, it's too easy to be cynical about the corporatisation of the sharing economy. True, the phenomenal spread of Airbnb and

Uber (market caps of $38 billion and $54 billion, respectively, at the time of writing) has had severe implications for town planning, labour exploitation and the environment. But the sharing economy spans a wide spectrum. There have been plenty of non-monetary schemes in recent years: community Local Exchange Trading Schemes (LETS) and time banking schemes for instance (where volunteers do unpaid work in the community in exchange for banked services in return) have flourished without money changing hands. They have been the social glue of many grassroots communities. The principle of reciprocity is still alive and kicking, and the sharing economy shows no sign of slowing down. So, given those two highly effective forms of collaboration, what might be next?

I believe we're now seeing a burgeoning of **collaborative creation** (sharing what we make) sometimes referred to as 'peer production'. As previously mentioned, there's nothing new about collaborative creation. What makes it different now, however, comes as a direct result of the previous phenomena of collaborative knowledge and collaborative consumption. Historically, if you had an idea, built a gizmo or knitted a quilt, it would be to serve your limited personal needs – if you were lucky, you might get asked to do another for a friend. The user-innovators who became producers did so by seeking an external venture capitalist, giving away big chunks of equity, and power, in exchange for variable levels of expansion. Now, there's an alternative.

Where are we headed?

In the medium-term, we may well see a further phase: collaborative creation may well beget **cooperative production** (sharing what we make at scale). Until the Covid-19 pandemic, this remained in the 'highly speculative' category – largely because of what we know of user-innovators' motivations. Research tells us that, for every James Dyson, who looks at a vacuum cleaner and thinks 'I could make a fortune making a better one of those', there are a dozen others who encounter a problem, figure out a solution, perhaps shared it with a small circle of fellow users but have no desire to go into production. We've figured it out, it meets our needs, so job done.

That all changed with Covid-19. Suddenly there was a universally felt crisis but with urgent different local needs. Enter 'cosmo-localism'. I know, it's a terrible term, but it looks and feels like cooperative production. The slogan of cosmo-localism is 'design globally, manufacture locally'. By using open-source methodology in the digital commons, that which is normally regarded as scarce (intellectual property) is made plentiful, and that which is often regarded as plentiful (materials and global supply chains) should be regarded as scarce and therefore made as close to the need as possible. So, during the coronavirus pandemic, designs for face shields were made open-source and FabLabs, Makerspaces and schools – anyone with a 3D printer – churned them out for local doctors' surgeries and hospitals. Medics who were desperately calling upon their governments to #GetUsPPE (personal protective equipment) were surprised and delighted that the solution lay within their neighbourhoods. During the pandemic, cooperative production, based upon cosmo-localism principles, had, very rapidly, become a viable, sustainable, alternative mode of production. Of course, it relies upon a loosening of the tight grip on copyright and regulatory standards, but it isn't just a cheaper and more environmentally friendly way to provide products and services at scale – it's also way faster. Let's take an example.

Sharing open-source blueprints (cosmo), and working from a series of 'shops' scattered throughout the USA (localism), the #Wikispeed members – car enthusiasts, working mothers, schoolkids and retirees – set themselves an interesting challenge. Could they collaboratively produce a prototype for an environmentally sustainable car that could achieve 100 miles per hour, running on 100 miles per gallon? The normal product design cycle for a major car manufacturer is 10 years. The Wikispeed group developed a prototype in *three months*. At the time of writing, the group is seeking crowdfunding to go from prototype to production, whilst also working on the design of a $100 'mini-home', for people sleeping rough, and a 'mini-factory', housed in a shipping container.

Writing about Wikispeed, *Forbes* magazine claimed that:

> [...] the implications of these radical management methods for manufacturing are revolutionary. The ability to drastically reduce the development time for new models and innovate more rapidly amounts to a phase change – another sign of the shift to the Creative Economy. It has the potential to transform not just the auto industry but every kind of manufacturing.

And that's the critical point. Harnessing the power of us is both an opportunity and a threat to the status quo. It's an opportunity to rewrite all the rules of business, education, politics, healthcare, social and personal development – the whole of life as we live it. It's also a threat, however, because what has historically held back groups who wanted to create and produce goods, services and campaigns were the twin gate-keepers of capitalism: access to capital and access to the means of production. Now, with peer-to-peer lending platforms, like Funding Circle and Zopa, and with desktop 3D printers costing under $1,000, that's no longer the case. So we can expect collaborative production to operate without the need to conform to the established norms. Indeed, it could be argued that we've actually had cooperative production since 1844.

The inexorable rise of co-ops

The town of Rochdale in North West England would never be described as pretty. I can personally testify to that: I bought a house there in the 1990s. It was a tiny, cramped, terraced house, squeezed between a pub and the Golden Star Chinese takeaway, and directly opposite Turners asbestos factory. All things considered, it wasn't my finest purchase. The town does, however, have a rich history and, at a meeting in 1844, in the Weavers Arms pub on Ashfield Road, 28 workers formed the world's first cooperative.[2] Comprising textile workers, shoemakers, cabinet makers and joiners, the Rochdale Pioneers, as they became known, had founding principles which have stood the test of time remarkably well:

1. Open membership.
2. Democratic control.
3. Dividend on purchase.
4. Limited interest on capital.
5. Political and religious neutrality.
6. Cash trading.
7. Promotion of education.

These principles have hardly changed as the cooperative movement grew from those 28 workers to an estimated 1 billion members,

---

2 The Cooperative Movement's earliest formation has many claimants, going back as far as 1498, with the founding of the Shore Porters Society in Aberdeen, Scotland. Scots have some justification in feeling overlooked as the home of cooperation. Many cooperatives – Fenwick Weavers Society (1769); Galashiels & Hawick (1839) – pre-dated their English rival. However, many of these early attempts floundered, and it is generally felt that the Rochdale Principles established the framework that enabled the global spread of the movement. As someone born in the shadow of Hadrian's Wall, I'd strongly recommend that we don't get involved in such cross-border disagreements. Who knows where it will end.

across 145 countries, in 3 million cooperatives, generating over *US$2 trillion* of revenue annually.

Cooperatives are possibly one of the least well-known social movements, so let me share some facts with you. Worldwide, 12% of the population have membership of a cooperative organisation and 10% of employees work for one. The Rochdale Pioneers envisaged the cooperative as a route to social and economic equity and, 175 years later, that still holds. Countries with strong co-ops comprise 8 of the top 12 countries in the social progress index, which measures basic human needs, equality of opportunity and access to knowledge.

In other words, cooperatives work.

But do they work in the context of this book? You might think cooperatives might be too hidebound, too much of a throwback, to be modern hotbeds of innovation. In that case, consider credit unions and mobile banking. Most people are familiar with credit unions: member-owned banks which specialise in helping people get small, short-term loans. For obvious reasons, their popularity has soared in the developing world. Organisations like the Grameen Bank – a cooperative founded by Nobel Prize Winner Muhammad Yunus – came up with the concept of micro-credit. Micro-credit loans are usually for very small amounts and are made available to people living in extreme poverty. They have repayment rates of 97% – higher than any other banking system – and though small, such loans have transformed the lives of millions of people. Despite their success, however, there are still 1.7 billion people around the world who have no access to a bank. It may take more than a day to travel to the nearest credit union. Yet 90% of those 1.7 billion people own a mobile phone (many of which are 'dumb' phones). The World Council of Credit Unions (WOCCU) is working with the Bill & Melinda Gates Foundation to make banking available to millions more people through the vehicle of simple text messages.

Mobile banking turns out to be a lightning rod for people-powered innovation. It's estimated that over half of the innovations in mobile banking in Africa came from users, and many of those have since been assimilated in more developed economies. One such example, according to von Hippel, actually prefaced mobile banking itself:

> People assume mobile banking is an innovation of mobile phone companies. How mobile banking began was with airtime cards. What users did initially to transfer money was to send their airtime card code to their village and have the local phone owner use that code. The airtime card code became a currency. You bought your airtime. You rang up the person in the village who had a phone. You gave her the code for a $10 card. She passed on, say, $9.00 to your family, and used the code for cheap calling. This was the basis of mobile banking. It also meant mobile agents were already in place when mobile phone companies took the innovation on.

So yes, cooperation *can* be just as innovative as corporatism.

Key points:

- The emergence of people-powered innovation is a recent result of a historical desire to cooperate, built upon the snowballing impact of collaborative knowledge, collaborative consumption and collaborative creation.
- People-powered innovation can be seen in social movements, in makerspaces, and in the more collaborative and enlightened workspaces.
- User-innovation has been underappreciated and poorly understood.

- During the era of industrialisation and mass production, we've seen the neglect of user-innovation in organisations, counterbalanced by an explosion of activity in informal and online communities.
- The coronavirus pandemic revealed the potential for cooperative production to solve urgent crises.
- The growth of cooperatives around the world has been based upon principles of self-help and self-reliance. Co-ops offer an alternative means of production based upon mutual support and collaboration, not competition.

Put simply, when groups of people get together to figure things out, in the right learning environment, under the right conditions, there is no limit to what they can achieve.

CASE STUDY: BREWDOG

'Don't start a business, start a crusade.'
James Watt

Having worked our way through the recent history of people-powered innovation and its complex terminology, we could all do with a drink. So, allow me to invite you to my brewery. To be accurate, I should declare that I only partly own the BrewDog brewery. And that's not particularly unique. Over 130,000 people (and counting) have a stake in BrewDog. The company call us 'Equity Punks' and I confess I handed over a decent proportion of my meagre freelance pension fund one night after sampling one too many of their products. These are not shares in a publicly listed company – although they may be by the time you read this. I'd known about this start-up upstart, with a penchant for upsetting the corporate world, for some time, and more recently read the book *Business for Punks* written by their co-founder, James Watt. But I only felt like it was a business to support financially after a conversation with the manager of the BrewDog bar in Dundee, Scotland. Over the course of a pint of their excellent signature brew, Punk IPA, he told me about the ways they supported personal development. He'd been an investor first and only later decided to work for the company. It turns out that a lot of people follow that path, because of the remarkable sense of community that they've built.

The story starts in 2007, where school friends James Watt and Martin Dickie had recently graduated from university – studying

Law and Brewing respectively. As a classic example of user-innovators, they leased a garage in Fraserburgh, near Aberdeen, with a bank loan and not much else apart from a passion for redefining what beer could be. Producing small batches, filling bottles by hand and selling at local markets, a good day was selling five cases. It was clearly unsustainable. A year later they entered samples of their beer into a competition run by supermarket behemoth Tesco and, on the point of liquidation, were told they'd won first, second, third *and* fourth place. Tesco placed orders for 2,000 cases per week, and they were up and running. Since then, BrewDog (founding employees: two men and a puppy) has grown at a staggering rate. In 2007, James and Martin sold 184,000 pints of beer. Ten years later, over 1,000 employees (and a dog) produce over 136 *million* bottles of beer, sold in supermarkets and BrewDog bars all over the world. Little wonder that they've been listed in the *Sunday Times* Fast Track 100 privately-run businesses for six successive years.

Carving out a reputation for 'blowing shit up' and being the Sex Pistols of craft beer has not harmed their marketing either. However, the punk label only goes so far. The punk music pioneers couldn't play their instruments. Technically, they were terrible. Then came musicians like Elvis Costello and The Police who adopted the aggression of punk but secretly really knew their craft. They were smart and knew how to market themselves. James and Martin might not thank me for saying so, but their knowledge of how to make great beer – and headlines – is more Elvis Costello than Sid Vicious.

In common with many of the impressive organisations I've visited, there is a simplicity to their structure and mission that enables them to make complicated things look easy. Martin handles beer production and James does everything else. That includes BrewDog Airline, TV programmes, over 70 bars around the world and their first hotel called DogHouse (onsite at their eco-brewery in Columbus, Ohio). BrewDog turn the phrase 'no previous experience' into a rallying cry. Underneath this portfolio, they are quintessentially a founder-run company with only two priorities: making great beer and looking after their community (employees and investors). As one of those investors, I was entitled to visit their base in Ellon, north of Aberdeen. So it was that I found myself on a cold, damp November evening (what the Scots would fabulously call 'dreich') walking, somewhat forlornly, through a featureless industrial estate.

I'd made the pilgrimage to the DogTap, the onsite bar/restaurant, expecting to see lots of beer nerds. I was quite taken aback by the sight of so many locals, kids and dogs. The decor could best be described as cosy industrial chic, mixed with 1950s Americana. No excessively loud music, board games stacked alongside beer manuals – it was just what a local pub should feel like. And then there's the beer. It's an apocryphal myth that the best Guinness is made with water from Dublin's River Liffey, so what would draught Punk IPA, poured only days and yards away from the source, taste like? Bloody gorgeous, that's what. I was yet to learn what freshness means in carbonated craft beer circles, but this was as fresh and flavourful as beer could be. I stayed rather longer than anticipated.

The next day was a chance to see how the business ran and to talk to Cameron Robertson, then Head of Engagement, and Allison Green, then People Director. Allison's office kept well-stocked samples, so as we chatted, we sipped on a bottle of Declassified Demi-God (a 14.1% ABV milk stout for the nerds among you). Allison is a direct yet friendly Northerner, with a forthrightness that's much needed, as essentially, she is James Watt's right-hand woman. She explained:

> We have a fairly flat structure, which means that James inter-feres in nearly everything – you would think he owned the company. He basically sets the direction for people and then throughout the rest of the year, I help people do those things.

Allison is acutely aware that BrewDog is a brand approaching cult-like status – its fans go to extraordinary lengths to turn their fandom into a job. She said:

> We get a lot of people asking to work at BrewDog, and we try to put them off. Working here is not like being in a Disney movie – they think it's going to be Disneyland. It's not. We're shit at some stuff, we have exactly the same problems that all businesses do, we just have better beer.

Indeed, it's not a theme park – more like a busy and very, very high-tech environment. It's now a 24/7 operation, brewing around the clock to meet demand, not just for the many varieties of beer (they've concocted over 400 different types) but also vodka, gin and whisky.

Throughout my visit, I was struck by how people working there wanted to tell me about their jobs – and beer. People and beer. So how do they look after their people? Well, if the list of benefits is anything to go by, very well indeed. With an appropriately bold ambition to be the best company to work for in the UK by 2020, BrewDog pay all of their people the living (not minimum) wage – perhaps not significant if you're in admin but hugely important if you're pulling pints, part-time, in one of their bars. Then there's the enhanced paternity/maternity leave, private healthcare, a very generous pension contribution, life assurance, subsidised childcare, a staff recognition programme, an on-site gym, staff discounts, a beer allowance and a whole host of 'crew treats'. There's also a novel 'pawternity' scheme (a week off work if you get a new dog), and 'dog years' (four weeks' paid sabbatical every five years). Although that's an impressive list of perks, it's their commitment to learning that sets them apart: every employee is encouraged to learn more about beer through an outsourced training programme with a salary hike if they complete it. They also have a self-managed education support fund – £500 per year to undertake short courses externally – plus financial support if employees choose to complete a degree in brewing. And the company has 'BrewDog Bites': a series of in-house workshops covering presentation skills, coaching, change management and many more.

In 2017, the company announced its 'Unicorn Fund' to considerable approval from its crew and Equity Punks. This is a profit share/corporate giving scheme whereby 10% of profits are shared across all employees and a further 10% goes to charities chosen by crew and punks alike, through the BrewDog Foundation.

Taken as a whole, these initiatives make BrewDog a highly desirable place to work. So it's mildly surprising to see some negative reviews on job recruitment sites like Glassdoor. Complaints centred on two aspects of BrewDog's culture – both of which are common in passion-led, founder-run organisations. The first is workload and work/life balance – in this, James Watt is a terrible role model. 'Driven' doesn't even begin to describe it. The second is the speed at which projects are initiated, then dropped, leading to an underlying sense of constant swirl. I asked Allison how new recruits felt upon joining BrewDog. To her credit, she was aware of the criticism and was working hard to fix it.

> Working here is really weird, and it doesn't matter how much we prepare people for the changes involved in working in a slightly chaotic, founder-led business, it still takes a while for people to get their heads around it. We say: 'Let's be the best place to work we can possibly be.' But we're in the high-performance business and if people don't perform, we do everything we can to help them, but we do exit people. When you work here, you become so invested that it's almost everything. And James, of course, is 100% invested in everything we do – all of the time. But if I didn't reply to an email from him at the weekend it's not a problem – he doesn't expect it. And that's the piece we

have to deal with in our teams. We have to keep reminding them that we're not curing cancer here – we're making beer.

It was at this point that the subject of our discussion, co-founder James Watt, walked in. From the tone of his book, I was expecting loud and abrasive. What I got was softly spoken and charming. James is one of those people whose speech patterns have a job to keep up with his speed of thought, which in his case is lightning-fast. It was an unexpected bonus to have a chance to talk. As BrewDog is growing exponentially, is it still possible to hold on to the punk ethic?

> Yes, I definitely think so. We see our business as punk in that we're rebelling against bland, mass-market tasteless industrial beers, but also by doing things on our own terms – a new type of company that's part community owned, that looks after its employees, that shares its profits with its employees – a company that does things differently. But it's easy to get caught up in this bubble, because we're all close to this business. We're less than 0.4% of the UK beer market, up against companies that are two and a half thousand times our size. So we're still tiny, still the outsider, still the rebel.

While Cameron poured some Zombie Cake (praline chocolate porter 5.5% ABV), James answered some Equity Punk nerdy questions about home brewing. Though I had no idea what he was talking about, it was a revealing moment of someone being animatedly, unashamedly, transparently in their element. I once spent a weekend in the company of the late Paul Allen, co-founder of Microsoft, and a bunch of education experts from around the globe. Paul only seemed to be loosely connected to the conversation, constantly tapping on his laptop. Eventually, I found out what he was doing that was so distracting. He was coding. At that time the world's fifth wealthiest man was writing code, for no apparent reason, other than fun. He couldn't *not* write code, any more than Stevie Wonder could stop writing songs. I think that James Watt and his pal Martin would still be home brewing if they either built BrewDog to be the world's biggest beer-maker, or if it all crashed and burned tomorrow (both outcomes are entirely possible). They actually live out their mission 'to make other people as passionate about great craft beer as we are'.

That's not to say that James isn't a savvy business owner. His book makes it clear that he has all the fundamentals (crusade before product; cash is king; fans, not customers; everything is marketing; forget dales; company culture is 33.3% of everything) in place. But he's acquired those skills for the sole purpose of living out the mission. Alongside that – for good or ill – comes a company culture that doesn't just reflect the personality of the founders. It is entirely the product of who they are, unencumbered by consensus or collaboration. A group of senior executives on a company retreat could never have collectively created the BrewDog Charter:

We Bleed Craft Beer – This is our true north.

**We Are Uncompromising –
If we don't love it, we don't do it. Ever.**

**We Blow Shit Up –
We are ambitious. We are relentless. We take risks.**

We Are Geeks – Learn obsessively, share evangelically.

Without Us, We Are Nothing – We. Are. BrewDog.

In a follow-up email, I asked James to reflect on the specifics of that culture. His answers are worth quoting at length as they contain great advice for any start-up organisation.

On radical transparency

> We release all our latest numbers weekly, so everyone across the business sees every single detail of our results on a week-by-week basis, and the responsibility is shared across the business. Our numbers don't lie, and ensuring everyone has access to them means everyone has the opportunity to affect them. We also share all our plans; we recently released a blueprint for the next Decade of Dog, ensuring all our plans are laid out in black and white for the world to see. And we even released all our recipes in DIY Dog, allowing anyone to brew home-brew-sized batches of our beers for themselves! Transparency is a huge part of our approach to comms. Open-sourcing our recipes opened the doors to invite anyone to have a go and brew their own BrewDog beer. Craft beer should be inclusive, and inviting people to try it themselves is the ultimate incarnation of this.

Imagine Coca-Cola releasing their recipe. They have kept it locked in a vault for almost a hundred years. Yet, if your mission is bigger than creating shareholder value, it makes absolute sense to share it. Besides, commercial rivals would probably not be able to recreate Punk IPA – lots of people watch kung fu movies, but that doesn't make them Bruce Lee.

On keeping it flat

> This is a constant source of consideration for us – we're maniacally obsessed with flat org structures and we'll always fiercely defend this. Bloated, top-heavy businesses offer little to no

autonomy, and as a result, no responsibility. With a flatter hierarchy, the ownership lives and breathes in everyone and results in much more buy in and tenacity from everyone across the business. As we grow globally, it's vital that we keep it as lean as we can.

On empowering employees

We hand our teams a high level of autonomy. Their ownership over their own successes and failures is critical to our development and growth – as we build our business internationally, we need to have awesome people on the ground, empowered to make decisions and impact the world around them with great craft beer. Tight restraints and limitations on our teams would only set us back as a company. Likewise, we hand a lot of decision-making over to our Equity Punk community who are consulted on everything, from what new beers to produce to how to market, name and design them. Trust is key to this and it works both ways – we trust our teams and our community and they trust us to support them, their future and our business's future.

The BrewDog Unicorn Fund is a key initiative for us which encourages trust, engagement and autonomy in particular – we empower every employee to make the right decisions to support growth of the business, and we reward them by sharing 10% of our profits equally. Every employee has a stake in the success of the business, and in order to maximise that, we tell them to go ahead and make decisions which will either result in cost savings or seize an opportunity for growth. There are countless examples of it working across the business, from employees negotiating better rates with suppliers or finding an ingenious way to wax dip bottles without the need for costly equipment, to setting up daytime ballet classes in our bars to encourage footfall and new customers at a time that would traditionally be quiet. Our team have embraced this way of working – and it only works because trust exists and is demonstrated, individuals are engaged in the concept and everyone has autonomy to take decisions – thinking like an entrepreneur.

Prior experience is overrated

James believes that building a start-up organisation, without the burden of previous experience, has worked to their advantage:

> We didn't have any business experience, which was probably a blessing as it meant we were not distracted by theory and the way things are meant to be done. We just made it up ourselves as we went along, and as a result we were probably more creative. Martin and I try to lead from the helm and set the example for the rest of the business on how to attack problems, how to take on challenges and how to innovate. Myself and the directors on our Mission Control (their version of a senior leadership team) are constantly inspired by other brewers in our industry as well as from business leaders from a broad range of backgrounds and industries.

A commitment to learning

Allison Green told me that, when James goes on holiday, he'll take 30+ books with him, and she knows that he will come back with hundreds of ideas. This is clearly a well-read, quick learner, and his expectation is that everyone in the company is perpetually learning. As James puts it:

> It is in our best interests to invest in our people. We encourage all staff to take the Cicerone beer exams to gain qualifications

in beer – something that expands the horizons of our staff [...] For leaders, we provide training courses away from the office and away from the day to day to give our future management team the chance to commit to their learning and development – these are active, alternative ways to learn and not traditional boring courses. We allow all staff the opportunity to undertake their own learning in their respective fields of expertise, which we pay for, and we strongly encourage internal promotion.

What sets BrewDog apart, however, is that its commitment to learning extends far beyond its paid employees. Building an open learning environment means engaging with *everyone* that connects with the organisation. As a user-innovator turned producer, James is determined to engage with BrewDog's own user-innovators:

> Shortening the distance between us and our community [...] means we can give people a window to our brewery and what goes on behind the scenes, leading to greater transparency. From #MashTag, where we hand the keys to our brewery over to our social-media followers for a week and brew whatever they tell us, to our beatnik brew days where we invite our Equity Punks to our brewery to brew their very own beers with us; all of these projects enable us to educate, evangelise and integrate communities within our craft.

From competitors to collaborators

Although BrewDog's output may be small compared to drinks giants like AB InBev (who produced 107 billion pints in 2017) they have become a big fish in the pond where they first learned to swim. To lose the loyalty of the small garage-breweries they once were could severely damage the brand. They've managed to retain the support of the craft beer community, however, through a determination to work with them and bring them to the attention of a larger audience: featuring guest beers in BrewDog bars and staging an annual festival (#Collabfest), where BrewDog bars team up with local 'competitor' brewers to create dozens of new beers. All of this is – depending upon your level of cynicism – either a shrewd marketing ploy or a demonstration of their bigger mission in creating new beers for beer drinkers to enjoy and learn from. As James observed:

> New ideas come from everywhere. Some come from our community and our social-media followers. Some come from our staff – one of our bar team members presented the idea for #Collabfest to us and we've never looked back. Collaboration and community sits at the heart of everything we do as we continue to drive forward our mission of making other people as passionate about craft beer as we are.

Having had a unique insight into James Watt's philosophy for BrewDog, do bear in mind that, although this *appears* to be the accumulated wisdom of a CEO with 40 years' experience, his journey – from fisherman/hobbyist, to the leader of a billion-dollar organisation – spans barely 10 years. During that decade, James and Martin have had more great ideas for building a new kind of business than most organisations have in a lifetime. The most notable has been the realisation of business as a community of learners, with a remarkable bond between founders and fans.

From consumers to communities

As Head of Engagement at BrewDog, Cameron Robertson had specific responsibility for those fans, through the Equity for Punks (EFP) programme and the Unicorn profit share/charitable giving scheme. Formerly a fan, then an Equity Punk himself, Cameron became an ever-present on the community forum. Eventually, someone figured out that he might as well be working for them, since he was such a pivotal presence on the forum. He poured a sample of Death or Glory (a cask-matured Belgian strong ale-style brew, 21% ABV, only available to Equity Punks – I have never tasted anything quite like it, warming and woody) and talked about his role within the company.

Cameron rapidly grew the role from initially looking after the EFP scheme to delivering the share scheme, the Unicorn charity and BrewDog airline, among other responsibilities. It's not a conventional job description at all, but, to borrow one of James Watt's maxims, BrewDog is 'happy being scrappy'.

For BrewDog, there isn't an arbitrary division between users and shareholders. Admittedly, things may change if the company floats on the stock market, but for now there's a real sense of community – which was down to Cameron's astuteness in making the forum a lively, vibrant, focal point for engagement, and James' determination to make 'internal = external'. A key part of that culture is not attempting to quash dissent.

As with any fast-growing initiative, it doesn't take long for 'tall poppy syndrome' to kick in. You only have to Google 'BrewDog + Hipster' to be met with a hail of insults. The founders turned this into a judo move, printing a range of T-shirts worn by staff, carrying the most scathing tweets ('Just a shit, hipster Wetherspoons', 'BrewDog bars are hipster cretin hangouts. I only force myself to go for the vegan burger', 'Nobody knew how to brew beer until this pair of twats graduated'). Similarly, forum users will often be highly provocative – not least because they know James Watt is himself one of the busiest posters.

Beneath the knockabout, however, there's a deep sense of engagement. Take DogTank, for example, a section of the forum dedicated to investor-generated ideas on how to improve the business – each week, three ideas are taken and voted upon. There are also plans to take people-powered innovation a stage further: there's a huge amount of latent knowledge within the beer fans in the forum, so the intention is to periodically take one of the more successful home brews submitted by fans and scale up production, with profits shared with the user-brewer.

A lively, open learning environment has two non-negotiables: transparency and reciprocity. Shortly after my visit, they staged one of their open days, inviting any microbrewers to come, so they could, as Cameron put it, share 'as much knowledge as we can in a day: international exports, selling to grocers, maintaining quality – that sort of stuff'. It's another example of their determination to support the community they still see themselves as part of – not just a self-help group but a vibrant example of knowledge exchange, driven by collegiality.

At this point, I thought my day at BrewDog was drawing to a close, but apparently not. A tour of the brewery followed, concluding with a visit to the microbiology and tasting rooms. I was shown instruments to measure various minute olfactory elements and told about acetaldehyde and the perils of dimethyl sulphide, but to be honest by this stage I'd tasted my fill and wasn't really able to take it all in. I just needed a nap.

'The future of business is to hide nothing. Involve everyone.'

Johnny Rotten, lead singer with the punk band Sex Pistols, once famously got paid to advertise English butter. It was seen by many as the moment punk sold out. Similarly, there are many BrewDog fans who fear the 'butter' moment is inevitable. The founders have been publicly critical of the many small craft beer makers who have been bought out by the 'monolithic' conglomerates and vow that BrewDog will never sell out. James openly talked about an imminent stock market launch, even if, as he says, 'it'll be the most unorthodox listing and we'll be the most unorthodox public company there's ever been'. It's unlikely that significant shareholders will feel comfortable with statements like the following:

> We are a high growth company. This creates amazing opportunities for us and our team members. This also creates a constant state of flux and a healthy dose of chaos. For us, the time to start worrying is when we don't have the chaos, because it will mean our growth has slowed. WE NEED TO EAT CHAOS FOR BREAKFAST.
>
> (BrewDog Culture Deck)

On the other hand, with turnover increasing 50%+ annually, a US foothold established, and new breweries planned for China, India and Australia, venture capitalists seeking more conformity might have to balance that against soaring stock value.

My own view is that the rebellious punk ethic will inevitably fade because, for all the stunts (they once brewed the world's strongest beer, 'The End of History' – a 55% ABV monster packaged in a stuffed squirrel or stoat, which generated publicity and anger in equal measure), the real strength of BrewDog isn't the punk attitude. No, the reason why James and Martin have created a robust business among an incredibly crowded market lies in their beliefs, in the culture they've fostered and through building a passionate, collaborative community including, but not restricted to, their 130,000 investors. Their website lists their beliefs: world-class craft beer; community ownership; independence; being a force for good in the world; radical transparency and being a great employer. Underpinning that is a commitment to a mission and the creation of an open learning environment that would be the envy of almost all bigger and longer-established organisations. That will take you a very long way.

Key points:

- 'Learn obsessively, share evangelically' – make learning experiential, make (some of) it self-directed, make it central to your employee engagement strategy.
- A dynamic open learning environment will more than offset a lack of experience.
- Build communities of practice within your users. Encourage peer production and co-decision making.
- If your purpose is something bigger than yourself (and it should be), make it tangible and visible.
- Have collaboration and community drive your mission.
- Top-heavy organisations kill autonomy, agency and a shared sense of responsibility – keep it flat.
- Sharing your learning widely doesn't just build your organisation's intellectual capital, it also builds your brand.
- Create platforms that allow customers to become fans and fans to become co-producers.

PART TWO

Mindset

Successful organisations need a range of mindsets.
Communities of user-innovators and peer producers
think differently to corporate hierarchies –
what can we learn from them?

CHAPTER FOUR

From Hackathons to Hashtags

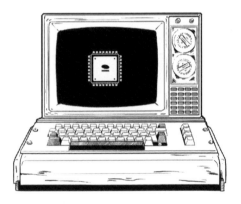

When it comes to shaping organisations through people-powered innovation, why does mindset matter? To the traditional organisation, understanding the mindset of your users – even your employees – didn't use to be a big priority. Many businesses went further. An organisation I used to work for had a policy of never commenting on external events, arguing that 'it was none of our business' and besides, when do you draw the line? The advent of corporate social responsibility (CSR) exposed some glaring inconsistencies and blind spots as organisations were expected to take a position on a bewilderingly wide range of issues. The hashtag generation insists upon a social contract, however: tell us what you stand for, and if we don't agree with your ethics, we'll take our business elsewhere. Misjudging the moral positioning of your users can have disastrous consequences, so now many large corporations employ 'ethical branding' consultants. In 2018, fashion multinational H&M, for reasons which seem unfathomable, put a picture of an African American child on their online store. The young boy was modelling a green sweatshirt bearing the slogan 'Coolest Monkey in the Jungle'. The reaction was predictable: Canadian artist The Weeknd immediately severed all connections with H&M and #boycottH&M was all over Twitter. Some companies have been accused – as were H&M in this instance – of manipulating controversy in order to raise their profile. The blunder is made, the retraction is swiftly issued, the social media hits are counted. I'd prefer to give them the benefit of the doubt.

The rule of thumb would seem to be this: the further away you are from your users, the greater the risk of a faux pas. Whilst even BrewDog have occasionally admitted to misjudging the mood of their community (and with a marketing policy that used to rely upon news coverage, not taking out ads, it was a fine line to tread), in general they understand their users' mindsets better than a corporation that spends a fortune on consumer analytics.

But why is mindset so important to innovative organisations? Simply this: in organisations that are seeking to work with user-innovators, or adopt the philosophies that make user-innovators so effective, what drives them and how they generate ideas is mission critical.

A tale of two mindsets

Communities that come together, united in a common purpose aren't necessarily a homogenous group. Indeed, for the more effective ones, it's precisely the difference in perspective that makes them ingenious. Nevertheless, they do share some common elements of mindset and, in general, these differ starkly from producer mindsets:

User-innovator mindset	Producer mindset
'What if?'	'Where's the market?'
Find usable, low-cost solutions	Get a return on investment
Driven by the desire for accelerated learning	Driven by the desire for predictable results
'It's my passion'	'It's my job/business'
Motivated by community and cooperation	Motivated by shareholders'/ stakeholders' demands

For the avoidance of any doubt, let me be clear: **there is no inherent superiority in the user-innovator mindset over the producer's way of seeing the world.** They each have their place. Five years ago, after a botched surgery, I was whisked into the emergency operating theatre with severe septic shock. As we now know, through the late stages of the coronavirus, sepsis is fatal in around half of all cases. Bodily organs are keeling over, like one of those domino stunts. So time is literally a matter of life and death. In that situation, I needed the surgeon to have the producer mindset. What I didn't need was him asking his team: 'Does anyone have any novel ideas that could save this patient's life?' Similarly, within days of researchers from Oxford University declaring their confidence in creating a Covid-19 vaccine, AstraZeneca, the global pharmaceutical giant, had set up supply and distribution chains to ensure that 2 billion people around the world would be vaccinated within weeks of approval being given. That's a pretty impressive producer's mindset.

In reality, highly innovative organisations need *both* mindsets, in a balanced form of co-existence. Unfortunately, many organisations over time squeeze out the user-innovator mindset, often unwittingly. This is when problems arise, where innovation goes to die. It's one of the reasons why large corporations often try to fragment organisational structures, creating small cells, so that they can hold on to the agility and sense of common endeavour that small communities display. Perhaps the greatest example of mass ingenuity to be found was Thomas Edison's 'Invention Factory' in Menlo Park, New Jersey. Edison himself was perhaps the greatest example of both mindsets at play. Gathering a small group of around 20 experimenters together, Edison was nevertheless a businessman at heart. That dual mindset ensured that in a six-year period, between 1876 and 1882, over 400 patents were filed and they invented the phonograph, the incandescent light bulb and electricity generating stations that powered the twentieth century.

When organisations lose the user-innovator mindset, collateral damage occurs in two forms. Firstly, the ability to identify problems that need to be fixed is missing – user-innovators tend to understand the needs of fellow users much better than producers can. Secondly, users innovate when the initial market for that innovation is bound to be insignificant. Producers tend to wait to see if there is demand before stepping in, and that's often too late.

So, having established the importance of the user mindset to organisations, how can it be put to good use?

Mindset beats skillset

Creating an organisational culture of open innovation, propagating mass ingenuity, is a quintessentially human endeavour. As we've seen through our brief foray into self-determination theory, motivation *matters*. In the organisations that I visited, one thing shone through above all else: establishing common purpose, getting the collective mindset right, is far more important than having the right skills in place. For one thing, as BrewDog has already demonstrated, experience can be overrated. For another, the most skilled people in the world won't perform unless the mindset is right. Still further, skills can always be imported, but a mindset must be grown. And, as if you needed any more reasons, a striking feature of people-powered innovation is that ***people often find solutions to problems that fit the skills that are to hand.*** (Witness the Riders For Health case study coming up.) Establishing the right organisational mindset precedes skills development, hands down.

Ingenuity moves fast – so long as it's open

We've already observed how collectives like #Wikispeed can outrun traditional automobile development timescales. This is, in no small measure, because they made their designs freely available. The move by the Chinese authorities – to release the genomic profile of the coronavirus – meant that small communities of user-innovators all around the world were able to immediately start to investigate possible treatments and vaccines. But it probably wouldn't have happened without the precedent of the Human Genome Project (HGP). As megaprojects go, this was pretty mega. Established by the US government in 1990, the quest to identify the entire genetic profile of a human was estimated to take 15 years. Using traditional research methods and 'closed' processes, it would have taken much longer. However, by ensuring that geneticists around the world worked collaboratively and under open-source principles, the entirety of DNA permutations was published in 10 years – five years ahead of schedule. The incredible advances we're witnessing today – in genetic testing, CRISPR gene-editing, DNA sequencing and immunology – can all be traced back to that decision to make the human genome data publicly available.

'First to market' is the holy grail in the knowledge-driven world we live in. IBM used to have three stages of testing before releasing software: the A-test was an internal process before a new product could be announced; the B-test was the stage of restricted user testing before the product went to manufacture; the C-stage was the final test before the product could go on sale. It was a lengthy process but it became the established norm for the IT industry. In 1984, however, WordVision went public with the draft B-test version of their word processing software for IBM PCs. They sold it as a 'Pioneer Edition'. By asking purchasers to use the software and report back any problems, they unwittingly pulled off a master-stroke – customers paid $50 to do the company's testing for them. It was so successful that C-stage testing effectively disappeared, and the B-test became the new way to release product – and so the phrase 'beta testing' was born. You're welcome.

These days, almost everyone invites users to feedback, report bugs and usability issues at the beta stage. It's a critical part of people-powered innovation. Google's mantra became 'everything is in beta' and some of their products are in 'perpetual beta'. Instead of this being the exception, it has now become standard practice, particularly in the tech sector. By engaging users, conventional development timelines have been slashed.

The *jugaad* mindset

In the street workshops and slums of India, user-innovators are found around every corner. They adopt the mindset (although some would say they have no choice) of '*jugaad*' innovation. Although there's no direct equivalent in English, *jugaad* has a couple of meanings: the first is 'good enough', the second is 'making the most of what you have'. Transplanting the passenger cabin from a lorry to a horse and cart in order to keep the driver dry during the wet season? *Jugaad*. The clay pot with water flowing through it to keep food cool during the summer heat becomes a *jugaad* fridge. You can Google thousands of examples, some of which are ingenious to the point of absurdity. And that's what makes *jugaad* – in India at least – a cause for contention, if not downright embarrassment. Many people echo the view of Indian journalist Manu Joseph when he wrote that 'the existence of *jugaad* is merely the evidence that the circumstances of a society are so bad that its smart people are doing what smart people in other civilizations do not have to do', while others complain that *jugaad* represents slack workmanship – an inability to finish the job properly.

I'm less concerned with the end products of *jugaad* thinking than with the philosophy behind it. It's often translated as 'frugal innovation', because solutions are found to fix a problem with minimal outlay, or to allow for easy replication and refinement. In the West, an increasing number of corporations have successfully adopted frugal innovation and user-innovators constantly display *jugaad* thinking.

The history of the skateboard is a classic *jugaad* process. The earliest skateboards, first seen in California and Hawaii, were a cheap solution to a problem: how do we practise surfing moves when there's no swell in the ocean? The initial tools of these 'asphalt surfers' were fairly basic – a chopped-off surfboard fitted with the rollers from a pair of old roller skates. In itself, this was also a *jugaad* solution: how do you practise skating when there's no ice rink available? The initial skateboards were basic but 'good enough', and their popularity soared. This presented the challenge of assimilation, which we'll come to in a moment. Of course, Manu Joseph has the right to claim that Western admiration of *jugaad* is frequently patronising and not applicable to large-scale corporations. But user-innovators around the world would probably have more affinity with Indian slum inventors than with large multinational R&D divisions.

Stay focused

There's an undeniably strong social element when user-innovators come together. Their *raison d'être* may be to find solutions to problems, but along the way strong relationships are formed. The most visible manifestation of these twin characteristics is the 'hackathon'.

The first event that called itself a hackathon took place in Calgary, Canada, in 1999, when a small group of open-source software developers came together to use cryptographic software as a way around the legal problems arising from draconian export regulations in the USA. With a theme as exciting as that, it's perhaps surprising that it wasn't the first, and last, hackathon. But the next decade saw a sharp rise in the popularity of hackathons and 'jams'. Music, video games, fashion design, education, culture jams, government, health and social welfare – pretty soon any problem, in any sphere of public and private life, was being hacked and jammed as a quick way to arrive at a solution. In case you've not attended one (I plead guilty to having organised a few myself), the format is usually that people are given a specific problem to solve over a fixed period – hours, days or weekends. Participants are required to share their prototypes at the event's culmination. Only later did a more competitive element emerge, when sponsors offered prizes to fix pre-determined problems.

In a 2015 study, researchers found that the motivations and principles driving participants were clear: 86% cited learning as the main goal; 82% valued the opportunity to network; 38% were attending because they wanted to achieve some form of social change. The next motivating factors came some way behind: 28% wanted to win prizes; 26% wanted to build a product; and, yes, 26% were attracted by the promise of free pizza. The most common guiding principles that have evolved around hackathons include:

- Stay focused on the output.
- Make events inclusive – welcome newcomers.

- Learning and sharing is important.
- So is sharing failures.
- Allow people to self-organise into groups.
- Group leaders are helpful, but not mandated.

(If you're inspired to host a hackathon, the definitive guide has been written by Joshua Tauberer: www.hackathon.guide.)

Hackathons adopted a methodology that would have seemed radical to the corporate world. But a process that was highly effective as well as deeply engaging meant that it was a matter of time before businesses, governments and venture capitalists would want a piece of the action. Facilitation gave way to assimilation – an idea that becomes successful runs the risk of being appropriated for other means, and hackathons were no exception. Soon, they were being used to test the viability of start-up companies, to create new product breakthroughs from proprietary companies, to lure talent to companies, or to simply tap into lots and lots of free pro-am expertise. NASA's annual Space Apps Challenge, for example, now draws 30,000 participants, lured by the prize of a trip to a space station (it's a step up from a slice of pizza, I guess). There's even a whole industry that's grown up, organising hackathons for large numbers of people who will happily pay $200 for the experience.

Is this necessarily a bad thing? No. And if you're the CEO of a company that is struggling to innovate, or simply needs more users to get involved in their product and service development, hackathons are a great tool. But they should come with a health warning: **once the mindset behind people-powered innovation becomes corrupted, the original user-innovators can feel like they're being played and will take their skillset elsewhere.**

There's much to be learned from the thought processes that have informed peer production and user-innovation. This chapter has concentrated upon aspects of motivation. Soon, we'll look at the value and attitudes underpinning people-powered innovation. It's worth pausing at this point, however, to acknowledge how much the landscape of innovation is changing. We used to allocate the responsibility for new ideas to R&D departments. With the advent of social technologies, our relationship with users has changed fundamentally. If mindsets align, then users can be a key resource, not simply in improving quality but in co-producing new products and services. They're going to do it anyway, so it's better to work with them than see them as competition.

Organisations that don't work with users are putting the cart before the horse, asking users 'What do you need?' Instead they should be asking user-innovators 'Can you help us fix some problems?' or 'What are you working on, and how can we help?' Successful futures rely upon producers and users innovating *together*, not separately. It's how millions of lives were saved during the AIDS epidemic. It's how the personal computer was created. And it's how you and your organisation can benefit from mass ingenuity.

CASE STUDY: RIDERS FOR HEALTH

'It's about seeing problems in a different way.'
Andrea Coleman

I first met Andrea Coleman, the co-founder of 'Riders for Health', on a study trip, hosted by Ashoka (a network of 'changemakers'). If you met Andrea in your local grocery store, you'd probably assume she was a kindly, sympathetic senior citizen, quietly enjoying her retirement. She has a gentle face and a soft-spoken manner. Watching her make an impassioned pitch to highly successful business leaders, however, I knew I had to interview her. When she was 19, she was one of only two females in the UK taking part in motorbike races, thus continuing a long family tradition of bikers. Motorcycle races were her life and, unsurprisingly, that's how she met her first husband, Tom.

Tragically, Tom was killed in a motorcycle accident and Andrea's reaction was to look for something more positive to come out of motorcycle racing:

> I didn't know how to just sit down and say 'I'm just going to feel terrible... I'm going to feel really bad. So my way to deal with it was to be really, really busy and create something. I felt the need to be doing something bigger than the sport (because) motorcycling is literally going round and round in circles.

She didn't know what that something would be, but with money raised through the sport, she was able to make a sizeable donation to Save the Children for their work in Africa. In return, they invited Andrea, journalist husband Barry Coleman and motorcycle legend Randy Mamola to visit Somalia in 1986, where she witnessed first-hand the desperate health problems experienced in rural communities. They were taken to vehicle graveyards where ambulances with less than 8,000 miles on the clock were up on blocks with steering wheels missing and they knew they had to try to help.

Eric von Hippel talks about the way user-innovators shape a problem to fit their skillset, and this was definitely the case with Andrea. If she'd been a pharmacist, she may have come up with a new vaccine programme. Andrea the motorcyclist looked at it and saw that access was the issue – these people could not get better if health workers had no transport. Except they had plenty of transport.

Andrea said: 'Big NGOs [non-governmental organisations] don't bother about vehicle maintenance – if it breaks down, they buy another one.' There was no shortage of trusts and foundations that were happy to put their logos on new vehicles they'd bought, but it was a harder sell to get them to pay for maintenance, running costs and logistics – the boring stuff. Andrea recounted a conversation she had with a Zambian health minister as recently as 2016, who matter-of-factly told her that the average life cycle of vehicles in healthcare was 18 months. She was appalled.

In 1986, Andrea, Barry and Randy founded Riders for Health, a non-governmental organisation dedicated to working in sub-Saharan African countries to ensure that people could get medical help no matter where they lived. First, they organised a maintenance programme for motorcycles in Lesotho, training local mechanics. The vehicles went five years without a single breakdown. Then she took out a loan for $3.5 million to buy a fleet of vehicles that could transport health workers to remote locations, ferry patients hundreds of miles to hospitals or rapidly carry blood samples to testing centres on motorbikes. This was an organisational gamble, but within five years Riders for Health in The Gambia paid back the entire loan.

In 2015, there was a devastating outbreak of Ebola in Liberia. Carrying blood samples usually involved journeys lasting days, frequent breakdowns and samples getting spoiled through heat and light contamination. They worked with a designer to create a new, safer carry bag and set up a complex relay system to ensure that the maximum time for a sample to reach a test centre would be no more than nine hours. Logistics was not seen as a high priority then, but when Riders for Health showed that six times as many patients could be seen through smarter scheduling and reliable vehicles, other countries soon asked for help. Riders for Health now employs 600 people and, over 30 years, has brought healthcare to 42 million Africans who otherwise would have been denied it. Little wonder that, in 2013, Andrea was named 'UK Woman of the Year'.

'I think we're unreasonable'

The mindset of Riders for Health is reflected in their three core values: practical, enterprising and collaborative. I asked Andrea what she meant by 'practical'. Her response showed an understandable frustration, often felt by social entrepreneurs working alongside aid agencies in crisis situations:

> There's a huge amount of academic study, rather than training people to roll up their sleeves and build capacity to fix things. Instead, they restate the problem, or they fix the problem for them and then walk away – it drives me nuts […] Everyone recruited to international development has to have a degree – why? Local empowerment is so important and you can't just have

a world filled with microbiologists and brain surgeons – you also need mechanics who want a 9–5 job without going to college. One major foundation spent $2.5 million working alongside us, studying need in rural health – they concluded that what women wanted was predictability – knowing that the health worker would arrive on Thursday, so they didn't go off and work the fields. I could have cried – $2.5 million to tell us what we already knew.

In a sign of its maturity, Riders For Health is now rightly staffed, and led, by Africans in their fields of operations: Liberia, Kenya, Zimbabwe, Zambia. The ownership may have changed, but the mission – 'to make the last mile the most important in healthcare delivery' – remains the same.

Andrea, who still rides motorcycles at an age when many of her peers need mobility scooters, has had a lifetime's experience of working with social entrepreneurs. She has some fascinating conclusions on their mindset:

Every social entrepreneur has a different set of characteristics to someone who works, say, for a charity. They're bloody-minded, there's something about wanting to change the world. There's a doggedness there […] *I think we're unreasonable*, we're not intimidated by the difficult thing. We're thinking 'This is unreasonable'. We're not just going to walk away from this. It's about seeing problems in a different way.

Having a bigger purpose, an unreasonable doggedness, a failure to be intimidated by big challenges, a tendency to see solutions through the skillset at hand and a willingness to bring in other skills when you don't have them – these are all key ingredients in the mindsets of user-innovators, practising mass ingenuity.

Key points:

- Focus on the mindset – ingenious innovators will shape a problem to fit the skillset.
- Know your limitations – surround yourself with people who have the skills you lack.
- Make your actions practical, enterprising and collaborative.
- Social enterprise demands unreasonable attitudes – the world won't change by itself.
- Be excited, not intimidated, by the scale of the challenge.

CHAPTER FIVE

When Needs Must – Why Lead Patients Aren't Waiting

We can't say we weren't warned. In 2015, Bill Gates gave a TED talk entitled 'The Next Outbreak? We're Not Ready'. It predicted the 2020 coronavirus pandemic in terrifying detail. In 2016, James Clapper, US Director of National Intelligence, reported:

> The populations of Asia and Africa are urbanizing and growing faster than those of any other region, according to the 15 UN [United Nations member states]. Emerging diseases against which humans have no pre-existing immunity or effective therapies pose significant risks of becoming pandemics.[1]

---

1 Statement of James R. Clapper, Director of National Intelligence before the House Permanent Select Committee on Intelligence. Hearing on

We were warned in 2017 when the outgoing administration of Barack Obama conducted an exercise that played out a global flu pandemic that brought international travel to a halt and collapsed stock markets – all with a vaccine many months from development. Almost all of the incoming administration staff either left or were fired a couple of years into Trump's presidency. In 2018, Trump closed the unit responsible for pandemics the day after its director, Luciana Borio, stated: 'The threat of pandemic flu is our number-one health security concern.'

The lack of preparedness wasn't restricted to the US administration, however. The UK's initial response to the crisis was to say that wide-scale testing – even for health workers – wasn't necessary. The EU offered to include Britain (still in Brexit transition) in a scheme to bulk-buy thousands of ventilators. The request was ignored and when asked why, a government spokesperson said: 'Well, we're no longer members of the EU.' A UK supplier to the National Health Service, Direct Access, offered to supply 5,000 ventilators and 50 million testing kits. Emails went unanswered and other countries snapped them up.

Flattening the curve

In the UK, it was only when projections of a quarter of a million deaths emerged that complacency turned to barely concealed panic. Around the world, state leaders ordered lockdowns, markets collapsed, borders were closed and citizens fought over toilet paper in supermarkets. Within weeks, the coronavirus had brought the entire world to its knees, with a third of the world's population under house quarantine by the end of March 2020. Intensive care units became overwhelmed, and we all had cause to thank the health workers who risked their own welfare in keeping the

---

Worldwide Threat Assessment of the U.S. Intelligence Community, 25 February 2016.

most vulnerable alive. Those governments who acted decisively and quickly saw the best initial results. Vietnam quarantined over 100,000 people in military camps and hotels. By the end of April 2020, they had 270 known cases of Covid-19 and no deaths – in a population of 97 million. By contrast, those governments that delayed lockdown, like the UK or the USA, were playing catch-up, to the tune of exponential growth.

Into the breach, caused through administrative complacency and lack of coordination, came an army of inventors and hackers. In Italy, Isinnova 3D printed a connector that turned snorkelling masks made by Decathlon into ventilator masks for doctors. The design was made open-source, so that anyone could follow their lead. In Spain, a group of engineers developed a cheap ventilator that came in two forms: one made of wood or acrylic for makers and FabLabs to manufacture, and a metal version for mass production. Helpful Engineering is an international group of over 3,000 volunteers working with the medical community to produce the equipment needed to safely combat Covid-19. #GetUsPPE is a decentralised US group of designers and makers producing face masks and other protective equipment. Their website even had a script so that volunteers could call their local hospital and offer to donate.

The *jugaad* ethic of 'good enough' was everywhere, as was open-sourced design. Safe, airlocked hatches for takeaway restaurants, repurposed sleep apnoea devices, gamers playing simulations that mimicked potential virus mutations… I could fill the rest of this book with examples. By the end of March 2020, there were so many projects that additional websites were needed simply to curate the range of initiatives. *Make* magazine summed up the global response:

> This uprising of action in response to COVID-19 demonstrates the ingenuity and talent that flourishes at the grassroots, along-side the resources of government and the corporate sector. It also fills a powerful desire for people to get involved and bring

whatever expertise they have to bear – technical, medical, social, political, legal. This movement inspires hope for the future. Leveraging open, collaborative innovation by grassroots makers at international and local levels can help solve not just for the coronavirus but teach us new ways to work together to solve other challenges too.

The maker community also expressed frustration, however, at the rigidity of the regulatory frameworks. Whilst it was self-evident that sub-standard ventilators may actually cause more harm than good, many projects looked to free up approved ventilators by using their assisted breathing solutions for less critical patients. *Make* presented the dilemma:

> Representatives of the American Association of Respiratory Care have expressed understandable concerns about whether a quality open-source device for clinical use could be designed and manufactured in less than 18 months, given time for development, testing and approval. But will America get to a moment when 'good enough' is enough?

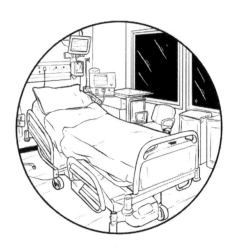

The Covid-19 outbreak merely brought to the fore something that was already becoming self-evident, at least to anyone with first-hand experience: the power of us finds its most vibrant expression in the field of public health. In less than a generation, people – patients – have gone from being largely unquestioning, deferring to the perceived wisdom of medical specialists, to being informed and challenging. It's unsettling for professionals and regulatory bodies, but it's not going away.

Earlier, I shared my experience of sepsis. It involved a period in an intensive care unit, where I received the best care possible. Bookending that trauma were not one but two cancer experiences (I never do things by halves). For men, colon and prostate are two of the most common cancers to suffer from. I viewed the experiences as my responsibility to learn as much as possible about my conditions. And yet I have talked in waiting rooms with (I think) elderly men *who couldn't even tell me which cancer they had.*

Thankfully, that's become a rare encounter, and instead, I've been able to tap into the accumulated knowledge of fellow patients. They combine professional levels of knowledge with first-hand experience. We refer to them as 'pro-ams' and I'm certain that I would not be alive today without their willingness to share their wisdom. Some, however, go further. 'Citizen scientists' turn research into potential therapies, often experimenting upon themselves and others. Why do they take such apparent risks? Because, in many cases, they have run out of options. I soon learned that nowhere is people-powered innovation and user-led ingenuity stronger than in those with life-threatening conditions.

So, you have been warned – some of the people I will introduce you to here have heart-breaking stories. But their responses have also been inspiring. Also, if you have any of the conditions featured here, please bear in mind that I'm not sharing them with you as any form of personal advice or endorsement. I'm simply not qualified to do that. What interests me are the motivations and methods that lie behind the medical solutions being sought – *not* the products and formulations they generated. I've always believed that each patient has to take responsibility for their own health, and I would never dream of making recommendations.

Understanding 'lead patients'

A common pattern among the patients and professionals I interviewed was the acceptance that, just as the coronavirus can't survive soap and water, neither will a fixed mindset survive an existential threat. My local hospital happens to have one of the largest oncology units in Europe. I interviewed, on the basis of anonymity, one of their leading immunologists. 'Why,' I asked, 'is so little attention paid to possible alternative cancer treatments when there are plenty of reports, both published and anecdotal, claiming they could be beneficial?' After a long pause, he replied:

> If you'd asked me that six months ago, I'd have said, 'Because there's no robust evidence to show they work.' However, three months ago, my brother-in-law was diagnosed with glioblastoma [a cancer of the brain, for which survival rates are crushingly low]. I found myself Googling apricot kernels, dodgy clinics in Mexico, health supplements, you name it. When the outlook is so bleak, you become rather more open-minded.

Sara Riggare is a Swedish researcher at Karolinska Institutet, who is living with Parkinson's disease. She's also researching the links between Eric von Hippel's theories on 'lead innovators' and self-care medicine. She defines 'lead patients' as patients (or family members) living with or caring for people who have serious illnesses, who have developed innovative strategies to maximise quality of life. Research suggests that up to 8% of patients with rare diseases have developed innovations that were unknown to the medical science community. According to Riggare, as many as 45% of patients could potentially become lead patients.

So that's two professionals who, having experienced chronic conditions first-hand, are determined to listen to lead patients and learn from their experiences. But, as we discovered in Chapter Three, we're moving from simply sharing what we know to sharing what we create. Take IT consultant and citizen scientist, **Tim Omer**.

Tic-Tac technology

Tim has lived with type 1 diabetes for over 20 years. He was frustrated that, even if he could afford a continuous glucose monitor (CGM) to get real-time data on his glucose levels, it would not talk to his mobile phone. He connected with the 'Nightscout' forum – an online community of parents (their hashtag is #WeAreNotWaiting) who wanted to see their diabetic children lead more normal lives, including the ability to safely engage in sleepovers at their friends' houses. Together they created open-source software that continuously monitors glucose levels. The key processing components in Tim's CGM sit in a discarded Tic-Tac box (this is true *jugaad* innovation) and the code Tim created drastically reduced costs, while ensuring that patients could avoid buying closed software.

You would think there'd be real commercial potential in such ingenious solutions, wouldn't you? So did Tim and Nightscout, and several producers were approached. Their response was: 'We'd need regulatory approval and probably a 10-year clinical trial period before we could go into production.' So, they decided to give the designs and operational guides away for free, on their website. As Tim said:

> As patients, we do not want to wait for the industry to regulate us, to tell us what we can and cannot do, on the devices that WE own, or the information they produce. We're not waiting anymore; we will innovate ourselves.

Buoyed by their success, Tim and Nightscout have been developing increasingly more ambitious projects. xDrip is their insulin pump that uses data from the CGM to administer the correct dosage of insulin. They also found a creative way around the nerdy exclusivity that sometimes hinders open-source software. As we've seen already, the most powerful learning associated with mass ingenuity has a strong social element, and here's more evidence: Nightscout established xDrip parties, where patients who knew how to build their own insulin pumps taught those who didn't.

At the time of writing, Tim is leading the development of a home-made artificial pancreas system (APS). There's something of a race taking place between patient-innovators and industry producers to get the first APS to market, and it's not hard to see why. The market in the USA alone for an all-in-one, automatic monitoring and dispensing system is estimated to be around $300 million. Industry analysts guess that the first commercial systems will cost around $8,000 to buy and several thousand dollars a year to run. Tim thinks it can be done for a fraction of that and wants to make his self-assembly kit available for free.

The stock response from the industry and legislators has always been: 'But you don't know what you're doing! You're taking risks with people's lives. You need to stop and leave it to the professionals.' Tim countered this argument at a conference at the Institute of Healthcare Improvement, in 2017:

> From a patient perspective, we're not going to stop. We have a condition to manage. We have access to very cheap electronics; we have a world-wide network of communications. We

have very ingenious, passionate and clever people and we're going to see more and more ambitious projects, more bespoke projects. We *should* be careful, we should review, we must be sure to scrutinise. But we should not be afraid. We should not be scared of what, as a patient, we're potentially able to achieve […] From a regulatory point of view, we need to understand that technology progression is measured in days, not years. There are patients out there who are leading and innovating in their care. Patient-to-patient community-led support is the *only* care path where the patient comes first.

Of course, there are risks. But patients with chronic serious illnesses have to take responsibility for their own conditions anyway. Diabetics have to decide on the correct amount of insulin to inject – too little or too much can have disastrous consequences. So isn't it better to have communities of support and innovation to work alongside medical practitioners?

The impatient patient

Much is made of technology-driven rapid advances in the field of healthcare – and with justification. Huge corporate dollars are being invested in biotechnology, machine learning and genomics. And we all need the pace of innovation to continue to accelerate – within acceptable safety guidelines. We should not, however, discount the growing numbers of citizen scientists who are collaborating, experimenting and making significant breakthroughs.

People like **Anna Vonnemann**, who developed ReMoD, a postural device that enabled her daughter, Dindia, to walk again after a paralysing stroke at birth. Or **Mat Bowtell,** the Melbourne-based engineer, who bought a 3D printer and now makes open-source prosthetic limbs for one Australian dollar apiece (their commercial equivalents sell for around $5,000). Matt could easily have sold his designs and made a small fortune. Instead, he insists upon making his designs widely available on his website (free3dhands.org.au) so that user-innovators can access them freely anywhere in the world.

Innovation without risk isn't innovation

We ought to remember that there's a long-established tradition of medical researchers – professional and amateur – experimenting on themselves. Indeed, some of the truly breakthrough treatments might never have surfaced without their courage (or recklessness, depending on which side of the ethical sofa you sit). Marie Curie, alongside her husband, Pierre, conducted experiments on radioactivity, most notably discovering polonium (named after her native Poland) and radium. It was said that she regularly walked around with test tubes of radium in her lab-coat pockets and later died of aplastic anaemia, attributed to prolonged exposure to radiation. Australian doctor Barry Marshall drank a broth with *Helicobacter pylori* mixed in to prove that ulcers weren't stress-induced or psychosomatic but were actually caused by bacteria in the gut. He chose not to tell the ethics committee at his hospital, knowing they would attempt to block him. His breakthrough discovery won him a Nobel Prize in physiology.

Given these predecessors, the contemporary rise of 'biohacking' (hobbyists carrying out genetic experiments) is, therefore, to be expected. The difference now is that, unlike Marshall, who didn't even tell his wife about his experiment, biohackers frequently livestream on social media. They're buying and selling CRISPR gene-editing kits (they start at just $159) and making their experiments more radical and easier to copy. Perhaps the best-known of these is **Josiah Zayner**, who edited his own genes using CRISPR and, for his next experiment/stunt, performed a faecal transplant to attempt to rid himself of debilitating gut issues. To the great annoyance of the academic community, the 'poop swap' worked.

So, we've arrived at a critical point. Gene editing is developing at frightening speed. It will soon be possible to 'print' genetic code at home on machines that cost a couple of thousand dollars. Burkina Faso is preparing to inject mosquitoes, in 2022, with edited genes that could potentially eliminate malaria. Such 'gene drives', in the wrong hands, also have the potential to be weaponised to unleash future global pandemics. It's inevitable that people with incurable conditions would be willing to take high personal risks. HIV patient **Tristan Roberts** did just that, injecting himself with the N6 gene, live on YouTube, in an attempt to rid himself of the side effects of the antiretroviral drugs he has to take. It didn't work, but, at the time of writing, he hasn't abandoned his quest. Who knows, in time we may come to view such biohackers as latter-day versions of Marie and Pierre Curie, or Barry Marshall.

There are, of course, significant risks in biohacking. But solutions won't come from driving it underground. As George Church, Harvard Professor of Genetics and widely seen as the father of gene editing, argued, in an interview with *Popular Science* magazine, the way to balance the risk/reward inherent in the safety debate is strict licensing, coupled with open education:

> You can't just hoard your ideas inside the ivory tower. You have to get them out into the world [...] We went from a world where almost nobody knew anything about computers to a world where almost all of us are computer geeks for a huge fraction of our day. And I'd like to see that happen with the digital world of biological molecules too.

Attempting to slow the progress of these biohackers, through arcane and unnecessary over-regulation, will be counter-productive. Far better for governments, corporations and regulatory bodies to adopt an approach of curious humility because, as Eric von Hippel has demonstrated, no one understands a problem better than the users. When it comes to health innovation, those problems are understood by relatively small numbers of patients. With the novel coronavirus outbreak, however, suddenly the entire world's population became interested in accelerating research and novel treatments. Our tolerance for risk became greater, as did our intolerance of institutional over-regulation and arrogance.

I'll close this section with two pro-ams who, driven by tragically sad personal circumstances, are successfully building bridges between the academic research world, and the lead patients who follow less conventional routes.

Pan Pantziarka is a warm and softly spoken Greek Cypriot scientist. His particular focus is the micro-environment that cancer cells need in order to flourish. He was keen for me to know that he'd had no formal medical training. His son, George, was diagnosed with his first cancer shortly after his first birthday and had three different cancers before his fifteenth birthday. He was diagnosed with hereditary Li–Fraumeni syndrome – a mercifully rare propensity to multiple cancers. In memory of George, Pan established the George Pantziarka TP53 Trust, a support and advocacy platform for the condition. The ReDo (Repurposing Drugs in Oncology) project has grown out of the Trust and aims to make patients aware of the use of existing and well-tolerated 'off-label' generic drugs to help starve cancers of the necessary growing conditions. These drugs are intended to support, not replace, existing conventional treatments. They all have well-documented anti-cancer properties, despite not being initially designed for that purpose. Most are extremely common and very cheap to manufacture: metformin (a diabetes drug); hydroxychloroquine (an anti-malaria treatment subsequently – and wrongly – touted by Donald Trump as the treatment that could end the coronavirus pandemic); cimetidine (an antacid); thalidomide (an immunomodulatory drug originally and infamously prescribed for pregnant women with early morning sickness, with disastrous results, now routinely prescribed for multiple myelomas). There have been 270 drugs already identified as 'safe' (i.e. having low toxicity), with 75% of them under expired patents and therefore cheap to manufacture.

So, why haven't we heard about them? Simply because most clinical drug trials are funded by large pharmaceutical companies who need a return on investment to cover their substantial development costs. There's no money to be made in generic (i.e. 'off-patent') drugs, even if they do have significant alternative uses in cancer treatments, so it's very difficult to get studies funded. Without the coronavirus pandemic, it's unlikely that we'd have even heard of hydroxychloroquine.

The movement for repurposing existing drugs has largely been overlooked by regulators and big pharmaceutical companies alike. Once it became clear that a Covid-19 vaccine wouldn't be available for at least a year, however, repurposed drugs suddenly became a regular topic for news reporters. Globally, over 1,100 accelerated trials were instigated, of which over 700 were investigating the efficacy of repurposed drugs. ReDo monitored every single one of them, presenting interim reports on their website.

I found another bridge-builder in a quiet neighbourhood in Eindhoven, Netherlands. **Daniel** was working as a scientist during the day and taking care of his wife, Mihaela, in the evenings and weekends. Like Pan, he has no medical qualifications but has the essential skills of a lead innovator: an urgent need, innate curiosity, a formidable desire to help people and a passion for learning. Growing up in Romania under the regime of the Communist dictator, Nicolae Ceaușescu, he realised the only way to build a better life would be to study in Western Europe. He arrived in the Dutch city of Nijmegen with 10 euros in his pocket and was accepted for a PhD in physics. In 2013, Daniel's mother had been diagnosed with colon cancer and his wife was found to have a rare and aggressive form of adrenocortical cancer and was given months to live. As Daniel put it: 'That is the strongest motivation you can have – to find a solution to their cancers.'

It's a commercial reality that relatively little research is carried out on rarer forms of cancer, and their situation became ever more desperate when the only thing the hospital would offer was chemotherapy, with only the promise that it might extend Mihaela's life by a few months, not years. So, Daniel, with his scientific background, set about learning everything he could about both the disease and potential treatments. Once they had enough understanding, they felt that he could start Mihaela on a course of treatment. But, as 'non-qualified' persons, weren't they concerned about the risks involved?

> When you step into the new, you have to take small steps – if you take a small step and something goes wrong, you can step back. People make mistakes because they move too fast. So that was our strategy – take small and informed steps; get information from as unbiased sources as possible, and then apply it. But, of course, there are risks and it was very painful: with one eye I was smiling – as we were seeing a response – but with another, I was crying. We were stepping into the unknown.

I visited Daniel and had the privilege of meeting Mihaela before she finally lost her battle with cancer, years beyond the hospital's prognosis. He showed me 'the pharmacy' – a shed in the garden with masses of pills, supplements and formulations. It's important to stress that Daniel wasn't just following treatments that were gathering attention on forums. He applied his scientific training to the process, only experimenting with treatments for which there were reputable peer-reviewed studies, where limited applications had been approved on compassionate grounds, not simply anecdotal evidence: 'What I learned was that you need to have filters to identify value because the world is full of anecdotal stories. But I have a very open mind, so I listened to everything.'

By now, Daniel had legions of cancer patients and carers who asked for advice, to the point where his own health was beginning to suffer. He established a not-for-profit foundation,[2] working with universities, institutes and foundations in Europe and the USA.

Lead patients and the war on complacency

And this is the critical point behind this book – we are witnessing a wave of user-innovation, which is too often being dismissed by established institutions. They have a choice. Ignore them, regulate them to the point of impotence or work with them. We'd all be better off if they chose the latter.

As these are matters of life and death, let me be clear: I'm not saying that 'big pharma' already has the cure for cancer, yet it's withholding it in the interests of shareholder profits. I'm not saying that eating mushrooms or goji berries or even *carrots* are the secrets *they* don't want you to know about. Anyone working to defeat this deadly disease would love to be the person who came up with a cure, whether it was on- or off-patent. But I am saying that producers like pharmaceutical companies have little incentive to look at widely available compounds that can be effective, simply because their *raison d'être* is to return a profit (while benefiting patients). So they're not able to fund large-scale studies into drugs in which they have no financial stake. That leaves a vacuum, which lead patient-innovators are having to step into. Why? Because needs must. They have skin in the game – either they, or their loved ones, are dying, so they will consider *anything*. The examples I've shared in this chapter highlight the need for a balance to be

2 The Mihaela Catalina Stanciu Foundation for Life – if you would like to support it, I can't think of a worthier cause.

struck – between bottom-up ingenuity and top-down statutory protection – and for doors to be kept open. And, as we've seen, in times of emergency, it is impossible for our national institutions to be able to respond as swiftly as an army of volunteer inventors, hackers and makers.

As with almost all of the industries featured in this book, the health industry tends to see the informed patient – let alone the user-innovator – as a threat, rather than the wonderful opportunity for collaboration that it should be. The response to that threat too often ranges from condescension to litigation (which is why I have changed some of the names of people I've interviewed). It's a tragedy, because the fruitful path would be to establish cooperative alliances. And unless you intend to shut down the internet, pro-am patients are the new normal. People are not going to *choose* to be uninformed about their health. So let's bring user-innovators and producers together. We shouldn't have to wait for moments of personal or national crises before we unleash the power of us.

Key points:

- The urgency faced by lead patients often ensures the most ingenious solutions.
- The Covid-19 pandemic has significantly recalibrated development and safety timescales.
- The pandemic has also brought together user-innovators, lead patients and producers in a powerful, effective alliance.
- Can we take those recalibrations, lessons learned and new alliances in the After Corona world?

CHAPTER SIX

The Values and Attitudes Driving the Power of Us

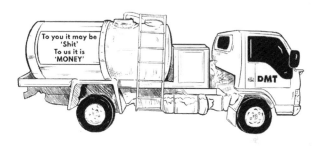

Isaac Durojaiye (also known as Otunba Gaddafi) was a very big man. Almost seven feet tall, weighing 300 pounds, he was also a very smart man. He moved from his native Nigeria to the UK to study graphic design. But something kept nagging at him to go back home and help his country. So he did. Finding work back in Lagos proved difficult and, given his physique, it was no surprise that he worked as a security guard. On one assignment, in 1991 – planning a wedding party – Isaac was astonished to see that there were likely to be two toilets to serve 10,000 guests. This was far from unusual for Nigeria – all but the super-wealthy would use any bush that could provide cover in order to defecate. As a big guy, Isaac was well aware of the lack of discretion and dignity in such a public spectacle.

So he was determined to find more portable toilets for the bride and groom's big day. Except he couldn't source any. This was his light bulb moment.

Isaac realised that people would be willing to pay a small amount to go about their business in private. So he set about building mobile toilets. And I do mean mobile – with wheels. Initially, there was little demand, so Isaac continued his security work. Working at an Interpol conference in 1999, he saw the lightweight Portaloos we all know from building sites and pop festivals, and imported 40 of them. Charging a nominal amount to use them, he was able to establish Dignified Mobile Toilets (DMT) in 2002 and rapidly grew the business. As a social entrepreneur, Isaac persuaded 'area boys' (gang leaders) and widows to keep the toilets clean in return for a small wage. DMT soon expanded to cover many major cities in West Africa, improving public sanitation and creating employment. In 2000, Nigeria had less than 500 public toilets. By 2011, there were more than 5,000, thanks almost entirely to Isaac and DMT.

But that's not all. At the time of his tragic death in 2012, Isaac was working on a plan to turn human waste into biogas fuel and the remaining pulp into fertiliser.

Little wonder that Isaac's slogan was 'Shit business is serious business'. The vehicles that collect the waste for processing had boldly emblazoned large lettering on their sides: 'To you it may be "shit" – to us it's MONEY'. To Isaac's workers, human poo was effectively their bread and butter (I really hope you're not eating anything right now), but it was also pushing the boundaries of science. We perhaps don't take seriously enough the consequences of not dealing with human waste. In Kenyan slums there are significant health risks from so-called 'flying toilets'. People living without household sanitation usually defecate into a plastic bag and then throw it into the streets. They're not only endangering public health; they're literally throwing money away – it's estimated that waste from Kenyan slums could generate 10,000 kilowatts of energy per day. Further, the poo-to-power process uses biodigesters to remove disease-causing pathogens from the excrement, making it safe to be used as fertiliser, and the process stops methane gas from escaping into the atmosphere. It's a win-win-win-win-win situation: preserving dignity, creating employment, combating global warming and generating an alternative fuel source. And it all started with a security guard trying to keep a bride and groom happy on their big day.

How values and attitudes shape the power of us

Chapter Four examined user-innovators' mindsets and how they frequently differ from producer mindsets. Chapter Five detailed the ways in which critical circumstances – personal as well as global – can propel people-powered innovation. This chapter delves into the values and attitudes that shape those mindsets, and how more mainstream organisations can learn from them. DMT wasn't dealing in excrement – it was dealing in values and attitudes: the human dignity of people in poverty mattered. Sub-Saharan Africa Africa is not helpless – it can play a vital part in limiting the worst effects of the climate emergency and finding local solutions to persistent unemployment improves public health and public safety.

Of course, communities of user-innovators don't have a monopoly on doing the right thing. But values and attitudes play a big role in firstly *connecting* people, and then not simply in *how* we figure things out but also *why*. So, while there are many more values and attitudes, the four that I found most frequently emerging, from both the desk research and the case study visits, were as follows:

1. **Foster communities, not competition.**
2. **Stay true to your roots.**
3. **Find your tribe.**
4. **Don't try to fake it.**

1. Foster communities, not competition

Mass ingenuity occurs when a community swarms over a problem to fix it more quickly. That didn't begin with hackathons, but it's remarkable how many processes, now commonly used in business, originated from a bunch of geeks. Take, for example, the Homebrew Computer Club which met in (the other) Menlo Park, California, in 1975. Word quickly got out that, although they looked like a bunch of hippies, the participants there were collaborating on some pretty cool stuff. Two of the regular hobbyists attending Homebrew (motto: 'Give to help others') were the two Steves – friends who would later become the founders of Apple Inc: Jobs and Wozniak. Consider that for a moment: the personal computer grew out of a weekly social gathering, not via a mission statement or a business plan. What was the specific problem they were trying to fix? Well, this may surprise you, but, at that time, it was impossible to walk into a shop and simply buy a computer. You had to build one yourself. That's why the Homebrew faithful congregated – not to give birth to the knowledge economy but just to build a computer for their own personal use. In an interview with cnet.com, Wozniak recalls the excitement he felt as circuit board data sheets were handed around:

> That night the full image of the Apple I popped in my head, and I knew that I'd have my own useful computer, [for] basically no money. I'd just add a microprocessor to my terminal, which had the human input and output. I'll never forget that first night.

That spirit of reciprocity defined the group, so it was not surprising that many of the early attendees of Homebrew club went on to lead microcomputing corporations, thus ensuring that Silicon Valley was located in California.

Given the somewhat unconventional, nerdy attitudes found within the Homebrew Computer Club, it was to be expected that there'd be no formal 'teachers' dispensing wisdom. Facilitation and peer learning defined the experience. Facilitators are the midwives of mass ingenuity. The sense of community was further enhanced by the free distribution of designs and codes being developed. It's therefore a supreme irony that Apple, which grew out of an open community of peer producers operating on open-source principles, subsequently pulled up the drawbridge, becoming a notoriously 'closed' company.

Decades after picking the brains (and codes) of Homebrew's participants, Steve Jobs launched the first iPhone. It hosted a small range of closed apps, all owned by Apple. Jobs appeared to work on the assumption that we'd all be grateful simply to be allowed to be the cool kids with the new phone (and he was largely correct in this assumption). Apple was subsequently alarmed to discover that roughly 1 in 4 of all iPhones had been 'jailbroken' – developers had hacked the phone so that it could host a variety of apps (most of them free to users) written with alternative software. Apple's response, initially, was to try and close such jailbreaks down. It was now in direct competition with the open-source community from which it had emerged.

That strategy didn't work, however, so they created the app store. This gave the *chimera* of being open-source, whilst retaining all the control and capturing all of the value (130 billion downloads and counting). It's at this point that I should introduce you to Benjamin Mako Hill. Benjamin may not be a household name, but I'm willing to bet that you've had cause to thank him (as have I, on *many* occasions). He is a fascinating cross between an academic and a user-innovator but is perhaps best known as the person who wrote the little bit of code that pops up to remind you to include the attachment to the email you just wrote. Naturally, he wrote it in open-source code, so that as many people as possible could be reminded, without paying for the reminder.

Mako Hill is an authority on the open-source software movement and has a three-stage chronology of its history:

1. Open-source software created a social movement.
2. It invented new forms of mass collaboration.
3. That collaboration was so successful that the proprietary world learned from it and is now outsmarting it.

And that, according to Mako Hill, should be a cause for celebration not resentment. Speaking of the development of the Apple app store, he said:

> They've learned from us (the free software community). The app store is *not* free software, and it's *not* peer production [...] It was an example of how big companies could create something that looked a lot like peer production and open-source without having to get their hands covered in freedom.

It must be said that there are many within the open-source community who find it hard to match Mako's Hill generosity. This process of 'strategic openness' – giving the appearance of being the good guys, while conveniently keeping the competition in check – is often ridiculed by those who are a little more sceptical about corporate mindsets. Let's return to BrewDog for a moment. There are some who see the collaborations I mentioned earlier – specifically, partnering with (by now) much smaller craft breweries to create new, shared recipes – as reinforcing the community of open learning from which they profited; giving back, in other words. Others might see it as a cynical marketing ploy while reminding the opposition who the big fish are in the pond. In short, another example of strategic openness.

Strategic openness isn't just practised by multinational corporations. You see it every time a school encourages the 'student voice' but limits students to designing a new badge for the school uniform rather than redesigning the curriculum. It's evident every time a company launches a crowdsourcing campaign but ringfences what their customers can comment upon. This inevitably leads us to the next value.

2. Stay true to your roots

User-innovators, by and large, are not in it for the money. It's quite rare for someone to have emerged from a tin-shed culture to a penthouse office. It's even rarer for those few who do to retain the respect of their founding community, as we'll see with Yvon Chouinard, CEO of Patagonia. So, a key currency within these communities is respectful attribution and staying true to your roots. That's what would distinguish, say, Benjamin Mako Hill from, say, Steve Jobs. And if you *don't* become the most profitable company in the world, forgetting where you came from can have real consequences.

Billabong gone…

The provenance of surfing innovations, everything from boards, to apparel, to culture, has deep roots in the user community. In 2013, I interviewed Rusty Miller. He's an authentic surfing legend: US Surfing Champion in 1965; the first surfer to discover the mountainous waves of Uluwatu, Bali; a surfing coach all his life, and still teaching in his 70s. He made clear to me how he thought that the distortion of surfing – from a grassroots philosophical movement, inspired by the graceful moves of its Hawaiian originators, to stunts, fast-cut videos and lifestyle magazine articles – was propagated by big businesses. None of this bothered companies like

Billabong, who made fortunes out of the crass commercialisation of the lifestyle. Ultimately, however, the custodians of the surfing ethos have longevity. Provenance matters, and the historic pioneer inventors are regarded with due respect, bordering on reverence.

That spirit of board shaping and peer production allowed Billabong (and Quicksilver and the like) to hop onto the wave of popularity and exploit it. By 2000, Billabong had become a publicly listed company. Ultimately, however, lead user-innovators (to use von Hippel's designation) like Rusty carried more weight within the surfing community. New converts to surfing realised that they didn't have to buy their kit from conglomerates. Instead they could choose to support shapers and makers – the artisans – who were authentically from that community. So, they took their custom elsewhere, and Billabong's fortunes went into freefall. By 2014, Billabong had sold its empire of shops for $1 a share. A similar fate befell MySpace. Originally a thriving user-led platform for new music, it was acquired by Rupert Murdoch, at which point the founding community of musicians packed up their tents and moved elsewhere. Murdoch lost over $550 million on the bet that user-innovators would be content with their archive being managed by a business mogul.

It's a historical fact though that Billabong and Quicksilver were founded by surfers. It seems that chasing the waves of popularity and profitability led to a loss of identity. The 'Billabong Effect' – or call it the 'MySpace Syndrome' – hangs around people-powered innovation like a bad rash. So the next attitude becomes key.

3. Find your tribe

Yochai Benkler, a Harvard Law School professor, has been described as 'the leading intellectual of the information age', and as long ago as 2005 he was giving TED talks on the growth of collaborative communities. He's been at this a while and frequently reminds audiences that the most commonly used software systems were created not by Microsoft, IBM or other tech giants but by collections of volunteers freely giving their spare time to develop free open-source software (Linux, Debian, Ubuntu, et al.). Benkler argues that collaborative communities engaged in peer production place great store in what he calls 'pro-social, intrinsic motivations' (are they making the lives of their community – or planet – better?) rather than financial, extrinsic drivers.

According to Benkler, having such tightly knit, pro-social values does not hinder efficiency or effectiveness. In fact, he believes it's quite the reverse, maintaining that these motivations ensure that 'commons-based innovation outpaces proprietary innovation' (communities outperform bureaucracies). This is quite a bold claim, so it's worth digging a little deeper into Benkler's explanation. He suggests that there are two properties within collaborative communities that aren't routinely found in commercial groupings. Firstly, there is **motivational diversity** (people have a variety of reasons for wanting to work together). As we saw with the analysis of motivations for people attending hackathons, some have a strong moral purpose, others want to learn, while still others just want to make friends with like-minded people. Secondly, effective collaborative communities have **social integrity**. This is a phrase which could be defined in multiple ways. Here's how Benkler sees social integrity: **offering a shared identity and social meaning that keeps teams as persistent learning networks with long-term direct and indirect reciprocity and mutual social recognition.** In other words, when people are figuring something out collectively, for love, not money, they:

- know who they are, and why they're together;
- want to learn from others – and share what they know, without the need for financial inducement or coercion;
- know that their contribution, and the contribution of others, will be recognised and valued.

Let me stress that this chapter is all about understanding why some groups work and others are just painful to be a part of. It's not about 'personal chemistry' or establishing a clear line of command. It's about understanding what drives them, what matters to them and how that helps them find solutions more quickly. Nor is there an assumption that you'll only find this useful if you happen to share a hobby with others. This is useful if you work with *any* group of people, and you are trying to help them become more effective.

4. Don't try to fake it

A few years ago, Campbell's Soup launched their 'Ideas for Innovation' portal, looking for ideas for new products. They seemed pleased with the 5,000 initial suggestions they received – a minor miracle, considering that they said it might take six months to respond, and that rejected ideas would not get an explanation for their failure. In one patently insincere attempt at crowdsourcing ideas, they managed to reverse all of Benkler's key characteristics of collaborative communities. There was no learning, no reciprocity and no social recognition. This is as superficial an illustration of people-powered innovation as sending innumerable requests to connect on LinkedIn, so that you can boast about the size of your network. People can see when you try to fake it.

Here's another example, involving another household brand: Couchsurfing.com (that's not the household brand – few people have even heard of it, let alone used it) was created in 2003, based upon open-collaboration principles. To this day, no one is allowed to charge visitors to sleep on their couch – Couchsurfing bans the exchange of money.

Airbnb (founded in 2008 and now very much a household brand) was originally set up along the same lines as Couchsurfing. The one big difference was that, as its popularity grew, a lot of money changed hands. Airbnb takes 3% of all bookings, so their $30 billion self-valuation is entirely plausible – or at least it was until the coronavirus lockdown kicked in. Airbnb has essentially, and cleverly, appropriated the tools of the commons (the ratings system, community forums) but beaten the commons at its own game. We're supposed to feel like we're supporting the sharing economy when we stay at an Airbnb property, but when hotels are being listed on the site – thus squeezing out the private homeowners – it's clearly a long way from Airbnb's founding principles. In reality, it's faking the values and attitudes of Couchsurfing. Why should they care if the money continues to pour in? I'd speculate that, with its community forum increasingly populated by disgruntled private hosts, and cities beginning to ban Airbnb from operating, people are starting to call 'faking it', and its MySpace moment may not be too far away.

So, now that we have explored the mindset, values and attitudes of highly ingenious collaborative communities, we can begin to see how the leadership and culture of the organisation determines their effectiveness. First though, let's look below at a not-for-profit organisation that deeply understands the mindsets of communities and helps lever the way groups think, feel and act to enable them to have more control of their lives and their immediate neighbourhoods.

Key points:

- Cultivating mass ingenuity is dependent upon the integrity of the group across various contexts: social, motivational, aspirational and facilitation.
- Collaborative communities can outperform mainstream institutions if they place values at the heart of their composition.

- Maintaining a commitment to the founding principles of the collaboratives you work with, or come from, will sustain their support and investment. Moving away from those shared values can have catastrophic consequences.
- Effective collaboration requires a spirit that values learning, reciprocity and social recognition.

CASE STUDY: REPOWERING

'We have a systems failure.'
Agamemnon Otero

Looking for a leader in a not-for-profit, I headed back home following a tip-off from my long-time friend and colleague, Mark Stevenson. He told me about a project based in South London and made me promise him I would ask Co-CEO Agamemnon Otero about his own back story. Now I know why.

Brixton is a district in London that came to global prominence during three days in April 1981. The Brixton riots saw a short but intense uprising of young black men against London's police. At that time, Brixton had some of the worst housing in the country and some of the highest unemployment rates – 65% of those without work were black; the police used the deeply unpopular practice of 'stop and search' and young black men were disproportionately singled out. During the Brixton riots, 280 police and 45 members of the public were injured, and 150 buildings were damaged, with an estimated 5,000 police involved. Copycat riots across the UK soon followed in areas where social deprivation was evident and racial tensions had been simmering. Brixton came to represent Britain's neglect of Afro-Caribbean communities.

These days Brixton is multi-racial and well into the process of gentrification. However, it did not escape from the spike in knife crime in London in 2018/19. That said, I've never personally felt unsafe in the area and so had no qualms about visiting Repowering's offices, housed in a modest building, directly opposite the legendary Brixton Academy music venue.

Repowering is a cooperative dedicated to empowering communities in London to control and generate energy. But that description doesn't do it justice. It's also a training and employment agency, an educational project, a community investment fund, a solar panel manufacturer, and the force behind 40 'energy gardens' at overground railway stations in London. Oh, and did I mention the UK's first two blockchain-powered peer-to-peer energy trading pilots? The dropping of 'London' from its title indicates an ambition to diversify and grow. When you meet Agamemnon, you can see why.

First, I promised you his back story: Agamemnon is an unusual name, and Otero's arrival into the world no less so. Agamemnon was a king from Greek mythology who famously sailed his troops to Troy to wage war against the Trojans. His name in Greek means 'steadfast, unbowed' (two handy qualities of leaders). *This* Agamemnon (Otero) had a father who made a living diving for rare metals in shipwrecks off the coasts of Uruguay and Brazil. When his mother was pregnant, Agamemnon used to kick constantly in her womb unless she was in water. So she spent the whole of her pregnancy bathing in a coastal port in Uruguay. That port was where one of Admiral Horatio Nelson's ships, *HMS Agamemnon*, was shipwrecked. 'So my name had to be Agamemnon.'

His remarkable early life continued. By the time he was 24 years old he had discovered his second cancer – stage-four testicular – while working as an artist-in-residence in the Highlands of Scotland. After intense chemotherapy, he lived in a small cottage on the Findhorn river: 'I'd come out of chemotherapy and go straight into the river, with salmon swimming over me, and I thought: *This is the perfect way to be dying – or living.*' The second cancer provoked a rethink of… Well, everything: family, friends, money, systems. He resolved to enjoy good health (and he looked a picture of just that when I met him) and to find a way to use his maker skills in bringing people together.

A means to an end

So, how did Agamemnon become involved in solar energy? Expecting a technical explanation of the centrality of renewable energy platforms within public policy, I was a little taken aback by his response:

> Solar is just a means to an end. This is the best solution right now, but in the future there will be better solutions. It's about finding a financial mechanism that provides a revenue stream to support well-being in communities […] London uses 13% of the UK's total energy generation; as a country we spend £117 billion a year on energy. Lambeth borough is spending £160 million a year on energy – and there's only 350,000 people living here! What if we invested that money into energy generation in a renewable, zero-carbon way? What if we grouped together to buy that energy? What if we did practical learning around the finance, technical, legal, media, marketing of how to own and manage that? In fellowship, yes, but building a succinct, clear, business case towards well-being.

And that, in a nutshell, is Repowering. It's a beautifully circular programme of self-sufficiency: a community fund is established, with a guaranteed 3–4% interest for investors, which pays for the making of solar panels, made by young local trainees (who gain skills, employment and a qualification along the way); the panels go on the rooftops of social housing blocks, schools and hospitals, discounting energy bills for occupiers; the surplus energy is sold back to the government, which then supports the administration costs of the new cooperative, self-sustaining community. Rinse and repeat. All over London (and soon, further afield).

The Energy Garden cooperative is similarly circular. People nominate overground train stations in London and track-side spaces to be gardened. The harvest is not only fruit and veg, but also energy. Solar panels are planted alongside edible gardens in and around stations; school kids learn about real food by growing vegetables and herbs, and about science by installing the panels; the energy generated helps pay for maintenance; the energy gardens generate sales of crops, honey, even beer (there's an Energy Garden Ale). As Agamemnon observes, the gardens transform drab stations: 'Once corridors of urban grey and we've turned them into arteries of support and health for a resilient city.' At the time of writing, energy gardens have greened over 20,000 square metres of London – that's about the same as New York's High Line.

Repowering's Co-CEO is Dr Afsheen Rashid. She joined Repowering after advising the UK government on energy and climate change. Together, Afsheen and Agamemnon bring a powerful mix of advocacy and vision, together with technology and business smarts. A cornerstone of Repowering's success, however, is a commitment to building relationships. Because they work primarily with people who form closely-knit collaborative communities, Afsheen and Agamemnon have a deep understanding of the mindset, values and attitudes that collaborative communities (as described in Chapter Six) are built upon. They understand the need to not fake it, to honour the tribe and to stay true to your founding principles. Agamemnon is acutely aware of the need to achieve financial viability, but it cannot be at the expense of the communities they serve. Businesses cannot be immune to the societal shifts they see around them. Speaking at the Atlas of the Future Conference, in 2019, he zeroed in on the crisis at the heart of the current turbulence:

> Right now, people feel disenfranchised. We have a systems
> failure. Young people don't feel invigorated to go out and take
> a space in society. It's not that they don't want to learn, it's
> that they feel there is not a way in. Adults feel excluded too.
> We believe that companies don't have to be divorced from
> community development – they should be at the heart of it.

After an hour in his company, I realised why this Uruguayan-born,
adopted Londoner, with movie-star looks and a mythical handle,
was awarded an honour (Member of the British Empire) by the
Queen. He sees connections where others see problems. He sees peer
production as a vehicle for societal transformation. This isn't just
people-powered money, or people-powered education and training,
or even people-powered energy. He's not Repowering electricity –
he's repowering *people*, and that's a much more significant force:

> My job is about how to facilitate – not do it for people – an
> egalitarian, sustainable, resilient future that feeds positivity
> back to that community. In some cases, we use batteries,
> solar thermal, biodigesters, whatever. We have paid accredited
> training for over 100 trainees, over 2,500 kids going through
> our schools' programmes. We're using art, dancing and acting
> to invigorate the concept of how to learn about sustainability,
> without being prescriptive about them being solar installers or
> gardeners. We have programmes that use gardening and solar
> to talk about things that are real: how to connect interperson-
> ally, running a business, communicating what you're doing.

Bringing user-innovators and producers together

One of Repowering's immediate targets is to eliminate the dreaded
electricity meters, loathed as symbols of lack of trust by people

on limited incomes. Their solution is to use community-owned blockchain technology to allow people to trade their surplus energy through supplying batteries. This is a UK first, and it's important to stress that it came about through a request from users to have more control of the energy they were now generating. They wanted to be able to buy energy from specific sources (say, the solar panels on their local school), so that community projects would benefit. They also wanted to be able to gift their excess energy, or sell it at a discount, to family members and friends. A complex collaboration between resident groups, Repowering, EDF (a national energy utility) and University College London have demonstrated mass ingenuity in a way that the *Financial Times* predicted will change the entire energy market, stating that 'households will increasingly buy their energy from local sources, such as neighbours or local businesses that generate their own electricity via solar panels or wind turbines'.

As a leader, however, the most important skill Agamemnon brings is engagement: knowing how to engage people in believing in themselves and their communities; knowing how to engage with politicians and investors in seeing beyond the return on investment (ROI); engaging young people in meaningful work; and, perhaps most importantly, knowing how to engage with people as the artist and maker he really is:

> The most demeaning piece of human existence is to not be a part of your own creation. If you want to demoralise someone, give them everything. Struggle is a beautiful thing. If you make a desk for your partner, you start off by thinking: 'If I make this thing, it'll be cheaper than going to IKEA.' After 15 hours, all of that's gone and it's about 'What is your purpose?' Is the process of building something for the person that you love empowering you as much as it is empowering them? Is this item beyond money? Everybody has that choice. What better

way to teach someone how solar energy works than to make the panels with them? Our kids had never grown the food on their plates from scratch. We took them into track-side garden spaces, picked the crops and hung the seeds upside down. In the spring, they shake the seed husks out over a whole garden, they've eaten the food and repropagated a field. THAT'S when they go: 'It's a cycle, and *I did this.*' Food becomes the direct link between their spiritual growth as a human and the consumption of nutrients.

At a time when learned helplessness is disproportionately affecting our urban communities, Repowering is telling a very different story. It's saying: 'No one is coming to save us. But no one needs to save us. We can do this ourselves – we have the *power of us.*' To help people find that voice is just about some of the most important work you can do. And, given the unprecedented set of challenges we're facing in the near future, it's never too soon to start.

Key points:

- Societal influences (like learned helplessness and a crisis of identity) will have an impact upon group mindsets, so don't perpetuate those deficits in the groups you lead.
- When people have greater control of their futures, they are capable of extraordinary feats of invention (as in the peer-to-peer trading platform).
- The sense of concern for others in the community, coupled with agencies whose technical expertise is founded upon the pursuit of a common good, is a powerful combination. If it can change a community, it can change a world.

PART THREE

Operating System

*The way your organisation operates will either feed
or starve its ability to innovate*

CHAPTER SEVEN

Building the Base of Mass Ingenuity

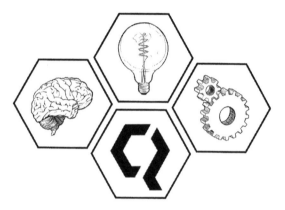

In every organisation, from a computer club to a multinational governmental alliance, there are two fundamentals that need to be in place if you want to thrive: structure and management. This applies just as much to people-powered innovation cultures as it would to a widget factory. The structure and management of an organisation reflects the mindset of its mission, values and purpose. And it builds the base for a culture where mass ingenuity thrives. This section isn't attempting a theoretical analysis of organisational development. Instead, it looks at how people-powered communities operate and shares some of the more radical perspectives that could transform any organisation.

It will hopefully challenge the way you think about your own organisation, and how it's structured and managed. This chapter starts with a reminder of why change isn't an option. Then we'll ask the three big questions shaping structural change, before addressing the question of where to begin. Learning plays such a fundamental role within innovative organisations. It's at the heart of the operating system – and because it's so important, we'll cover it in the next chapter.

Do we *have* to change?

With so much discomfort surrounding any kind of organisational change, there would need to be some very good reasons to warrant significant disruption to the way we work, communicate and innovate. Fortunately, we're spoiled for choice. Thomas L. Friedman's book *Thank You for Being Late* lists the three major accelerations that we're currently living through: technology, globalisation and climate change. Heather E. McGowan (who we met in Chapter Two) and her co-author Chris Shipley, chronicle the scope and speed of these changes. Their book *The Adaptation Advantage* investigates the areas where change is needed most, including education, personal identity, cultural norms, the world of work and global power. They list the five biggest global companies at 50-year inflection points: in 1917, all five were from the 'extractive economy'; in 1967, the top five came from the manufacturing sectors; in 2017, the top five were all from the knowledge/data economy. Their conclusion is that *everything* is changing, and at an accelerating speed. So why should organisations be immune?

The death of the org chart

There once was a world where knowledge and authority trickled down from above. Corporations were long-established, large and complex. So dividing activity into departments and having clear lines of command and control had a kind of internal logic. Laying it out in a neat diagram enabled employees to see how they fitted into the bigger picture. The problem was that, even then, it was also hopelessly inefficient. And everyone knew that it wasn't *really* how decisions were taken – that was a much more subjective, personality-led, prejudicial process. But, now that companies are smaller and need to be more adaptable and nimbler, the traditional org chart is well past its use-by date. In a moment, we'll meet some of the smarter organisations who threw it away some time ago.

The death of the job description

There used to be a time when the function of a particular job was relatively static. The ideal candidate would, therefore, have a predictable set of previous experiences. Their qualifications would act as a filter, because applications far outnumbered vacancies. Even then, however, it was a blunt tool and besides, that 'get-out-of-jail' card ('Any other duties deemed appropriate by your line manager') could always be played when necessary. Then global employers like Google and EY severed the connection between a degree and recruitment. Companies were required to refocus and reorientate on a monthly basis. Furthermore, when an employee's personal network is more valuable than their past experience, companies were getting better hires through using LinkedIn and other social-media platforms.

So, if you want the best people in your organisation, you really don't have much choice but to think differently about your organisational operating system. In a survey undertaken by Deloitte in 2014, 78% of millennials said they wanted to work for a company that encouraged innovation and creative thinking, yet most said they were not getting this at their current company. When asked why not, the top two reasons given were management (63%) and organisational structures and procedures (61%).

There are other, better ways of rebooting your organisation. When you want to get the best ideas from your people, you can take inspiration from the hobbyists, hackers and pro-ams who make change happen for intrinsic reasons, rather than extrinsic rewards. Their operating systems are people-powered not least because, as the roots of the word 'amateur' suggest, they do it for love not money.

The structure and management of innovation: three big questions

1. 'Who's in?'

Consider the challenge facing Procter & Gamble (P&G) at the turn of the millennium. Throughout the twentieth century, P&G had grown rapidly, building a wide range of industry-standard brands, specialising in personal healthcare and household goods. This growth came largely from within the company – they grew their R&D team to around 8,000 employees globally. The disruption to the industry brought on by new technologies, however, meant that even 8,000 wasn't enough to keep up with the pace of innovation. As the new century dawned, P&G's stock value had fallen, from $118 a share to $52. Not many CEOs would know how to arrest that decline. The newly installed boss, A. G. Lafley, issued a bold challenge: reinvent the innovation strategy by bringing half of all new ideas in from the outside.

The porous organisation

This is how P&G's radical 'Connect and Develop' (C&D) programme was born. It's often wrongly represented as an outsourcing policy, when in point of fact it's a really good example of *insourcing*.

Over the next 10 years, C&D doubled P&G's innovation rates, contributing 35% of all new innovations (not quite hitting Lafley's target, but pretty good, all the same). It transformed the company's attitude from 'only invented here' to 'proudly found elsewhere' and was a pioneer in what is now known as 'open innovation'. And C&D succeeds because the barriers to entry are virtually non-existent. On their website, they list technical challenges they've encountered or new development areas that need to grow. If you have an idea, all you have to do is fill in a form. If your solution or new idea is accepted, you are brought into the company on an associate basis.

2. 'Who's in charge?'

What if I told you that there was a company in Silicon Valley that had no hierarchy: their teams were entirely self-managed and had total control of their own budgets; roles and responsibilities were determined by the small teams who actually did the work; remuneration was decided not by bosses but by committee; and there was no Human Resources (HR) department to handle disputes – only an expectation that employees in conflict would figure it out for themselves. What kind of a company would you expect that to be? A tech start-up? A software giant?

The answer is that it's a tomato processing plant. Actually, not just any tomato processing plant – it's the largest in the world. If you've ever eaten a pizza, you've probably sampled Morning Star's product. Employing 600 full-time staff plus around 4,000 seasonal recruits, it is the global market leader, the big tomato, generating annual revenues of around $1 billion.

It's a good example of a new organisational structure which has gained popularity in recent years. It's called *holacracy*. The derivation of holacracy is not, as you'd expect, Ancient Greece. According to Brian Robertson, advocate and author of the book

Holacracy, the term originated in a sci-fi novel written by Arthur Koestler in 1967, *Ghost in the Machine*. For obvious reasons, it's more commonly described as 'self-management'.

The self-managed organisation

In practice, no two organisations implement self-management in the same way. How and how much self-management you champion would depend upon your history, culture and mission. There have been a number of myths surrounding holacracy that haven't helped its cause. 'Where's the structure/org chart?', 'How can you make decisions if no one is in charge?' and 'You can't make a decision until everyone agrees' are just some of the misconceptions. The reality is that there *are* structures – in the form of overlapping circles of activity – and decisions are made by the circles, who usually have a 'lead link'. As for the absence of management, within Morning Star there are many more managers than in a traditional organisation, because *everyone* is responsible, and therefore *everyone* is a manager. Instead of accountability flowing upwards, it flows sideways. Roles are held accountable by a *Colleague Letter of Understanding* which specifies the expectations, deliverables and goals of each employee.

I know that you're thinking this is a recipe for chaos. And, in truth, there have been some attempts at self-managed teams that have been just that. However, two of the most prominent companies to switch to self-management, Valve (the world's biggest video games developer) and Zappos (the world's biggest online shoe retailer), have seen that, when implemented well, self-management enhances what Harvard Professor Teresa Amabile calls 'the quality of the inner work life'. Amabile defines this as 'making daily progress in meaningful work' and the link to self-management is fairly obvious. If you're effectively in control of your own work, making your own decisions and accountable only to your peers, the chances are that you are going to feel fulfilled by what you do.

Holacracy is just one example, albeit a radical one, of new structural models that are emerging to ensure that people feel included in setting the direction of the organisation and monitoring its course. In a self-managed workplace – and high levels of self-direction were apparent in all of the organisations I studied – the benefits accumulate. People are more engaged and happier. Productivity goes up. People accept greater accountability ('with great freedom comes great responsibility') and leadership becomes distributed. Team members become more motivated and encouraged to learn. In the Deloitte study I cited earlier, their conclusion was that 'companies that eschew conventional hierarchies and give more freedom to employees tend to attract young independent-minded talent'. The degree to which you devolve the capacity to make decisions will depend upon a range of circumstances, not least whether your people feel ready for it. But it is clearly an idea whose time has come. Even in the most traditional of organisations (we'll conclude with a civil service department in the Middle East), changes are afoot. The teacher-powered schools movement in the USA is growing rapidly by ensuring that teachers make more of their own decisions – thus helping to stem the alarming rates of attrition within the profession.

3. 'Who have we left out?'

Let's return to the wisdom of Yochai Benkler for a moment. In an essay, published in 2017, entitled 'Peer production, the commons, and the future of the firm', Benkler argued that collaborative communities present a real threat to established commercial organisations, concluding that:

> The best people to solve a given problem are unlikely to work for the firm facing the problem [...] models of innovation that allow diverse people, from diverse settings to work col-

laboratively on the problem will lead to better outcomes than production models.

Let that sink in for a moment. If he's right (and I believe he is), he's saying that organisations trying to figure things out without opening the doors to outsiders are making a big mistake. Indeed, in the essay, he goes so far as to question whether 'firms' have a future at all.

Inclusion and diversity

The impulse to include can come from a number of sources: to some it's just the humane thing to do, while for others it can be the route to organisational loyalty, yet for some people – the smart ones – it's a prerequisite to innovation. It's a mistake to see inclusion as merely a recruitment policy. If you want to tap into the power of us, you need to see the potential for inclusion everywhere: in your members, in your stakeholders and *especially* in your users. P&G's Connect and Develop may have provided a spectacularly successful way of bringing user-innovators into the producer mindset of the corporation, but it also tended to exclude a much-overlooked demographic.

James Surowiecki's *Wisdom of Crowds* famously demonstrated that larger groups of people can make smarter decisions than individuals – however gifted – but *only* if there's diversity within its membership. Noticing a high proportion of early retirees from its company, P&G could see that a significant proportion of its intellectual capacity was being lost – and if it was happening to them, it was probably happening to others. YourEncore is a clever way of retaining that knowledge. From a modest start in 2003, it now hosts over 12,000 retired professionals from life sciences and consumer goods industries, happy to work occasionally to bring 'A world of experience to make a difference in the world' (as their motto has it). Soon we'll examine diversity more fully through the sparks & honey case study. In *Rebel Ideas: The Power of Diverse Thinking*, Matthew Syed argues that all successful organisations need to put diversity at the front of their innovation strategy, not just because it's the right thing to do, but also because a lack of diverse thinking blocks teams from even fully understanding the problem at hand. As Syed maintains:

> The first step for any group seeking to tackle a tough challenge […] is not to learn more about the problem itself. It is not to probe deeper into its various dimensions. Rather it is to take a step back and ask: where are the gaps in our collective thinking? Are we beset by conceptual blinkers? Has homophily[1] pulled us into one tight corner of the problem space? Unless this deeper question is confronted, organisations run the risk of a pervasive glitch in group deliberation: examining a problem, looking ever-deeper, while doing little more than reinforcing their blind spots. We need to address cognitive diversity before tackling our biggest challenges. It is only then that team deliberation can lead not to mirroring but to enlightenment.

So diversity is a smart move if you're genuinely trying to innovate, and hopefully by now I've convinced you of the need to change. There's still one final question to ask:

Where do we start?

There was a common philosophy in every one of the case study organisations I visited: **when developing the power of us, it's more important to think about what you take away than what you add.** Most organisations do the opposite, adding complexity upon

---

1 Homophily is the tendency for people to be attracted to those who are similar to themselves.

complications, until the number of barnacles that are attached to the hull of the ship completely obscures the shape, speed and direction of travel. People working in organisations become resentful of these accumulations of practices and procedures, not least because they can be interpreted to suit individual, contradictory needs. They become even more resentful when things have become so complicated that the dreaded 'restructure' is mandated from above. It isn't just because it makes people anxious: too often it's a tool adopted by management to weed out the personalities that don't fit.

So, I'll finish this chapter with two stories of how change was brought to an organisation, in order to make it more people-powered. The first may be considered too radical for most – even though it started 40 years ago – but it's packed with inspiration. You see, most of the building blocks of people-powered operating systems were hewn by Ricardo Semler some time ago. In case you haven't read his wonderful books, *Maverick* and *The Seven-Day Weekend*, here's a profile of this Brazilian genius:

At just 21, in 1980, Semler took over the reins from his father at the SEMCO Group, a manufacturer of maritime centrifuges – and only maritime centrifuges (it's OK, I had to look it up too). SEMCO is still based in Sao Paolo, Brazil. With such a narrow, though highly specialised, portfolio, it was obvious to Semler that they needed to get some new ideas. On his first day in charge, it's reported that young Semler fired 60% of the senior leaders at SEMCO and set about diversifying the company. This was the start of possibly the most radical, visionary, yet successful experiment in industrial democracy for 100 years. For the next 20 years, the more the business diversified (including HR consultancy, heavy industrial machinery, accounting software, payroll services), the more stripped down its management structures became. They ditched their mission statement (no one believes them anyway); they ditched their org chart; they got staff to set their own salaries (most pitched them lower than the market rate); entrepreneurial employees were encouraged to leave to set up their own business and work with SEMCO as partners (long before we'd heard the word 'frenemies'); SEMCO's structure became atomised in small autonomous satellite teams (Sao Paulo's traffic is horrendous); most significantly, during Semler's 20-year tenure as CEO, SEMCO's annual revenue grew from $4 million to $212 million. Giving a TED talk in 2014, he summarised the entire strategy into a single paragraph:

> We looked at it and we said, let's devolve to these people, let's give these people a company where we take away all the boarding school aspects of this is when you arrive, this is how you dress, this is how you go to meetings, this is what you say, this is what you don't say, and let's see what's left. And so, the question we were asking was, how can we be taking care of people? People are the only thing we have.

In order to realise his dream of 'participative management', Semler urged every remaining employee to ask *why* existing practices were in place and then insisted that managers devolved the solutions back to employees. There are very few examples of what we now consider to be progressive workplace leadership that can't be traced back to Ricardo Semler.

Having secured SEMCO's future, he successfully applied his participative management principles to education, in establishing the Lumiar schools in Brazil. Despite his multiple successes, Semler's actions, almost 40 years after their initiation, are still considered 'radical'. It appears that trusting people to manage themselves is still a scary proposition.

Making the shift

The second example of a starting point is taken from a more traditional sector, in a very traditional location. The Knowledge and Human Development Authority (KHDA) sits on the edge of Dubai, almost in the desert. In a region that's growing exponentially, its government is anxious to keep ahead of the game. I had heard about the Rahhal initiative – a restructuring of education and training that acknowledges informal as well as formal learning, and the entitlement to learning throughout a lifetime – but I became even more interested in how a branch of the civil service could transform itself, in the way that KHDA is seeking to do.

So it was, on a searingly hot day in August, that I found myself in a complex that was more Google than government administration building. All open plan, with treadmills, ping-pong tables, walking tracks, sugar-free snacks, the full nine yards. I was there to meet with the people behind Rahhal, Hind Al Mualla (Chief of Creativity, Happiness and Innovation) and Dr Abdulla Al Karam (Director General of KHDA). I was curious to see why the organisation – essentially a regulatory body for independent schools – had created this working environment, and how they'd gone about it. Dr Al Karam explained how their 12-year journey had brought them to a unique position for a government agency: totally non-hierarchical, self-managed teams:

> We started with the hardware – we tried a 'no doors' policy. Gradually we built a completely open (physical) environment. Some were unhappy, worried about noise – but they were fewer than 10%. That was just the hardware – what about the operating software? We knew it couldn't be hierarchical. So we got rid of the org chart. Then we cancelled Human Resources because they only make people unhappy.

And so it continued. KHDA now operates in a similar way to Morning Star. There are no layers of management, only circles of activity. What used to be HR is now known as the 'Humans of KHDA' circle, involving 20% of the organisation in recruitment, induction and performance management. The 'Thrive' circle has responsibility for well-being and self-directed learning initiatives, the 'EXOG' (Exponential Organisational Growth) circle looks for future innovations and the Delight circle replaces what used to be the customer service function.

Whilst there were understandable teething problems (these are civil servants, after all), the results have been affirming. And Al Karam explained that they were merely getting ahead of the inevitable:

> If you don't have self-management within five years, you won't be able to attract talent. So we've done it while it's still an option. Doing the hardware part is easy, but the significant impact comes when you change the operating system. When you don't have a line manager, when decisions are distributed, it improves efficiency, it improves transparency. But the real reason we've gone to self-management is simply because we feel it is better for our well-being.

Dr Abdulla and his team at KHDA illustrate a common theme throughout these case studies: we cannot expect end users, customers, students, employees to do anything we wouldn't do for ourselves. And their well-being is the starting point, not a happy by-product.

Making structures and systems people-powered

Most people reading this book will position themselves at the producer end of the user-innovator/producer continuum I described earlier. The likelihood is that you're either a producer or you work for a producer. If you've made it this far, it's reasonable to assume that you want to develop the power of us within your organisation.

It's always possible (though unlikely) that you aren't in a position to make your organisation porous, its membership diverse, its entry barriers low enough to welcome users. In that case, Chapter Twelve will provide some tools for bringing user-innovator thinking into your organisation.

Please don't forget, however, that the best way to be infected with the user-innovator mindset is to actually bring user-innovators into the organisation. Through C&D, P&G did it. Valve did it by growing a developer community that creates limitless virtual-reality environments with them. SEMCO, Morning Star and KHDA did it by embedding participative management in their structure. And you can too. Find the customers who are user-innovators. Make your students and parents the people who help you rethink your learning programmes. Turn consumers into co-creators, rather than simply talking to them.

But there's nothing to stop you from bringing them into your structure AND adopting their mindset!

Key points:

- The pace of change is such that organisational systems can't respond to the needs of their people and their users – radical change isn't just needed; it has become inevitable.

- In order to flourish through the power of us, organisations need to become innovation ecosystems, prioritising inclusion and diversity, becoming more porous and lowering entry barriers.

- Since people are more ingenious when they have more control over how decisions are made, the more innovative organisations are instigating self-management principles, according to their capacity for devolution. Small, autonomous teams will invariably outperform hierarchical silos.

- Blanket change can be overwhelming – start small, change one part of the operating software, protect the experiment and monitor carefully.

- The producer-mindset is the dominant mindset in organisations – you can balance this though by incorporating user-innovator thinking – even better if you can make structural changes so that user-innovators become part of your organisation.

CASE STUDY: SPARKS & HONEY

'The human's role is to teach
the machines to be more intelligent.'
Annalie Killian

For a century, 'Madison Avenue' has been a metonym for the advertising industry. It wasn't just used to describe an economic sector – it stood for an *attitude*. If you've seen the TV drama series *Mad Men*, you'll know this. It's what the writer William Safire described as 'gimmicky, slick use of the communications media to play on emotions'.

And so it was that I found myself on Madison Avenue, slap-bang in the middle of Manhattan, New York City, to visit sparks & honey (the lower case is intentional), an organisation that would have hitherto been known as an advertising agency but is, in fact – and this is not hyperbolic – the epitome of the knowledge revolution.

Except I wasn't *quite* on Madison Avenue. I was a block away, on Fifth Avenue, surrounded by policemen and protesters. The reason why I couldn't get to the sparks & honey office, a mere 100 yards away, was because the newly elected US President, The Donald, was in town for a fundraiser. I watched as the procession of at least 60 vehicles passed by and people with placards screamed obscenities at anything with tinted windows, just to be sure. After 20 minutes, I asked one of the policemen how long it might be before I could cross the road. 'We don't know – maybe four, five, hours' was the clipped response.

So I called Annalie.

Annalie Killian is one of the world's great fixers, so a presidential blockade was a mere bagatelle. Juggling social media and Google Maps, Annalie worked out how the locals were circumnavigating road blocks, guided me by phone, charmed New York's finest ('He works here, Officer, and he has a *really* important meeting to attend') and I was in. So much for 'lockdown'.

The episode, as I was to discover, was emblematic of the human/machine interface we're all going to be grappling with and an illustration of what sparks & honey are about: using real-time data mixed with human connections to navigate disruption.

Tangible intangibles

There was a time when everyone knew what you did, and what you did determined where you were. 'Advertising agencies' worked with brands to sell stuff and, if you were big enough, you were based on Madison Avenue. Then came the internet, and from that came the knowledge economy. Brands were no longer solely marketed through traditional media (newspapers, television, radio) and the nature of advertising changed fundamentally. Instead of 'outbound' messaging – pushing products and services to the widest possible audience – the shift to digital meant that 'inbound' messaging – engaging people in a two-way conversation – became cheaper, more targeted and therefore more effective. This shift reconfigured marketing. Now, pretty much anyone could set up in business. Rents in Brooklyn are cheaper than in Manhattan, proximity to tech companies becomes paramount, and so Madison Avenue is no longer the 'must-be' place in which to base yourself.

Furthermore, once you're dealing in knowledge, not just persuasion, a less tangible stock-in-trade becomes possible. Had they been around 10 years ago, sparks & honey would probably have defined their function as an ad agency. Now, they call themselves a 'cultural consultancy' whose goal is to help 'people and institutions understand and shape culture by making change visible, measurable and actionable'. Ahead of my visit, I came across a quote from the founder, Terry Young, which sums up the disruptive intention driving the company: 'I loved the idea, from the very beginning, of being a founder, an entrepreneur in advertising, on Madison Avenue – but can you redefine what the industry is, in exact contrast to what it was in the 1960s?'

Meeting Terry Young in the flesh is about as far away from the Don Draper stereotype (from *Mad Men*) as you can get. Modestly dressed and modestly spoken, he chatted with me in the open office which doubles as a TV studio. He explained how the company had navigated that evolution:

> When we started, in 2012, the vision was to understand human behaviour and therefore make an impact in advertising […] now, the impact is the whole world. It's how do we understand what makes people tick, and how does that become new products, new innovations, new business models? Now we're looking much broader – two-thirds of what we do is outside of the marketing and advertising realm.

There are two immediate signs that sparks & honey is as far removed from the ruthless, slick culture of the advertising industry of the 1960s as you can imagine. The first is the 'open manifesto' that adorns the entrance to their office. It reads more like the declaration of a socialist democracy than a mission statement:

> We believe the future is not just *about* us. But about *all* of us. We believe in inclusiveness. And in business that stands for something bigger than profits […] Our fortunes and futures are inextricably linked, and the time of secrecy, guardedness and closed doors is past […] We believe in business where people

take ownership. Where people bring themselves to work with all their humanity, diversity and passions, free of judgment, and are valued and rewarded for their candour, for their eclectic, exhilarating, unpredictable ideas, abilities and viewpoints.

The second is the daily culture briefing that's held every midday for an hour to a curated live audience of 50 or so people and livestreamed on Facebook. It isn't just the tone of it – witty, fast-paced, inclusive – it's the breath-taking eclecticism and topicality of it. Anything that has surfaced in the previous 24 hours that's culturally interesting is shared, rated, connected and tagged in real time by data scientists, all artfully presented by the two 'briefers'. Culturally, nothing is too highbrow, nor too low, to be left out: the aesthetics of food packaging, licking cane toads to get stoned, consumer financial conservatism, corporate tax avoidance scandals, supermodels carrying books to accessorise their outfits. On the day I attended, they squeezed over 40 cultural 'signals' into less than an hour. Just observing it was exhausting. And tomorrow they do it all again. And the next day.

But it's clearly worth the effort, as is the fact that they're essentially giving away free samples. The daily briefings, and other open events, attract over 5,000 visitors a year to sparks & honey's offices, and many more online. It's part calling card, part training, part PR event. The people attending are sparks & honey staff (everyone takes part, every day), would-be clients, contacts of previous clients, college students and old guys like me wishing they were 30 years younger and twice as smart. Remember when you read that, in the future, today's students would be getting jobs *that hadn't even been invented yet,* and you heard yourself saying 'Yeah, what kind of jobs?' Well, sparks & honey kinds of jobs. Many people might struggle to imagine what a culture briefer, or a human network director actually *does,* but make no mistake – we are not talking about the economics of thin air here; sparks & honey have consistently enjoyed 70% per annum revenue growth since they were founded. And I shall now attempt to explain how they do it.

The power of augmented intelligence

To really understand how this company can thrive by digesting a blizzard of ephemera – and why sparks & honey is a kind of canary in the coal mine for the future of work – you have to meet Q, an always-on, 24/7, 'cultural intelligence platform' that sits at the heart of sparks & honey. It gorges itself on over 1 million 'signals' a day. These signals can come from anywhere: a host of social-media sites, newspaper articles, research papers, patent files, sparks & honey's human network of culture scouts and advisors all over the globe, and, of course, the daily briefings. What's really striking is the intricate dance between humans and machines taking place here. Signals are fed into Q, automatically and manually by humans. Making sense of emerging patterns is achieved in the following ways:

1. Experts train Q to sift, connect and sort signals into 'taxonomies' (another function of the daily briefing).
2. Emerging patterns (called 'elements of culture') are scored using a number of criteria: energy (how fast is it moving?), prediction (how long will it last?) and reach (how many people will be exposed to it?).
3. If an element has enough energy, prediction and reach, sparks & honey will commission an 'intelligence report' from an expert advisor. Most of their revenue seems to come from organisations asking them to study and advise upon such trends and emerging fields.

Although sparks & honey wouldn't (yet) describe their approach as 'big data', there's still a significant amount of data being processed – signals can date from as far back as 1852 – and can range from major societal shifts to transient internet memes. Culture is essentially a giant accumulation of personal biases. So their approach is to introduce as much bias as possible, through their extensive human network, thus hopefully balancing the biases. Organisations in the business of cultural trend-spotting need to adopt a stochastic approach, acknowledging that so-called 'black swan' events (random and unpredictable) are more common when you're dealing with people. Bias and unpredictability mean there's a greater probability of 'shit happening' (this is why it's said there are only two kinds of social forecasters: those that are lucky and those that are wrong). sparks & honey and Q, working their data dance, try to improve their luck by highly sophisticated statistical analysis but still accept they can't always predict precisely.

Data divinity?

By now I had a nagging doubt that, while all this stuff was really interesting – and it's been a long time since I was so absorbed for three days – I still couldn't see how processing a million+ signals a day could generate enough income to house a fast-growing business with a prime site in New York City.

I needed a concrete example: let's take eSports. If you have teenage kids, you'll be familiar with this phenomenon, even though it seems counter-intuitive, at least on the surface. Why would millions of young people watch other young people play video games? Wouldn't you rather spend that time playing rather than watching? Well, video gaming as a spectator sport has become a big business. Back in 2013, however, it was just a few scattered signals. Q picked up on it, and sparks & honey commissioned a more in-depth report: 'eSports: The biggest sport you've probably never heard of'. The report brought attention to the 300 million eSports fans who follow competitive video gaming. It shone a light upon companies like Twitch.TV, specialising in televising video gaming, and recently sold to Amazon for close to $1 billion. There have even been high-level negotiations taking place to make eSports a demonstration event at the 2024 Olympics.

If you're scratching your head at this point, wondering how this phenomenon has *completely passed you by*, you get why companies like sparks & honey exist. After the report came out, major brands began queuing up to commission sparks & honey to help with their eSports strategy. eSports, however, is just the beginning. Main-streaming marijuana, engaging with millennial mothers through social media – culture is *everything* we do, so sparks & honey now finds itself in a very different space. In 2017, it worked with the US Department of Defense. Could they help them identify the earliest signs that young people were being radicalised? I wish I could tell you more about this intriguing project but, for obvious reasons, it's classified.

From ads to ambiguity

The more sparks & honey people I spoke to, the more it seemed that the organisation was fully committed to the complicated often ambiguous world of 'no easy solutions', rather than the simpler directness associated with traditional marketing and communications. That seems to be partly a product of Terry Young's own background. Somewhat unusually, he took a mid-career break, before founding sparks & honey, to volunteer for the Peace Corps, spending two years supporting social enterprises in the recently established Kazakhstan. He was dealing with a very different kind of cultural change, but it was an experience that has clearly helped inform sparks & honey's developing purpose. This is complex work:

> We're in the horizontal business of understanding both sides of
> an issue. But we also want to point a company in the preferred

future direction and those preferred futures tend to have something we also care about. With the Department of Defense project, we're looking at what's happening with ISIS – it's a tough topic to be involved in, and you're asking yourself some really challenging questions. And you're also doing it with the government, which can make you feel a little uncomfortable at times. But at the end of the day, we know that it's better for us to save lives.

Another of the 'no easy solutions' they're grappling with (in their daily work, not just forensically) is how humans relate to automation and artificial intelligence. They're only at the start of these investigations, but they are already sure of one thing: the impact of automation on the job market has barely begun. And there's very little we can do about it except adapt and try to ensure that automation provides a competitive edge, albeit to a smaller workforce.

Speaking about how that ambiguity would transform the industry, Terry made a prediction in an interview with *AdAge*:

> If you take an agency that has 100 people, within five years, those 100 will need to be 30, and the other 70% (of work) will be automated. Those people that remain, however, are going to be able to do things better, smarter, faster. Using traditional frameworks, an analysis might have taken us three weeks. Using the technology we have, we can now turn it around in 24 hours.

Cognitive diversity: a keystone for mass ingenuity

By this time, I felt like I had a good grasp of how the company was not only bridging two sectors (advertising and strategic consultancy) but also balancing profit with a broader social purpose. I still needed to understand how it built a culture of learning and nurtured its people. The people with key responsibility here are the Managing Director, Sharon Foo, and the aforementioned Annalie Killian.

I first met Annalie in 2013, at her home in Sydney. She was curating the 'Amplify' festival for her then employer, AMP – a major wealth-management company in Australasia. A couple of years after that, Annalie decided that she needed a new personal challenge. So she moved to New York City, just like that. In middle age, with nothing more than her considerable talent and extensive networks, that easily qualifies as 'a brave move'. But it's one that hasn't caused her a moment of regret. Just like the song says, Annalie could 'make it anywhere'.

Within a few months, the rapidly expanding sparks & honey had appointed her as Director of Human Networks. By the time I caught up with her, she'd become Vice President of Strategic Partnerships.

Sharon Foo was born in Singapore. Annalie is South African. Both have worked in several countries, and together they bring a wealth of experience and global awareness. A challenge for many tech-led companies is how to build a workforce that reflects their client base. I visited Google once, toured the entire Sydney campus and didn't meet anyone who was older than mid-30s. I expected a similar demographic at sparks & honey, but I was taken aback at just how diverse their staff are. Organisations don't get to be diverse by accident, and sparks & honey has made diversity, alongside openness, two of its foundational strategies. It's a powerful combination. And a necessity when trying to predict cultural shifts. Simply recruiting the smartest brains isn't enough, as Sharon explained:

> We've been talking a lot about IQ [intelligence quotient] and EQ [emotional quotient]. At sparks & honey, the IQ index is extraordinarily high, but EQ needs to be equally high. Diversity in ages and race and nationalities helps to bring about that empathetic leadership and sensitivity.

Annalie went further, emphasising the business imperative of bringing a wide range of abilities to identify new opportunities:

> We have an advisory board member who lives with a disability; she's wheelchair-bound. On one of the first days she came here, she opened us up on the size of the market opportunity that is entirely overlooked by marketers. As a consequence of that, it informed one of our research reports called 'The Economics of Ability'. As a result of her being on our board, it changed our perspective. We recently had a major piece of work with a global cosmetic company. As we put the team together, we included not only this member of our board but also people of an older age.

Never too old

This brings us to one of the most striking examples of sparks & honey's inclusivity strategy: their 'Senior Cultural Apprenticeship Program'. It's a fascinating take on the concept of apprenticeship: applicants need to have a *minimum* of 30 years' experience, are expected to work with the 'millennial strategists' and contribute to the daily culture briefing. There aren't too many tech-led companies that specifically target this demographic. sparks & honey's inaugural Senior Cultural Apprentices, Gwen Kelly and Sharon Lewis, are typical of the cognitive surplus that's available, but underutilised, in these 'bonus years'. Together, their marketing executive experience encompasses Walmart, Citibank, Amex, Saks Fifth Avenue and more – who wouldn't want that kind of experience around the place?

As Paul Butler, sparks & honey's Chief Operating Officer, explained, this is less about 'giving back' than gaining an edge:

> When we recruit, we're fortunate enough to get great levels of experience and education. But we're also looking to get 'cogni-

tive diversity' – we're looking for people who've demonstrated an ability to think in different ways. I've worked in companies where people were largely between 18 and 45 – we're in the process now of looking for people who'll bring something that typically companies don't recruit for: wisdom.

Indeed. The global auction for talent isn't really interested in diversity. As a CEO of what's still a relatively small staff, Terry Young has been intentional in getting the widest cognitive diversity on-board, spanning cultural backgrounds, ethnicities, sexual orientation, gender and age: 'It's this diversity of experience that leads to diversity of thought, which continues to have the most significant impact on our client work and how we're able to look at culture from so many different angles.'

If sparks & honey's competitive advantage only lay in the breadth of the demographics of its employees, that would still be no small achievement. But it's the creation of the human network – its ecosystem – that not only makes the organisation porous but will also be its legacy. There are three tiers to the human network:

1. They have the type of advisory board that one might expect: C-suiters, thought leaders and entrepreneurs.
2. Persons of influence: subject matter experts, academics, artists, start-up founders, who might be approached for a very particular insight.
3. The global scout network – this consists of over 200 people, from 20 countries, plus 5,000 guests who attend the daily briefing and many organisational partnerships.

Annalie explained why, and how, it developed:

> We started with the open philosophy as a design principle. Since we're a small company, how do we scale openness? That's how

we came up with the network – it's like a cloud of creativity that sits around the organisation – we've got humans in the cloud instead of data. I was attracted to it because I think it's one of the options in the design of organisations in the future. We'll see organisations having fewer and fewer permanent employees, but they'll scale up and down either through freelancers or through networks.

The contribution of emerging ideas and cultural signals from people ranging from CEOs to well-informed college students is a prize asset, so a significant part of Annalie's job is maintaining this collaborative community. Her great skill is to incentivise them – through enhancing their CVs or commissioning them to do research – and to connect them in meaningful ways. Earlier, when we examined mass ingenuity's enabling conditions, I shared Yochai Benkler's conviction that collaborative communities relied upon motivational diversity and social integrity, not status or salary. Well, here's mass ingenuity in living colour. Annalie has embedded reciprocity and mutual social recognition – the foundations of social integrity – through the entire network. And it works beautifully, democratically, globally. It harnesses the power of employees to pro-ams, hobbyists and learners all around the world. In just the same way as the process of beta-testing software is now seen as integral to new product development in the tech industry, what sparks & honey are doing, through their human ingenuity in the cloud, will become the organisational norm of the future – we simply won't know any other way.

And this is what makes sparks & honey a stellar people-powered organisation. It would be too easy to stereotype it as a place where the insatiable hunger of Q, the artificial intelligence platform, has to be fed by the humans. As Annalie said: 'We're a 100% human-powered organization. Everything here is designed by humans, and strategies are built by humans. The human's role is to teach the machines to be more intelligent.'

Hold that thought. Because that's a beautiful way of casting that relationship. Machines can already do many things better than humans – but they'll never know what it *is* to be human.

I asked Paul if other sectors could learn from their transition from advertising agency to strategically focused, globally concerned consultancy. His conclusion was clear:

> What we're trying to do is to solve the big questions about humanity. A lot of the thinking is displayed on our walls. We have the UN's 17 sustainable development goals right next to our mega-trends. It reminds us that what we do is very much connected to these larger questions: equality, poverty, climate. We keep these front and center, so that the work we've done – whether it's around gender, or ability, or economics, are tied in to those goals […] how do we teach young people to think about broader emotional, human decisions that have to be reconciled, where real choices have to be made, as opposed to just thinking about business and the competition?

It was almost time to go. Mercifully, Trump's fundraising circus had by now decamped, and Manhattan's streets had been returned to New Yorkers. Because of the way the day had started, it struck me that I'd seen two irreconcilable futures for America. Donald Trump came to power on a promise that couldn't be delivered: to return jobs to a nostalgic, industrial past, through a policy of economic isolationism, and to throw democracy into reverse gear. Seen from another place, Terry Young is clear-eyed about the inevitability of automation taking jobs. But he sees sparks & honey's future driving three elements of a more human-centred and more open future: Firstly, by augmenting human wisdom with the technology to enable scale; secondly, by investigating possible futures through the lens of culture; thirdly, by licensing out their cultural intelligence platform, they will open up the previously closed business of cultural consultancy. We can't allow ourselves to be naive about the tensions inherent in this ambition – sparks & honey is, after all, owned by the media conglomerate Omnicom. But the potential of the knowledge and insights generated by a large global human network of cultural scouts, supported by cutting-edge AI, seems to be an essentially democratic vision. That can only be a good thing.

Key points:

- An open, porous organisation sees external expertise as the well that never runs dry. Build networks and invest heavily in relationships.
- Recruit for curiosity and empathy – EQ is as important as IQ.
- Organisations that harvest the cognitive surplus of their users and fans will learn much quicker than those that don't.
- Automation is inevitable – take the opportunity it affords to build on the things that make us human. What makes us human is also what will make us employable.
- Working on the things that define us as humans – creativity, cultural understanding, empathy, diversity – will pay innovation dividends.
- Organisations that focus upon 'solving big questions about humanity' will build user loyalty and hold on to talented staff.
- The knowledge age will blur the boundaries between disciplines and redefine industries. If your organisation commits to the motivational diversity and social integrity that feeds collaborative communities, you will be well placed to thrive.

CHAPTER EIGHT

Open Learning = Open Innovation

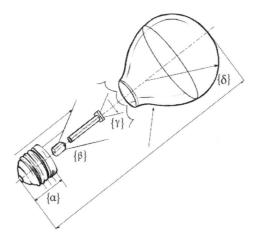

As sparks & honey graphically demonstrates, there is so much knowledge and data that swirls around contemporary life that the *only* way an organisation can thrive through innovation is to become what used to be described as a 'learning organisation'. Companies used to proudly declare themselves in this way when, in reality, they'd simply found a system for knowledge management. Now, even the most basic user forums have sophisticated knowledge management systems. Some deal with staggering amounts of information: in 2018, the UK's Mumsnet forum ('by parents for parents') had 1.3 billion page views, with posts from

119 million unique users. Their ability to leverage that wealth of information means that they have 10,000 Mumsnet 'influencers', regularly run advocacy campaigns, generate a turnover of over £8 million a year and no self-respecting prospective Prime Minister would turn down an invitation to speak to their base.

Simply processing or managing knowledge, however, does not make for a learning organisation. For that to occur, there needs to be a clear connection between the knowledge flowing in and out of the organisation, and the products and services they create. Many organisations would argue that learning can still occur even in organisations where confidentiality and secrecy dominate. While this may be true, the lessons of the past decade, and especially the period 'During Corona', suggest that closed learning systems will not be able to keep up with either the pace of knowledge flows or the pace of change.

First, let's see what makes learning and innovation 'open'.

The open learning environment

The concept of an open learning environment has been around for a very long time. Although not part of the popular mythology, Thomas Edison, while developing the phonograph and light bulb, would regularly host 'open house' sessions, open to the general public, in order to share their learning. But open learning only really became scalable with the advent of social technologies. Suddenly the barriers to participation were lowered. As a result, knowledge – something that used to trickle down from expert to novice – now spreads through peer-to-peer networks. Companies used to disclose knowledge on a 'need to know' basis – now the smarter ones don't have any secrets. Instead, they practise *radical transparency*.

Open learning has reached the point, socially, where it's now just part of our daily lives (think of the knowledge you exchange with friends and family every day, through media platforms). Most organisations would claim to have open learning environments, but they're actually practising another version of 'strategic openness'. The differences between open and closed learning environments are quite stark:

Closed learning environments	Open learning environments
Knowledge flows vertically downwards	Knowledge flows horizontally
Learning is linked to status	Everyone has access to learning
Learning happens in silos	Learning flows across boundaries
Knowledge is proprietary – the default position is 'don't share'	Knowledge is cultural – the default position is 'share freely'
Learning is delivered formally	Learning is socially cohesive

Open innovation

The term 'open innovation' was first coined, in 2006, by Professor Henry Chesbrough. He defines it as: 'the use of purposive inflows and outflows of knowledge to accelerate internal innovation and expand the markets for external use of innovation'.[1] That doesn't exactly trip off the tongue, so let's add the forms it can take and the benefits that can accrue.

1 Chesbrough, H. (2006) *Open Innovation: The New Imperative For Creating And Profiting From Technology*. Harvard Business School Press.

Chesbrough talks about the *directional flow* of innovation as 'outside-in' (bringing new ideas/people into our organisation to work on a specific challenge) or 'inside-out' (sending our people and ideas outside the organisation to create new applications or new audiences). Chesbrough says that the relationships can be business-to-business (B2B) or business-to-customer (B2C – though we've been using the term 'user' to signify consumers who also produce things: 'prosumers'). According to open innovation champions Innoget, the benefits are clear:

- Not all the smart people work for us, so we must find and tap into the knowledge and expertise of bright individuals outside our company.
- External R&D can create significant value: internal R&D is needed to claim some portion of that value.
- We don't have to originate the research in order to profit from it.
- If we make the best use of internal and external ideas, we will win.
- We should profit from others' use of our IP, and we should buy others' IP whenever it advances our business model.

Viewed like this, an open learning environment becomes a prerequisite to open innovation. Stefan Lindegaard's *The Open Innovation Revolution* points to a further prerequisite: the need to be 'institutionally humble'. Lindegaard cites a number of important cultural attitudes, essential in open organisations:

- a willingness to accept that not all the smart people work for your organisation;
- a willingness to find smart people outside your organisation (including your users) and a desire to work with them, listen to them;

- a willingness to share learning, not just internally, but with the external world;
- a willingness to embrace, not just tolerate, failure;
- a willingness to see research and development as something that happens externally, not just internally;
- an understanding that open innovation raises intellectual property issues – attribution matters and appropriate rewards for new ideas will pay off hugely.

For many organisations, that's quite a cultural shift. At the start of the millennium, knowledge was seen as a prized asset – whether you attended school or traded stocks, it was the difference between you and your competitors. You 'owned' knowledge, and therefore the imperative lay in keeping it from others. The CEO of a venture capital and asset management business that I interviewed described the extraordinary lengths they used to go to in order to keep new portfolios under wraps. Now, they regard that as a futile illusion.

Open innovation comes in many shapes and sizes

The methods organisations adopt to foster open innovation are numerous. Some have already been shared: hackathons, crowd-sourcing, collaborations with start-ups (BrewDog's #Collabfest beers) or innovation platforms (the most successful of which is still arguably Procter & Gamble's Connect and Develop). Perhaps the most popular is the 'open innovation challenge', where a cash prize goes to the first, or most effective, solution. Netflix offered US$1 million to anyone that could improve their suggestive filter logarithm ('because you watched…') by 10%. Forty thousand teams from 186 countries competed, with the prize going to one who only secured an 8% improvement – which shows how important filter logarithms are to Netflix. Richard Branson's Virgin Earth Challenge was launched in 2007, offering a $25 million cash prize to the team that could come up with a sustainable and economically viable way of extracting greenhouse gases from the atmosphere. Sadly, it is yet to be claimed.

When it comes to the really audacious challenges, it's hard to imagine any solutions being found in a closed innovation setting. So it's been no surprise to see the abundance of collaborations arising from the global response to Covid-19. Sciencebusiness. net set up a live blog, starting mid-March 2020, to chronicle just some of the open innovation collaborations taking place. I strongly urge you to take a look – it will give you hope for the future. Similarly, the aforementioned Innoget group immediately created a platform where needs arising from Covid-19 could be matched with opportunities to seek solutions. Yet another open innovation champion, Prepr, set up a global challenge, #BeyondCovid, to come up with innovative solutions in the fields of prevention, business, education and community. It was open to anyone – students, start-ups, citizens, researchers – anyone with a stake in mitigating the after-effects of the coronavirus. And that's all of us.

Before returning to the implications for open innovation in the way organisations learn, let's see what we're already learning from innovation at a time of pandemic.

The global insistence upon openness is overwhelming

Set aside the abject performance of authoritarian governments in failing to control the outbreak[2] compared with open, transparent democracies. When China sought to initially conceal the genetic profile of the virus, the world demanded otherwise. Within four weeks of the detection of the first case in Wuhan, research labs

---

2 At the time of writing the five countries with the highest death tolls, according to Johns Hopkins University, are: USA, Brazil, Russia, the UK and India – all initially sought to dismiss the danger and minimise the risk of inaction.

around the world had fully sequenced *and publicly released* the entire genomic profile of Covid-19. To reach that milestone during the SARS epidemic of 2002 took more than a year.

A global crisis demands a promiscuous response

The unlikeliest of bedfellows – across commerce, sport, citizen scientists, academia and public health – came together. The president of the Ford corporation instructed his engineers to be 'scrappy and creative' with whoever they could find to collaborate with. Siemens made their enormous Additive Manufacturing Network (being able to design and print 3D solutions anywhere in the world) available to anyone.

Act first, think later

At the outset of the pandemic, on 14 March 2020, Michael Ryan, executive director of the World Health Organization's Emergencies Programme, said something as chilling as it proved to be prescient. Warning of the dangers of inaction, he said:

> If you need to be right before you move, you will never win. Perfection is the enemy of the good when it comes to emergency management. Speed trumps perfection, and the problem in society we have at the moment is everyone is afraid of making a mistake – everyone is afraid of the consequence of error. But the greatest error is not to move. The greatest error is to be paralyzed by the fear of failure.

One can only wonder how different things might have been had more leaders acknowledged this philosophy. The *Harvard Business Review*, writing about the open innovation challenges during Covid-19, concluded that 'the biggest barrier to successful Open

Innovation is simply the reticence to commit to it'. In a single quote, Ryan brought together many of the themes of this book: a learned helplessness, a fear of failure, innovation that is 'good enough', the need to be on the front foot of change… So how do we sincerely learn from the pandemic and make a better world after it passes? One of the messages is surely that we have valued knowledge protection at the expense of social enterprise – or else why weren't the kind of promiscuous partnerships seen during Covid already happening?

The very precepts of learning need to be rethought. Knowledge that doesn't inform change is passive, inert. Our young people need to see learning not as a hoop to be jumped through but as a catalyst for change; learning should be a process of exploration, experimentation, evaluation and execution – not a passive appreciation of the great minds of our civilisations; most importantly, it is not a 'phase' of life to be slotted in-between childhood and the world of work. It will need to be a lifelong pursuit. And, like the other elements of our operating system, it works when there's a degree of self-management. Remember BrewDog giving employees £500 to spend on whatever they thought they needed to learn? Or sparks & honey using the human network to shape their 'curriculum'? Or Ricardo Semler adapting the principles of self-management to the formal context of schools in Brazil?

The lifelong learning revolution is finally here

The challenge remains: when so much of organisational learning still adheres to outmoded and passive models – the top-down transmission of 'training' – where do we look for a new vision of lifelong learning? My visit to KHDA in Dubai presented one vision. The insight of Rajeeb Dey, CEO of Learnerbly, shaped another. Rajeeb has a CV that most people twice his age would be proud of. Born of Asian parents, he resisted the family tradition of medicine to pursue an entrepreneurial path. He graduated from Oxford with a first-class honours degree in economics and management. He set up Enternships.com, which was a platform to enable school and university students to gain entrepreneurial work placements. At the grand old age of 26, he founded 'Start-Up Britain', a campaign to build an entrepreneurial response to the global financial crash of 2008, with the backing of the then UK Prime Minister, David Cameron.

Now he runs a start-up called Learnerbly, a platform that enables organisations to manage the learning and development of their people: from formal training events and conferences to recommended books. Learnerbly offers a sliding scale of engagement. Small start-ups may look to Learnerbly to deliver all their learning and development (L&D) needs, or they may simply need an administrative system for managing organisational learning. Learnerbly operates in the space between the old paradigm of workplace training in classrooms and the somewhat daunting prospect (for employers) of autonomous, self-determined learning.

I was particularly interested in his work on enterprise. These are skills that we all need – not just organisational leaders. They're also skills that should be developed from an early age but which far too many schools ignore – simply because they neither feature in the curriculum, nor do they appear on standardised tests. Rajeeb set up his first organisation (now known as Student Voice) when he was 17 because he saw that UK students were not getting what they needed from their schooling. Indeed, no one was even *asking* them what they wanted. After running the Entrepreneurship Society at Oxford University, his next platform, Enternships.com, matched recent graduates to developing companies to get their careers kick-started and has now been folded into Learnerbly to provide a wrap-around skills development programme: 'I felt that university students and graduates had no exposure to the world of start-ups, or even entrepreneurship as a career path.'

With so many innovative solutions, born out of so many opportunities, spotted in such a short time (he's still in his early 30s), it should come as no surprise that Rajeeb Dey was listed as one of the youngest ever 'Young Global Leaders' by the World Economic Forum and honoured by the Queen for services to entrepreneurship. Not bad for someone who considers himself an 'accidental entrepreneur': 'I didn't really know what an entrepreneur was; I just wanted to do something positive.' His mission now is to make sure future young entrepreneurs don't happen by accident: 'There needs to be a revolution in how we think about lifelong learning, and we need to make sure that everyone is equipped with the tools, attitude and the mindset to continuously reinvent themselves.'

Rajeeb Dey, to a large extent, is ingeniously plugging the gaps of an out-of-date education system. He's on a one-man mission to make sure the future skills we *all* will need – self-management, enterprise, adaptability – are widely available.

It still surprises me that CEOs often fail to connect the dots between autonomy, mindset, learning and innovation. Grassroots collectives of user-innovators, although not always articulating those connections, have it built into their DNA. Thankfully, the new knowledge economy organisations are starting to make them interdependent functions of 'how we do things here'. They look outside-in as well as inside-out. They gain control by giving away control. They make sure that the serendipity of learning isn't left to chance. And they make innovation open, so that they can be truly open to innovate.

If you're trying to make your organisation more innovative, and more agile, let **'knowledge, networks and learning'** be your mantra. And these three can *only* happen in open environments, through open approaches to innovation and with open minds.

Key points:

- The ubiquity of knowledge makes the task of keeping organisational secrets almost impossible.
- Innovative organisations have welcomed the opportunity to make knowledge and learning open.
- Closed learning systems still exist, but the experience of the coronavirus pandemic has exposed their inadequacy.
- Open innovation has become the go-to mechanism for organisations dedicated to keeping up with the pace of change. Those who adapt best to this shift already have a commitment to open learning.
- An agility in learning, and the humility to reach out to wherever good ideas emerge from, remain the biggest assets any organisation can possess.

CASE STUDY: LIGER LEADERSHIP ACADEMY

'You're involved in something bigger than yourself.'
Dom Sharpe

Context is everything. It's not possible to comprehend the mind-boggling learning environment that is the Liger Leadership Academy in Phnom Penh, Cambodia, without understanding the recent history and culture of the place, and the people who are dedicated to making life better there.

The rise of communism in Cambodia can be traced back to the 1940s French colonial period. Cambodia's plight mirrored that of Vietnam. By the early 1970s, the US-backed government was locked in a bitter war with the resistance army, the communist-backed Khmer Rouge. When the Khmer Rouge 'army' rolled into the capital, Phnom Penh, on 17 April 1975, they were met with flag-waving citizens, glad to finally be free. Within hours, however, the capital was evacuated. People were given no time to gather their belongings, having been told that an American attack was imminent, but reassured that they'd be back home in 3–4 days. For hundreds of thousands, it was the last time they'd see their homes. What happened next is still shocking, not least because to most of us in the affluent West, little was known about the Khmer Rouge regime, or the genocide that killed around 2 million Cambodians: almost 25% of the population. Sadly, the overwhelming sense you get when you are in Cambodia is that few people want to talk about it, even now. There have been no truth and reconciliation hearings, and the Khmer Rouge themselves were still in existence up until 1999. The Cambodian government-in-exile (which included the Khmer Rouge) still had representation at the United Nations, backed by people like Margaret Thatcher, who famously said: 'You'll find that the more reasonable ones of the Khmer Rouge will have to play some part in the future government.' As recently as 2018, two Khmer Rouge leaders, Nuon Chea and Khieu Samphan, were finally found to be guilty of genocide. This is still very raw, very recent.

During the 1980s, Westerners were kept out of Cambodia, undoubtedly hindering its reconnection to the world. However, by the turn of the century, Cambodia was opening up. Trevor and Agnieszka Gile were running an investment company out of Seattle and fell in love with the country after a visit in 2002. They returned home and established the Liger Charitable Foundation, giving it 30% of their business profits. The Liger Leadership Academy has been their flagship programme, opening its doors to students in 2012.

With a mission to find and educate changemakers of Cambodia's future, Liger could easily have become a school for the gifted children of a growing middle class. However, Trevor Gile avoided that trap. Speaking in an interview for *Forbes* magazine in 2018, he articulated Liger's unique selling point: 'We didn't want to be a private school for privileged kids; we wanted to give a chance to kids who otherwise wouldn't have one.' To their great credit, Trevor and Agnieszka were giving back with vision and purpose – and they needed leaders with the same vision and purpose. In Jeff Holte and Dom Sharpe (who we shall meet in a moment) they made inspired choices. Of all the learning environments I've experienced, Liger is one of the best.

Context meets need

So much for the opportunity and context. There have, however, been many well-meaning attempts to support Cambodia's attempts at reconstruction. It would have been easy for the Liger initiative to have followed formulaic guidelines: build schools that provide a basic education to as many children as possible through NGOs. Or simply give money, in the form of foreign aid, to the government to do more of the same. Liger doesn't follow that path. On the day I arrived in Phnom Penh, the national newspaper carried a report from the Association of Southeast Asian Nations (ASEAN) on the impact of artificial intelligence. The report predicted that 28 million jobs would be lost in the region, with those in agriculture and service at most risk – the place of refuge for Cambodia's lower-educated, lower-skilled youth. Cambodia's challenge, moving forward, is to ensure that it's not preparing its young people for an agrarian, even industrial, past. The need was for a future-focused flagship education initiative, an exemplar of what could be possible. What was needed in its leadership was a mix of pragmatism, optimism and ambition. Pragmatism because, even with the generous support of its benefactors, this is not a resource-rich school. Additionally, it may be a start-up school, but it has to sit within the same highly regulated, statutory national frameworks that other Cambodian schools operate under. As for the ambition, that needed people in it for the long haul but with a steadfast determination to leapfrog a century of educational development. Meet Jeff and Dom.

'We built the whole curriculum around our goal'

Liger Learning Academy is located 12 kilometres south of Phnom Penh city centre, amid banana and mango plantations. From the moment you enter the lush green campus, there's a sense of calm everywhere. Remember, this entire country has post-traumatic stress disorder. Then there's the size: Liger is a boarding school that accommodates 110 students aged 10–16 years old, plus a few visiting teachers (known as facilitators at Liger). By most school standards, that's tiny. There's a palpable sense of family here, in a land of orphans. Then there's the mission: Liger is an unashamedly selective school, but it's not typical of the genre. The overt aim, of developing future change agents, has made some form of selection inevitable. But to ensure equity, Liger has an exhaustive student recruitment process, and all student costs are covered by the Foundation. Every three years, Jeff and Dom visit remote provinces all over Cambodia, identifying students that demonstrate potential in areas like curiosity, entrepreneurship, collaboration and creativity. Inevitably, a process that aims to recruit 55 students once every three years, has 10–15,000 students being assessed for suitability. It's little wonder, therefore, that parents of admitted students feel like they've won the golden ticket, and Liger has had only one student withdraw in the six years since opening.

In any powerfully open organisation, leaders have to model the behaviours and mindsets they expect to see in others. Dom embodies the educator-as-entrepreneur he seeks to uncover in his students. He may look like he'd be just as happy surfing in his native Tasmania, but his commitment to rebuilding Cambodia is as genuine as it is long-held. Having first visited the country with the intention of adopting a Cambodian orphan, he soon realised: 'This wasn't a case of taking one child out of the country – there was some heavy lifting needing to be done here. Rather than take a child out, we realised we were forever connected to it.'

Jeff provides the curriculum leadership, having previously worked in schools in the USA, China, Qatar and the Democratic Republic of Congo. Crucially, Jeff was setting up collaborative international projects when email was a novelty: students growing plants in different countries, then sharing growth rates via emails; students exchanging emails with seniors at rest homes and then meeting face-to-face. 'There were always tears […] and it changed my whole perspective on what's possible in learning. Everything is connected, the world is connected, people are connected.' As we'll soon see, these early connections were foundational to the thinking that inspired Liger.

So these two contagiously infectious leaders came together to build a Liger Learning programme that would help move the entire country forward. As Jeff says: 'Because of Cambodia's recent past, this is a perfect laboratory to experiment in, in order to create globally minded leaders.' For Dom, it's also about understanding the national opportunity:

> It's all well and good to say that education is a right when you live in the West. Come here and everyone will tell you it's a privilege. The biggest resource lacking in Cambodia right now is human resource – and that's what we're developing here.

I'm waiting to be served my evening meal in a student apartment at Liger. It's a little unnerving: 15-year-olds often have a limited menu when they self-cater. And the conversation with adolescents can often be a little, well, stilted. I needn't have worried. Not only was the food delicious, the 4–6 students who occupy the boarding accommodation in this apartment (simple but comfortable) are regular hosts to overseas visitors. It's part of the policy of network-building here: the future belongs to those with the best networks. So we spent a very engaging evening, sharing cultural references across age and geographic boundaries, discussing music, Brexit, the rise in populism, what was trending on YouTube. And then it hit me: just a few years ago, these students couldn't speak a single word of English. Many of them would not have gone outside their rural province in Cambodia, let alone venture to the capital city, or represent their school internationally. And yet, here they were, just a few short years after leaving their remote monocultural village, completely at ease talking to a stranger about social entrepreneur-ship in an international context. How did *that* happen?

A clue lies in one of the design principles at Liger: **opportunity-based learning**. Earlier in the day, I watched while students held a Skype conversation with two NASA scientists they'd met on one of the many projects that students undertake during their time at Liger. Working in partnership with Marine Conservation Cambodia, the students were finding innovative ways to recolonise overfished areas of Cambodia's coastline. (I'm glad you asked – they're 15-year-olds.) While there, they met up with an American scientist, who talked with them about the CubeSat project, which NASA describes as:

> small satellite payloads built by universities, high schools and non-profit organizations to fly on upcoming launches […] a low-cost pathway to conduct scientific investigations and technology demonstrations in space, thus enabling students,

teachers and faculty to obtain hands-on flight hardware development experience.

These tiny cubes hitch a ride on NASA spacecraft. Now, this will come as a surprise to no one: Cambodia has no space programme. So when Jeff heard of the opportunity to launch the country's first satellite (albeit a tiny one), he saw another opportunity. Hence the Skype conversation. And, yes, there were moments of embarrassed silence. And some hard questions from the scientists: 'How are you going to fund this? What kind of observations do you want to carry out? What's your project plan?' Even if nothing comes of the project – and Jeff admits it's the most ambitious project they've yet contemplated – the learning that took place in that one-hour conversation with global experts was enormous. Most Liger students come from remote villages and have experienced fairly rudimentary elementary education – if at all. Yet here they were, trying to figure out how to launch Cambodia's first-ever satellite. It's *literally* rocket science.

They must have a pretty great science teacher to guide them through this, right? Well, actually, the facilitator in charge at Liger was a recent graduate from an engineering university in the USA with no teaching qualification, on a one-year internship. So how do they make learning work in those circumstances? Jeff firmly believes that you can facilitate learning without being an expert in the given field. Indeed, it's often an advantage. Dom gives a specific project by way of illustration. Liger is currently trying to help remote villages farm fish sustainably. Using 3–4 small fish ponds, and a process similar to crop rotation, families could potentially have fish all year round:

> I don't know if it will work. But we can try it here. And if it works here, it might work in the village. That facilitator has never built fish ponds before, so he's going to have to be very

innovative. If he was an expert, he'd be constantly telling kids: 'No, that's wrong, that's not how you do it.'

However, achieving great results – as Liger unquestionably does – is only going to be possible if this thing we call 'school' is actually a **community of learners**. Jeff explains it through describing another ambitious project:

> Our math teacher has been here since we started. He's a brilliant teacher and we get very high math scores. But he also has to do projects, so the first book we produced was a book on the economy of Cambodia, which is now currently being read by more than a million students. When he first did that project, he said: 'I don't know anything about economics, I don't know how to write a book, I don't know anything about desktop publishing.' But he did it, and it's being sold in bookstores, and it's in every school in Cambodia. This year he's working on volume two, and he feels a lot more confident! He still doesn't know much about economics and nothing about desktop publishing. But the students do – and there are economists to interview all over the country. So you have to figure it out as a group – how are you going to do this big thing together? So we're facilitators, but we're all students too.

Now we're getting to the glue that holds the whole thing together: an intense expectation of collaboration, coupled with a culture where failure is fearless. Dom explains how that works, contractually and culturally:

> We carefully screen people before they come here – we always say to incoming staff: 'You need to be comfortable with being uncomfortable.' The contract says you'll spend a lot of time out of your classroom, a lot of time out of Phnom Penh, some time

out of the country and most of your time out of your comfort zone – if you're not happy with that sentence, don't read the rest of it. Every seven weeks, we have a workday where facilitators go into each other's projects and problem-solve issues arising, make connections, seek opportunities for further collaboration. Here at Liger, we like to say that 'failure isn't accepted, it's expected!' If you haven't failed here, you haven't done enough. Science is nothing if it's not about failure. Every failed experiment brings you closer to the cure. It's a hard mindset to instil in people: the outcome of a project might fail, but it doesn't mean the learning did. You'll learn more if it fails than you would if the teacher hits the target by doing it for the kids. Everybody says 'failure's good', but when it happens, nobody likes it. It's important for me to admit to failure, publicly. So I do. And I acknowledge that it doesn't feel good, but it's a necessary part of life. That's a hard thing for facilitators, because education is built around success.

No set curriculum, opportunity-based, experiential learning, facilitators not teachers, projects that fail… To many people this would be a radically dangerous experiment. And Jeff and Dom are at pains to insist that these are solutions that work for their context – they're not trying to spark a revolution in conventional schooling, and their solutions wouldn't necessarily work for others. However, to dismiss Liger as merely an outlier would be to miss the point: there are aspects of what happens at Liger that already exist in schools all over the world.

Learning, at its heart, is simple. It's just that over time we have institutionalised it, commodified it and quantified it to the point where we often lose sight of that simplicity. When the Cambodian Secretary of State for Education visited Liger, he asked Dom: 'How do you get children interested in learning?' It's a question every parent may have found themselves asking. Dom's answer was that learning isn't something you need to make a child adapt to: 'Make *learning* interesting. In order for learning to be interesting, they've got to be engaged, they've got to be involved, they've got to have some sort of say in what they're learning.'

Scaffolding experiences

There's nothing new about experiential learning. We've known since the Ancient Greeks that we learn by doing. But that definition is inadequate, not least because it misses something that Liger has placed front and centre: the basic unit of currency is 'the experience'. Experiences serve as triggers for the acquisition of theoretical knowledge. They build a sense of agency – and confidence. They create the context within which problems can be identified and then solved.

As I reflected upon some younger students describing their travels around Cambodia, Jeff described the currency of experience to me:

> We scaffold learning, but not in the traditional way of adding one piece of knowledge to the previous one. Instead we build experiences, so that they are trusted to do more ambitious work. Imagine you're a 12-year-old, and you're going to a part of Cambodia that you've never been to before, to interview people you've never met before. 'Hello, we're writing a book about Cambodia's geography in English and Khmer – can we ask you some questions?' That's huge. So, start small, just do one interview at first; go as a group – we ramp it up over time, until it becomes an authentic experience. And the first time they do it and it works, and the person didn't get mad at them, they're like 'Wow, it really worked!' and they're ramped up… forever.

The global learning commons in action

The potential of open learning environments is, thankfully, becoming more widely understood, but there's an aspect to it that many conventional learning spaces – in either the workplace or the school or college – fail to grasp: the learning power of a vibrant network. Perhaps the most powerful skill that students at Liger gain is the one that Professor Guy Claxton has described as 'knowing what to do when you don't know what to do'. For these students, the answer is simple – turn to your network. Jeff describes the power of what I've previously termed 'the global learning commons' through a news story:

> There was a footprint found of a dinosaur here, and there were apparently no dinosaurs in Cambodia. Our kids said: 'Well, that's pretty interesting.' Now, there are no palaeontologists in Cambodia. But there were at least 30 palaeontologists that our kids contacted around the world. They didn't all write back or respond, but five did. So our kids had a million questions for them. Nowadays, we have the tools to mine this wisdom – but we don't have the mindset to think about 'How do you open up the entire curriculum, the entire knowledge base, to the entire world?' Our students will always remember those interactions with palaeontologists, but if I had them read a book on palaeontology, they wouldn't remember any of it a year from now.

The network that both Liger and its students are building is not just a global address book of experts. On the second day of my visit, I watched while a grateful leader of a privately run neighbourhood school handed over a cheque for US$6,000 to the students (any fees earned go towards an educational fund for Liger students). The students had acted as consultants to design activities for the Bambujaya school's third-grade curriculum. Students have also acted as consultants to the government, designed film-making courses and trained teachers in science, technology, engineering and math (STEM). They've written reports on public health issues, studying dengue fever, HIV, improving dental health – it's an extensive list. They even operate a bike tour – I met 15-year-old Chhoeu Chhoeun, the marketing manager of 'Journeys of Change', who told me about the culture, local history and faith healing I'd be missing out on if I didn't book a slot on the tour. You should do it if you're ever in Phnom Penh.

Simple structures beget complex learning

By now you might be getting a sense of the extraordinary achievement that Jeff and Dom have engineered. To be capable of such depth of learning, and to carry out these ambitious, high-impact projects requires a simplicity of design. Formal learning organisations are notoriously good at incorporating complexity into, well, everything: the schedule, their back-office systems, their assessment regime, how they maintain discipline. Sometimes it's a complexity that's externally imposed; at other times it just accumulates over time. To Jeff, it inevitably gets in the way:

> I've spent my whole life trying to create learning environments that are really powerful and really engaging. If we have 1,200 hours, roughly, for each school student in a typical year, how do you spend those really wisely, doing the things that you really need to learn how to do later in your life? We have to be kind of futurists for them – not just doing what we've always done, but what they're going to need for the next 10–20 years. We have to guess what their lives are going to be like in 20 years' time, and then make those learning experiences that will be useful. And if you do that, then it will be interesting. I don't particularly like school, but LEARNING IS INTERESTING!

So I've spent my whole life trying to figure out how to make school fit learning better.

There's only one way to become a leader...

When it's put like that, you realise that, structurally, they keep everything as simple as possible so that their focus can grapple with these profound questions. I had to remind myself that the great conversations I had with the students was in a language many of them didn't know until a few years ago. They're also taking US SAT tests in that language (and outscoring their American peers) and being offered places at universities from around the world. Liger was established to build leadership skills in order to rebuild the nation. You don't get that by being good at filling in multiple-choice tests, so I still had one big question for these two contrarians: 'How do you teach leadership and how do you measure it?' Jeff jumped in:

> To become a leader, you should practise being a leader. If you want to do big things in your life, you should practise doing big things, and what's amazing is that even very young kids can do amazing things. We take on highly complex projects, because when you get into life, that's what you will need to do if you want to be a leader. In today's world, leadership skills are just common skills people will need in the future. We have to work together, collaborate, talk to each other in a world that's becoming more connected – so why not practise that while you're here? Every year we have students write an essay 'How did I change Cambodia this year?' And it's mind-blowing what they've done. I guess somebody could score that if they really wanted to […] but we're measuring their impact every year.

For Jeff, the fact that they're already making a mark in their community, their country, through their projects, means that their commitment to Cambodia is strong: 'Our founder's real measure is that they have an impact in this country years down the line. What we didn't anticipate is that they'd make change happen along the way. They're making change happen now.'

Dom added:

> I always said our goal here was not to 'Westernise' Liger students. They are more Cambodian as a result of coming here than they would otherwise have been. I've always said that they'll know more about Cambodia – the history, culture, the present, what's coming – than they ever would if they'd just stayed in their village back home. And how can you change the country if you don't understand it? This is becoming an attractive country for companies to base themselves – tech companies included. But who's going to run these businesses? Who's going to have the ability, the passion, the ethics? The Liger students. The whole thing about Liger is that you're involved in something bigger than yourself.

I thought about those parting words on my final day in Phnom Penh. I had been trying to avoid going to the mass burial grounds of the Killing Fields site, just outside Phnom Penh, but I felt I had to. It's everything you'd expect it to be: horrifying, incomprehensible, sombre. But also somewhat surprisingly 'unfinished'. And that's the best way to describe Cambodia's response to the Pol Pot years and its future direction – it's unfinished. As I write, the photographer who documented the torture at Tuol Sleng has announced that he is setting up a new political party, to apparently little surprise or condemnation. Members of the Khmer Rouge are still working for the government. And the Khmer Rouge tribunal, at the time of writing, continues to grind the wheels of justice. It began in 2006, has cost an estimated $300 million (and counting) and has made just three convictions.

The tuk-tuk driver who haggled over the fare from the Killing Fields abruptly stopped no more than halfway back to my hotel. He insisted upon near-full payment, assuring me that his replacement would do the rest of the trip – for the remaining $2. My new driver was about the age of the senior students at Liger. He seemed happy enough with the arrangement. I wondered if he still would be in 10 years' time. This is a country that one can unhesitatingly say deserves a break – in more ways than one. To move it from where it is to where it deserves to be, and undoubtedly has the potential to reach, will demand a new generation with vision, entrepreneurship and a strong sense of social justice. That Liger is creating those citizens is genuinely inspiring.

Key points:

- Simple design principles beget complex thinking.
- See opportunities for authentic learning experiences, not as a distraction from the curriculum – make opportunities *become* the curriculum.
- Don't be disingenuous about collaboration and failure-tolerance – they only work when you give them the commitment, time, actions and support they need to drive your culture.
- Create experiences where learners solve problems that matter outside themselves.
- There are experts to be found all over the world. Use them.
- Powerful learning is built through scaffolding experiences (not just knowledge) and through building networks.

PART FOUR

Leadership

*Developing bottom-up innovation requires
a radically different model of leadership*

CHAPTER NINE

Architects, Not Surgeons

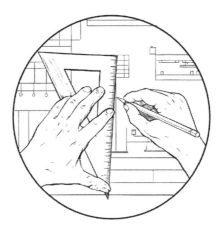

Capitalism is in a bad way. In fact, it's been in a bad way for quite some time. All it might take is a global pandemic to finish it off entirely.

Let's examine the universally agreed standard when judging the health of capitalism: profitability. At the risk of getting bogged down in the weeds of economic theory – no two economists ever seem to agree with each other – the immutable law of economics, coined by Karl Marx and known as 'the tendency of the rate of profit to fall' (TRPF) has been consistently demonstrated. Somewhat inconveniently, the rate of profit, in pretty much every developed economy for the past 70 years, has steadily fallen. By way of example, the US rate of profit in the corporate world, in 1952, stood at around 43%. By 2013, it was just over 25%.

Productivity fares no better. In a sharply perceptive 2017 report for Deloitte, Dr Rumki Majumdar attempted to explain the 'productivity paradox'. She highlighted the fact that, despite 30 years of phenomenal improvement in information technology, productivity has actually *decreased* steadily during the same period. Dr Majumdar argued that blaming the fall in productivity during the past 15 years on the global financial crisis was much too simplistic – productivity was already falling before 2007; the global financial crisis simply accelerated the decline. World productivity growth was 3.9% in 2006. By 2016, it had fallen to 1.6%.

Perhaps part of the cause lies in stubbornly low employee engagement levels (only 13% declared themselves as engaged by their work in the Gallup global survey of 2016, and that figure had been like that for a decade).

Capitalism After Corona

Add to that mix the psychological and economic after-effects of the coronavirus recovery. At the time of writing, the global 'magic money tree' was printing money for bailouts and corporate protection schemes to the tune of US$6 *trillion* dollars.[1] Additionally, people were openly questioning the value of judging the prosperity of societies solely by the strength of their gross domestic product (GDP) – shouldn't health be a key marker? And everywhere saw a reappraisal of the economic value of the people who risked the most during Covid (key workers) whilst generally being paid the least.

In short, productivity, profitability and employee engagement had been on a steadily downward trajectory for the past 70 years. On top of this, the collateral damage of the pandemic was

1 By the time you are reading these words, the final toll will surely be significantly higher.

prompting some commentators to declare that the 'supernova' of capitalism was about to burn itself out.

Leading our way out of it

On the other hand, capitalism still seems to be the least bad option when considering economic systems. And the picture is always one of economic swings and roundabouts. Extractive industries may be in (hopefully terminal) decline, but the knowledge sector boomed through the early twenty-first century. And with that boom came new models of leadership (for one thing, they didn't all wear trousers).

Spending time with James Watt at BrewDog's HQ in Ellon is a reminder that, in the words of Frédéric Laloux, author of *Reinventing Organizations*: 'The general rule seems to be that the level of consciousness of an organization cannot exceed the level of consciousness of its leader.' That consciousness, viewed over a 40-year span, has clearly changed. James and fellow co-founder, Martin, are creating an organisation that corresponds with how they want the world to be. So are Terry Young and the leadership team at sparks & honey. BrewDog have guarded their independence tenaciously, refusing to be taken over by monopolistic brewing giants. Their strength has been to remain true to their founding principles, even while the context, size and reach of BrewDog bears no relation to the days when they were selling beer from the trunk of their cars: make good beer for good people; look after your employees; take a stand and be a force for good; community ownership.

The reality is that even the most people-powered organisations are heavily reliant upon the attributes and skills of their leaders – although, ironically, the goal is usually to make them less reliant. The strategies may differ from those observed in more conventional leadership, and the relationships almost certainly will. In the *Hügelkultur* cultivation of mass ingenuity that we started with, the emphasis become less managerial and more horticultural. If the basics of the right mindset and operational software are in place, the leader's role is to be acutely aware of the changing context and to feed the right nutrients into the growing medium, so that innovation is fed by the root system and not by a top-down process of fertilisation. That growing medium is more commonly described as the culture of the organisation and it's the leader's role to ensure that it's as healthy as it can possibly be. There are eight key ingredients in that culture, and we'll share the cultural toolkit in Section Five.

Before that, this section will look at changing leadership styles – with a particular focus on leaders who prioritise people-powered innovation – and we have case studies from two of the best exemplars of that role.

We live in interesting times for organisational leadership. What worked a few weeks ago becomes problematic today, because the external context is never static. When Colin Kaepernick, the US American football quarterback famously 'took the knee' in refusing to stand for the national anthem before a game in 2016, he took a stand that cost him his career and led to multiple death threats. The National Football League's Chief, Roger Goodell, caved in to pressure from Donald Trump by insisting that no player could take the knee, which then meant that no club was willing to sign Kaepernick. By 2018, Kaepernick was a civil rights activist, promoting the then controversial #BlackLivesMatter campaign.

Nike took a different ethical position to Goodell and ran TV ads with Kaepernick saying 'Believe in something. Even if it means sacrificing everything.' TV ads. Two years after Goodell implemented the national anthem policy, George Floyd was brutally murdered by Minneapolis police, and the #BlackLivesMatter campaign ignited protests across the world. A different kind of pressure – from his employees (players) and fans – forced Goodell into an apology for not listening to players' concerns of racism and urged everyone to speak out in protest. Few people believed that Goodell was sincere on either occasion and he was widely accused of hypocrisy, while Nike were lauded for taking a consistent stand. Contexts and consciousness may change – moral positions should rarely fluctuate.

In *Reinventing Organizations*, Frédéric Laloux sets the emergent leadership styles in an historical context of consciousness, dating back over 100,000 years. He argues that the shifts in consciousness are evolutionary and assigns colours to them:

Colour (Category)	Characteristics	Leadership style	Examples
Red (Impulsive)	• Constant exercise of power by the chief to keep troops in line • Fear is the glue of the organization • Highly reactive, short-term focus	Predatory	Mafia Street gangs
Amber (Conformist)	• Formal roles within a hierarchical pyramid • Top-down command and control • Future is repetition of the past	Paternalistic/ authoritative	Church Government agencies Military Public school systems

Colour (Category)	Characteristics	Leadership style	Examples
Orange (Achiever)	• Goal is to beat competition; achieve profit and growth • Management by objectives (command and control the what; freedom on the how)	Goal-oriented/ decisive	Multinational companies Charter schools (academies in the UK)
Green (Pluralistic)	• Classic pyramid structure • Focus on culture and empowerment to achieve extraordinary employee motivation	Consensual/ participative service	Southwest Airlines Ben & Jerry's
Teal (Evolutionary)	• Self-management replaces hierarchical pyramid • Organisation as a living entity, with its own evolutionary purpose	Distributed/ purpose as motivator and yardstick	Patagonia

(Adapted from *Reinventing Organizations* by Frédéric Laloux)

Laloux's attempt to place organisational management into a 'theory of everything' has been dismissed as cod New Age psychology and pseudoscience but there clearly was resonance among his audience of organisational leaders. The popularity of writers/speakers like Seth Godin and Simon Sinek suggest that there is a shift away from the traditional model of CEO as hero taking place.

The community builder

Another analysis of leadership styles came with the publication of a study in the *Harvard Business Review*, in 2017, by Alex Hill, Lis Mellon, Ben Laker and Jules Goddard. Unusually, the study examined leadership styles, and their impact, in UK schools. Although the context was how leaders can turn around failing schools, there are obvious parallels with almost any kind of organisation. Briefly, the authors placed leaders into one of five categories:

- **Surgeons** – incisive, high-profile, they quickly identify what isn't working, focusing on performance. They cut resources in failing areas and redirect them to get quick wins, emphasising discipline and hard work.
- **Soldiers** – favour efficiency and order. They obsess over waste, cutting non-essential activities, and bolster morale by telling people they're lucky to have a job, urging them to do more with less.
- **Accountants** – resourceful, systematic. They believe in growing their way out of trouble and are usually believers in financial strength and make acquisitions and finding new revenue streams a priority.
- **Philosophers** – eloquent, love to debate. They think of themselves as experienced practitioners rather than leaders. They are always seeking out new ideas and approaches but mainly as an intellectual pursuit.

- **Architects** – quietly humble, focused on purpose. They frequently have an industrial background but gravitate towards education, to build community and seek incremental improvement.

As someone who has spent a long time in education, I could easily assign leaders I've known into one category or another – but the taxonomy also works for CEOs I've known in public and private spheres. So what impact do these diverse leadership traits make, and what legacy do they leave?

- Surgeon-leaders dramatically improve results during their tenure and get handsomely rewarded for it (typically 50% more than the other leaders), with more of them receiving public honours (knighthoods, etc.) than any of the others. Performance improvements, however, are unsustainable and fall as quickly as they rise. By this time, however, the surgeon has moved on to the next patient, leaving someone else to clear up the mess.
- Soldiers see financial improvements, but test scores stay the same. Morale plummets as staff fear for their jobs. Once soldiers move on, staff are left exhausted and unmotivated, and costs quickly rise again.
- Accountants often see financial stability achieved – even after they leave. Since test scores aren't their prime focus, they barely change during the accountant's tenure.
- Philosophers tend to be initially popular with staff, as their concerns are listened to and discussed. Eventually, however, the lack of improvement – either financial or performance-related – frustrates, and someone else needs to turn the ship around.

And what of architect-leaders? Well, the report found that this was the *only* leadership style that saw sustainable improvement, even after they left. There was slow progress in the first couple of years as architects engaged with the community and built the right environment. By the third year, however, metrics improved and continued to do so. Architects remain low-profile, receive the least compensation of the categories, and are 'more concerned with the legacy they leave than how things look whilst they're there'.

Zero CEO heroes

For too long the model of leadership has been the heroic figure, working longer hours than anyone else, wielding carrots and sticks in equal measure, and being the confident risk-taker who doesn't know what stress is. Surgeons can't build a culture of innovation, because they *are* 'the ideas person' who transforms the organisation. Being the heroic CEO may stroke the ego for a while, but eventually it just becomes exhausting. Running around *being seen*, hoping some of that innovative genius will rub off onto others, progress chasing and micro-managing decision-making. The challenge to leaders of organisations everywhere is this: imagine how transformational it would be if you gave people the freedom to self-organise and to imagine their own solutions to complex problems? Aside from the impact upon the organisation, and the fulfilment of users and employees, it would make your job a hell of a lot easier.

The traits of architectural leadership

1. Humility

We've seen a plethora of books recently that advocate a more empathic, humanist style of leadership. Titles like *Leaders Eat Last*, *Emotional Intelligence*, and *Ego Is the Enemy* point to a realignment in management styles – from instructive order-giver to listening community-builder. In the race to hire creative millennials, the brutal reality is that simply offering more money in exchange for employee retention won't cut it anymore.

A couple of years ago, I was asked to facilitate a gathering of some of the UK's major employers. They wanted a presentation on why millennials don't have the skills they needed and what could bring about change. I thought they'd missed the point entirely. So, instead, I did a provocation entitled 'Why the smart millennials won't work for "the man"'. I shared evidence that listed the attributes that millennials looked for in great organisations: inclusive leadership, transparency, empathy, ethical purpose, commitment to diversity, radical candour. And humility. Lots of humility.

2. Morality

It isn't simply in the global auction for skills that CEO ethics have an impact upon performance. Increasingly, customers will only spend their hard-earned cash on products that have passed the ethical smell-test. Some CEOs (like Patagonia's Yvon Chouinard) would feel comfortable being described as an activist, but even the more reticent have to recognise the change that's taking place. When we have lost faith in governments – especially in times of crises – we need to trust in *something*, and that transfer of trust has gone to our workplace leaders. As Brian Moynihan, Bank of America's CEO, said in 2018: 'Our jobs as CEOs now include driving what we think is right. It's not exactly political activism, but it is action on issues beyond business.' As we saw with Colin Kaepernick's protest and the murder of George Floyd, being morally neutral is no longer an option. By the same token, if users and customers suspect that your morals are at the whim of market demand, or external political pressures, your credibility will be shot.

3. Vulnerability

When President Obama made a speech about gun control in January 2016, in the wake of yet more gun violence, he found himself wiping tears away when recalling the mass killing four years previously in Sandy Hook Elementary School. It's perhaps a sign of the times that the conspiracy theorists on social media were immediately claiming that, far from wiping tears away, the gesture was, in fact, made to insert an unnamed substance into his eye ducts that would trigger tears. It was as if the public could not accept the notion that the country's CEO had emotions and made no attempt to hide his vulnerability. Michelle Obama – Grammy-award winner, acclaimed lawyer, author and former First Lady – frequently talks about dealing with 'imposter syndrome':

> I've sat on a lot of boards, I've been around some of the most important tables in the land, and let me tell you, there are a lot of people who don't belong there. At first, I thought it was me who didn't belong, but then I realised, nope, it's not me, it's that guy.

So if displaying vulnerability is good enough for the Obamas, it's good enough for the rest of us. Indeed, when it comes to leading organisations through the new landscape, it's a foolish leader who thinks they've got all the answers. And if they do, where's the incentive for anyone to innovate? In a complex and turbulent world – even more so post-Covid – we can no longer see vulnerability as a sign of weakness. As author and business consultant, Heather E. McGowan, put it when we talked in 2017:

> If you were a leader of an organisation 10–15 years ago, the chances are that you had the experience of everyone you managed

(you'd sat in their chair). When it came to making a decision, you had most of their knowledge. So you could make a decision based upon a certain level of confidence, and that certainty gave you an identity. Now we're looking at having people in that organisation with skills and knowledge that you may not have. So you have to think differently about how to make decisions, because you have to defer to people who report to you.

4. Enableability

OK, I know it probably isn't even a word, but you know what it means. A CEO friend of mine chairs his weekly director's meetings by very noticeably checking messages and texts on the phone. After I watched this unconventional approach, I asked if having his head buried in his phone isn't, well, a little disrespectful?

'I'm listening to every word that's being said,' he replied, 'and from time to time, I'll say something. But if I'm visibly in charge, I'll be the one they'll all look to before they speak.'

Adopting such a technique requires a great deal of self-confidence, but, in a people-powered organisation, a leader's first requirement is to enable others to do his/her work. Nothing else comes close. As we will see with the two CEO case studies in this section, occasionally absenting yourself from the centrifugal force that often shapes decision-making is just about the most liberating and sustainable thing you can do.

5. Security

Google built their success upon data. Not just the data they process on our behalf, but also the data they process daily in order to inform internal effectiveness. Given the exponential rise in collaborative working, they naturally sought to find the formula that would ensure that teams achieved peak ingenuity and peak engagement. So they crunched the numbers over a two-year study, involving 180 teams within Google to discover why some teams just worked and others didn't. The most important factor? Something they call 'psychological safety'. Being able to speak your mind or voice an opinion without fear of censure or ridicule was the most valuable team trait. By a country mile. So it's to be expected that the architectural leader will instil a strong sense of security among ALL team-workers. At the end of this section, we'll meet a leader who inherited an insecure environment and look at how he reversed that culture by making people feel secure at work. As it happens, he also had buckets of the final trait…

6. Curiosity

Good leaders model the behaviour they want to see from the people they work with. A restless curiosity typified the leaders I met and, since it's the most important characteristic knowledge-based organisations look for when hiring, it becomes a prerequisite of leadership. The typical CEO reads, on average, 60 books per year – they're a well-read profession. The number that can turn that sense of curiosity into a dynamic culture of organisational learning is considerable. As this is such an important requirement in people-powered organisations, I've dedicated the next chapter to it.

To be clear, I'm not suggesting that qualities like competence, absorbing data, exercising good judgement and the rest are somehow secondary to the above traits. Leading a people-powered environment is a *more* complex endeavour than in traditional 'command-and-control' organisations, because you need all the above *as well as* the stuff they study on MBA programmes. But as we're about to see through understanding one of the most supported brands in the world, it's worth the effort.

Key points:

- A societal post Covid-19 re-evaluation is likely to reprioritise what counts in measures of prosperity.
- Leaders of the knowledge revolution have had different traits, including moral and ethical consciousness, facilitating others and factors associated with 'servant leadership' – the demand for these new leadership approaches is spreading to all industrial sectors, even the political world.
- The best leaders model the qualities they wish to see in their people: curiosity, a thirst for learning, psychological safety, moral authority and transparent vulnerability.

CASE STUDY: PATAGONIA

'We were just growing for the sake of growing – which is bullshit.'
Yvon Chouinard

Malinda and Yvon Chouinard own all of the shares in outdoor wear specialist Patagonia. This economic independence is key to its fearless, and highly vocal, moral authority. It is a company whose activism is probably better known than its products. Yvon founded the company in 1973, when he began making rock-climbing pitons for his friends. When he wasn't climbing or surfing, he tinkered around in a tin shed, virtually giving his innovations away to his fellow 'dirtbags'. In those days, he and Malinda simply saw their work as a means to an end: to enable them to indulge their outdoor passions. Yvon is a classic example of the user-innovator, working with his pals to make better climbing equipment than the stuff that was commercially available.

Eric von Hippel describes the three phases of user-innovation: in phase one, users innovate to create the products or services they want for themselves (Yvon Chouinard and friends made climbing equipment, initially, for their own use); during phase two, other users test and adapt these innovations and the original user-innovations are either adopted or rejected. In both these phases, the market is too small for mainstream producers to get involved – it's considered too risky. It's only in phase three, with proven demand, that mainstream producers get involved and the original user-innovator has a difficult choice to make: cash in, sell their business, patents or designs to a more dominant partner, or hold on to the original vision and take on those dominant businesses/organisations. Yvon and Malinda chose the latter path. There are very few user-innovators who can also take the support of their community with them through all three phases. The Chouinards did just that. Yvon was always determined to control the means of production, even as the business started to take on the industry giants. Selling out to a bigger company was never an option. And it was all because of their founding purpose. They simply weren't willing to see their values and mission diluted in the quest for shareholder dividends.

By 2018, Patagonia was rated the sixth most innovative company in the world. In 2017, revenue was estimated to be $750 million, which probably makes Yvon a billionaire – a term he refuses to accept. It has employee turnover rates of 4% (described by business analysts as 'freakishly low'), partly due to the owner's instructions to employees to go surfing whenever the swell is up. It's why they refuse to move their headquarters – it's only two blocks from the ocean.

It's a company that appears to have it all, and the secret lies in its mission to 'save the planet'. It has become a highly profitable company by *not* chasing profits. Chouinard once famously said 'I couldn't give a shit about how much money we make', yet every time it does something to make a social impact, revenues go up. How? By exercising moral leadership. By retaining the loyalty and support of users and staying true to its bigger mission.

In 2011, after the founders realised that Patagonia was contributing to the overabundance of 'stuff' in the world, they did something quite exceptional. On Black Friday, always the biggest day of the year for sales, Patagonia took a full-page ad in the *New York Times* showing one of its fleeces, with the message: 'Don't buy this jacket'. It launched a reuse and repair service (now known as 'Worn Wear') and promised to fix any Patagonia garment. By

2015, Worn Wear was repairing 40,000 garments a year – that's 40,000 future sales lost. But even after allowing for their pledge to give 100% of all Black Friday sales to environmental causes, sales figures still went up.

Cynics and sceptics have tried for years to find flaws in Patagonia's 'too good to be true' model, but they've not been able to. In truth, these days it's hard to define Patagonia – is it a commercial business or a campaigning group of activists? In reality, each blurs into the other, and that's intentional. Patagonia's Environmental Internships Programme pays staff for up to two months to work on development projects in improving communities. Tin Shed Ventures is Patagonia's venture capital arm. It only supports environmental innovators: recycling fishing nets to make skateboards; regenerative agriculture; textile cleaning processes that don't use water; e-commerce platforms for reusing garments. Sometimes these innovations make it back into Patagonia's internal product development, but they chiefly serve to keep Patagonia grounded in the spirit of peer production that Yvon Chouinard loves so much.

It all could have been very different. Malinda and Yvon had their 'Billabong moment' in the early 1990s, as Yvon recalls with typical bluntness: 'I was faced with the prospect of owning a billion-dollar company, with thousands of employees making "outdoor-like" clothing for posers. I realised we were just growing for the sake of growing, which is bullshit.'

Instead of distancing themselves from the hacker/tinkering community that supported their early growth, Patagonia made activism the core purpose of the business. The appointment of Rose Marcario as CEO turbo-charged the organisation's commitment. In 2018, Marcario led a coalition of Native American tribes and grassroots groups in order to sue the US President. Trump withdrew protected status from 2 million acres of Native American tribal lands in Utah, offering them up to oil, mining and logging companies. Many corporations would consider suing the president to be a colossal act of self-harm. As Patagonia's lawyer Hilary Dessouky described it: 'It took exactly one email to the board. And the response was instant: yes, absolutely, go for it.'

Marcario herself wants to go still further – to redefine what a business could, and should, be. And even a cursory listing of their 'non-core' initiatives is breath-taking: Patagonia employees volunteer time and muscle through their Environmental Internship Programme, working in communities threatened by environmental vandalism. The company has a self-imposed 1% sales tax, with revenues given to environmental activist groups. Patagonia Action Works is a platform matching citizens who want to be environmental activists to a range of advocacy groups. Patagonia Films highlights areas of the world under threat. There seems to be no end to the ideas that come from their employees and leaders. Meanwhile, the company's performance during this period of ramped-up activism has been phenomenal. And yet, the *tripling* of profits, since Marcario's appointment, is almost an afterthought – not their reason for existence.

At a time when organisations are having to rethink their relationships with users, when corporate social responsibility has to be much more than a bumper sticker, Malinda and Yvon Chouinard have been trailblazing a path from tin-shed peer production to humane care for employees (I haven't even touched upon Malinda's ground-breaking onsite childcare for employees, decades ahead of the field).

The Patagonia story is a series of paradoxes. They built a highly profitable business by not caring about profit. They told their fans not to buy their products, yet even more of them did just that. They built a work ethic around not being there (to this day, Yvon still practises 'management by absence', spending half the year fishing). They reclassified customers as fellow environmental activists and they are challenging their competitors to do the same. They are world-class experts in designing an organisational

Hügelkultur. Yvon has even produced a 'how-to' guide – *Let My People Go Surfing: The Education of a Reluctant Businessman.* It should be required reading for any entrepreneur.

The Chouinards continue to be the best advertisements for their products and for an outdoor life. Yvon is in his 80s and shows no sign of slowing down. The recent shift in the company mission ('Patagonia is in business to save our home planet') was provoked by the accelerating global peril: 'I decided to make a very simple statement, because in reality, if we want to save the planet, every single company in the world has to do the same thing. And I thought, well, let's be the first.'

That is what real leadership looks like.

Key points:

- Organisations rarely survive the transition from user-innovation to production. When they do, it is because they have remained constant to their founding mission and the community they came from.
- Patagonia benefits from extraordinary loyalty because they insist upon seeing customers as fellow users – what their users do matters as much as what they purchase.
- Believing in something bigger than yourself – and directing all your activity to that purpose – means labour blends with leisure and work is always fun.
- Demonstrate trust – as Patagonia does with its 'Let My People Go Surfing' flexitime – and the rewards will be substantial.

CHAPTER TEN

The CEO as Lead Learner

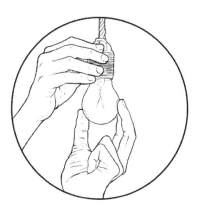

It's tempting to reduce this chapter to a single paragraph. When it comes to the importance of learning to the organisation, Peter Senge, in *The Fifth Discipline,* beautifully encapsulates the leader's motivation:

> Real learning gets to the heart of what it means to be human. Through learning we recreate ourselves. Through learning we become able to do something we never were able to do. Through learning we reperceive the world and our relationship to it. Through learning we extend our capacity to create, to be part of the generative process of life. There is within each of us a deep hunger for this type of learning.

In this single quote, we glimpse both the historical challenges of organisational learning and the way to change it, so that it stops being 'a function' and starts driving the organisation. Too often, CEOs delegate the responsibility for learning to a notch considerably further down the food chain. What kind of a message does that send? The CEOs featured in this book model the learning that they want to see throughout the organisation. Let's break the quotation down, so that we shed light on the very best practices.

- *Real learning.* Training is not a synonym for learning. A session of 'death by PowerPoint' will not *get to the heart of what it means to be human.* Real learning is not passively receiving information. Instead it is, in the words of Brew-Dog's James Watt, using 'active, alternative ways to learn, and not traditional boring courses'. Real learning is also rarely formal (though the classroom-based model of 'stand and deliver' is still the prevalent vehicle in most traditional settings). The daily lunchtime briefings at sparks & honey are good examples of how to make learning active.

- *Through learning we recreate ourselves.* Organisations with stellar learning environments allow for degrees of self-directed learning, because they know that we learn faster and better when we choose what we learn. The philosophy shapes Learnerbly's platform for organisations and also through CEO Rajeeb Dey's approach to his team's personal development. Learning is a key facet of human development. It can move us and trigger change. Compare the likelihood of hearing someone say 'I had to go on a compulsory course – it changed me forever', with 'After watching a TED Talk, I started digging deeper into the subject. I wanted to know more – it really made me think differently'.

- *Through learning we become able to do something we never were able to do.* Too often learning is 'prescribed' (by a line manager) to correct an employee's perceived weaknesses. As Morning Star discovered, its real power lies in making you even better at what you were already good at. The leader who is a visible learner (like Ricardo Semler) moulds a strengths-based organisation. They have not 'arrived' at a state of personal mastery; they're just further along the road. As it plays a critical role in creating 'serendipitous ingenuity', we will explore strengths-based learning further in Chapter Eleven.

- *Through learning we reperceive the world and our relationship to it.* The responses to the coronavirus outbreak by the case study organisations stretched their knowledge into new disciplines in order to be of service. Patagonia's Environmental Internships Programme is a good example of how organisational learning can often be more powerful when it is not simply 'learning how to be a more effective worker'. Equally, such opportunities to learn in new locations help determine our *'ikigai'* (a Japanese concept of finding your reason for being).

- *Through learning we extend our capacity to create, to be part of the generative process of life.* Agamemnon Otero's commitment to repowering communities – through the food they grow and the energy they generate – owes much of its success to the learning that young people experience in the 'generative process' of crop production. As a leader, Otero had the vision to see that the solar panels themselves were little more than a manifestation of learning. Through extending their capacity to create food and power, communities would learn how to take control of their lives.

- *There is within each of us a deep hunger for this type of learning.* As a result of the Industrial Revolution, learning became commandeered by societies in order to increase production. It distorted its true purpose. With the coming of the Knowledge Revolution, we've been presented with the opportunity to reaffirm what we've instinctively known to be true: that *purposeful* learning – the kind we all have a deep hunger for, seeks to make the world, and ourselves, better.

Without a dynamic and visibly valued culture of learning, people-powered innovation will remain out of reach. The organisations I visited all had a strong culture of learning. Their CEOs were, to a man and woman, lead learners in every sense of the phrase. Many of those lead learners had user-innovator backgrounds; the rest had taken time to understand the mindset that exists within that community. As a result, there was a deep sense of humility evident in the conversation held with them. And humility is non-negotiable, not least because, as Heather E. McGowan said earlier, leaders can no longer claim to have sat in every employee's seat. So instead of calling it 'servant leadership', let's just call it 'lead learnership' – because that's what you're going to need. See the disruption and the resulting turbulence in the wake of the pandemic as an opportunity to become the lead learner – not the font of all wisdom – within your organisation and remember the three most powerful words a leader can say: 'I don't know.'

That isn't my idea – it comes from the lead learner of an organisation that is our next, and final, case study. He's one of the most humble leaders I've met, so I'll say it on his behalf: it might seem an unlikely source, but he has created one of the best learning environments I've ever seen.

Key points:

- Leaders seeking to generate mass ingenuity must visibly commit to learning – and be the 'lead learner' within their organisation.

- Learning is much more than a 'function' of an organisation – it is an opportunity for personal growth and the search for meaning.
- Learning should build strengths within individuals, not attempt to fix weaknesses.
- The real purpose of organisational learning is to make the organisation less reliant upon its leaders.

CASE STUDY: WD-40 COMPANY

'Changing silos of knowledge into fields of learning.'
Garry Ridge

You can learn a great deal from a leader by how they communicate with you. Garry Ridge has an email signature that immediately puts you at ease: 'I may be working in a different time zone to you, and I am sending this message now because I am working. I don't expect that you will respond to, or action, it outside of your preferred working times.'

And below that comes his favourite quote, usually attributed to Michelangelo: '*Ancora imparo*', loosely translated as: 'Yet, I am learning.' Then there was the personal welcome when I arrived at the WD-40 Company global headquarters in San Diego: 'G'day, David. Welcome to WD-40 Company. I've set aside as much time as you need.'

No fancy office, no personal assistant, just Garry. As you can probably tell from his greeting, Garry isn't a native Californian. He's Australian, and the first thing he wanted to share, as he showed me around, was the tepee and the other visible nods to indigenous cultures. WD-40 Company doesn't have employees, it has 'a tribe'. The tour also taught me the origin of the products we all use 'to eliminate squeaks, smells and dirt'. The history is a perfect fit for Garry's passion for learning.

WD-40 Company was originally called the Rocket Chemical Company (RCC). Controversy surrounds the identity of the inventor – it could even possibly be the result of mistaken identity between two Norms. One proposal is that a San Diegan chemist, Norm Lawson, created the lubricant and sold it to RCC for $500. WD-40 Company's own website claims that it was *another* chemist – Norm *Larsen* – who invented it. Either way, Lawson or Larsen was trying to concoct a lubricant that would prevent water, and therefore rust, from getting into one of the early fledgling rockets. The Atlas rocket wasn't a huge success, exploding a number of times before being retired from service. And the need for a 'water displacement' (WD) lubricant had a similarly unfortunate run of luck. There were 39 unsuccessful attempts to create the right formula, before success was achieved on the 40th attempt. Hence, WD-40. It was only when employees started taking the lubricant home to fix a variety of household problems that John (Jack) Barry, the then CEO, put it in a can and subsequently renamed the company after its sole product.

And for the first 40 years of its life, that was pretty much it: one company, one (highly successful) product. And its very success, in becoming an iconic American brand, became the problem. Garry worked for the company for 10 years before becoming its CEO. At that point, 90% of its sales came from the USA, and 100% of its profits went into shareholder dividends – there was basically nothing else for them to spend their money on. Now, over 60% of WD-40 Company's revenues come from countries outside the USA; compounded annual growth in shareholder return over the past five years has been 23%. As for those failed 39 previous attempts, they were, as Garry loves to describe them, 'learning moments'.

Transforming an icon

As we settled into his office, festooned with brainstorm jottings ('It's all about the people, rejoicing in an abundance of worthwhile work'; 'The powerful words: I don't know, I don't understand'), I asked Garry to tell me about his upbringing in Australia:

> I was the youngest in a family of four. We grew up in Five Dock, Sydney, and as I grew up, I was always curious. I wasn't the best athlete, but I was always curious about business. I started working at a young age, delivering milk, then a paper boy, then working in retail stores – I was just curious. There used to be a TV professor back home, Professor Julius Sumner Miller, and he always used to end his experiments with the words 'Why is it so?'. And that became a kind of mantra for me as I grew up.

After studying at a vocational college, he found work in marketing, sales and then more general management. He was clearly on a fast track, because three years after moving to the USA, he became CEO of WD-40 Company. At that time, the success of the company was creating fearful employees, afraid to innovate, afraid to admit mistakes. So he led by example:

> When I took over as CEO it was a great organisation. However, we needed to change. We had silos of information: the more you knew and the less information you shared, the more power you had. I described it as changing silos of knowledge into fields of learning. It took people a little while to learn that not knowing was not a platform for punishment; it was a platform for enrichment. It took people a couple of years to feel like heroes for being vulnerable and step out there. We changed the vocabulary. And once we got that in place, the learning started to happen.

Nowadays, Garry's insistence on replacing the word 'failure' with 'learning moment' has become the stuff of management legend. But what does he define as a learning moment?

It's a positive or negative outcome of any situation that has to be openly and freely shared to benefit all. The reason I always say that is because I want to take the fear of not knowing out of the equation.

So employees are required to share their learning as widely as possible, free from fear or censure. The learning moment grew out of the four organisational pillars of WD-40 Company's culture: care, candour, accountability and responsibility.

Caring for you is not just treating you with respect and dignity – it's making sure you have a robust business plan, all the things that we need for the organisation to work.

Candour is simple: no lying, no faking, no hiding. I believe most people don't lie; most people fake and hide. So we can be in a meeting where we say: 'There feels like a little bit of faking going on here. What's causing that?'

Accountability, which is where the core of learning is, is: 'What do you expect of me, and what do I expect of you?' Our job as a leader is to sweep the things out of the way that stop you going where you want to go. And a big thing that gets in the way is not having a culture of learning and teaching. We have to provide that base of learning and teaching to enable that person to move forward. In the last four years, we've had 27,000 hours of classroom learning in this company.

The responsibility pillar is made real by asking every employee to sign up to the WD-40 Company's 'Maniac Pledge':

I am responsible for taking action, asking questions, getting answers and making decisions. I won't wait for someone to tell me. If I need to know, I'm responsible for asking. I have no right to be offended that I didn't 'get this sooner'. If I'm doing something others should know about, I'm responsible for telling them.

You can call me 'Al'

That balance between care, candour, accountability and responsibility is what has transformed WD-40 Company's employee engagement numbers. During Garry's tenure they've gone from the low 40s to the current 93% – that's an unparalleled number. Yet they've achieved that high score for over a decade. As we turned to engagement, Garry's tone noticeably hardened:

> We should be *ashamed* that 70% of people go to work every day and don't like their job. And we're very slow learners. Aristotle said: 'Pleasure in the job puts perfection in the work.' That was 384 BC! And whose fault is it? It's Al's fault, the soul-sucking CEO.

At this juncture, I should introduce Al, not least since he'd been sitting on the sofa during our entire interview. He must have been feeling distinctly uncomfortable at this point, but since he's a two-foot high doll, it wasn't obvious. Al sits there to remind Garry of everything he opposes: the soul-sucking CEO that puts himself before everything, and everyone, else:

> Al knows everything. He worked so hard to get to the role of CEO – who's going to know more than Al? So what does that do? It shuts down all of the creative thinking, all of the innovation. People just go numb. Employee engagement goes down. Al's number one attribute is that his ego eats his empathy, instead of his empathy eating his ego.

I shared with Garry the Surgeon-to-Architect taxonomy of leadership from the *Harvard Business Review* mentioned earlier

– it seemed so obvious that Al is the surgeon, while Garry is the architect.

> We had to build the trust first. Consistency of leadership is so important – tone at the top is so important. You don't have to like this company – that's OK. But if you're not happy, please go somewhere where you can be happy. Because our most important objective is that you're happy.

Coming from other CEOs (say Al), this might sound like a slightly sinister exercise in faux-sincerity, but the quest for authenticity is foundational to Garry's leadership style – alongside the primacy of building a culture of learning:

> A couple of things became clear to me. One, I was consciously incompetent, and two, I learned the three most important words I've ever learned: 'I don't know.' And I got very comfortable with those words. I looked for a way that I could confirm what I thought I knew and learn what I didn't know. So I went back to school. I went to the University of San Diego, doing a master's degree in Leadership, and that was an amazing experience – it gave me the balls to go and do what my gut told me to do.

Garry now teaches at the University and has encouraged 30 other employees to complete their masters, fully paid for.

'Everyone has to be a teacher and a learner'

The centrality of learning – to the organisation and to Garry personally – can't be overstated. He told me that Parnassus, one of the major shareholders in WD-40, had held a 10% investment in the company for over 15 years, purely on the basis of the culture of learning there. It's also a key attraction to younger employees:

What do millennials want? They want a place where they can be better today than they were yesterday, through learning. They're so inquisitive. A lot of people think it's about free food and shuffleboard in the canteen. No, they love to learn.

The main vehicle for learning is the Learning Laboratory, in which everyone has a right to enrol. There are three distinct areas:

- the competency lab – essential skills (trust-building, effective presentations, project leadership, etc.);
- the leadership lab – learning by doing (talent acquisition, leadership psychology, organisational theory);
- the faculty lab – skills development for teachers (presentational skills, adult learning, facilitating learning).

Garry underlines what we all should know: you can't *make* anyone learn anything. But a leader's job is to create a culture that makes learning irresistible:

I want people to be inquisitive; I want people to ask questions and take chances. My job is to create a company of learners. I like to ask my people and myself: 'When's the last time you did something for the first time?'

All good. But I was curious to know how this hotbed of learning fed into a company that, until recently, had but a single product line. Does innovation need to be a priority? Garry, very politely, corrected me:

You might just see a blue and yellow can, but during the last five years we've launched a whole range of new products, we've innovated with our delivery systems, formula innovation. We invest $11 million a year in our innovation development group. A number of years ago, when we weren't innovative, and we only had one product, I formed a group called Team Tomorrow, who could ONLY focus on revenues in the future. And they broke our model because we hadn't done anything new in 40 years.

'Innovation isn't just bringing out something new'

With a brand so ubiquitous, almost cult-like, as that blue and yellow can, it's easy to overlook the fact that some parts of the world are so-far impervious to its 2,000 documented uses:

> Innovation isn't just bringing out something new, it's about making what you have of better value to the end user. We're going to add $200 million of revenue to that can in the next seven years, because, today, people in China are meeting that can for the first time.

Or the ingenious way they've made squirting lubricant onto a squeaky door into a cultural experience:

> People will use WD-40 for the most oblique things, because we're an honest product and we rarely let the user down. They take chewing gum out of the carpet; we get people telling us they use it for arthritis – don't do that! We say we're in the memories business. People think of WD-40 and say: 'I remember when… I remember the smell of it with my dad under the car.' […] The second of our company values is to create positive lasting memories. When our innovation group is working on new delivery systems, we can say: 'Help me understand what positive lasting memories that will create.'

And you thought it was just a can under the sink?

'Opportunities are abundant. Focus is a gift'

I was starting to feel guilty about the time he was giving me. Didn't he have some major clients to meet? He seemed to be genuinely happy to talk about learning. And, make no mistake, this may be the CEO of one of the world's leading brands, but, more than that, he's just a really good human. He leads the way he lives – and his Australian roots play a key part in that. He was visibly moved when talking about his mother, who passed three months short of her centenary. He recalled how he would fly back from San Diego every year for her birthday to be met with a perpetual cup of tea and a lecture about staying grounded ('Remember, Garry, even the Queen sits down to pee'). When she passed, the only thing Garry took from her house was a single cup and saucer, to remind him to be like her: 'We only have to know two things to say to our mothers: "Yes, Mum." And two words to say to each other: "Thank you."'

And this sense of care is palpable. As Garry said:

> We're not just a company, we're a tribe; a tribe that puts a premium on meaningful work – work that means something to us, our customers and the world at large. Those are the conditions under which talented people do magnificent things.

The educator in me had to ask the question that had been nagging me throughout our meeting: as a natural educator, hadn't he originally wanted to be a teacher? He laughed: 'Funnily enough, I thought about being a minister of religion. I'm not religious, just spiritual. But I think you're right – the number one responsibility of a leader is to be a learner and a teacher.' And that's when it struck me – Garry Ridge is able to build a culture where people feel supported, empowered to take risks, to innovate, but they know there's a 'holy priest' willing them to do it. Garry himself quoted Simon Sinek in his aspiration: 'Leadership is not about being in charge; it's about taking care of the people in your charge.'

As he escorted me out, I had one outstanding question: How much of WD-40 Company's success is due to his presence?

> I hope less and less each day. I planted the seed, the tree's grown and a lot of people are sitting under it. When I leave, I'm convinced that, though that person won't be me, the culture will be so strong, and my successor will have been here a long time, they'll know that it's all about the people. If the champagne truck happened to hit me tomorrow, we'll be OK.

Garry is a visionary example of a lead learner who kickstarted innovation in a 60-year old business that couldn't help but make money, with little incentive to change. He represents the leadership needed for our time – and not just in the business world. The ego-driven dynamic leaders – embodied in his couch-surfing doll, Al – may still be with us, but their days are increasingly numbered.

Key points:

- A learning environment cannot exist in a culture of fear – turn admissions of failures into 'learning moments'.
- Innovation is much more than creating new products.
- Creating learning entitlements signals the importance of learning to the organisation.
- There is no room for ego or faking it in a dynamic learning environment.

PART FIVE

The People-Powered Innovation Toolkit

What practical steps can you take to make sure you have the right mindset, culture and distributed leadership in place?

CHAPTER ELEVEN

Unleashing the Power of Us

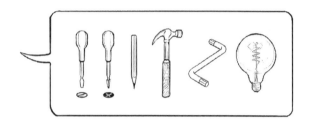

Economists argue that data is now more valuable than oil. If that's true, what price can you put on mass ingenuity? However intangible people-powered innovation may seem to be, I'd invite you to consider the potential benefits. You will increase engagement, build a learning culture that will retain your best talent, ensure that workers are happy and see purpose in their work *and* transform the innovation levels of your organisation. Mihaly Csikszentmihalyi described the 'flow' state when individuals are at their peak of creativity, when extrinsic factors (time, money, recognition) fade to black. Having people drive the organisation – rather than the reverse – could create that sense of flow across *every* individual belonging to that organisation.

Too many organisational leaders are lulled into thinking that if it's not a top-down initiative, it's probably ineffective and not going to deliver a return on investment. Trying to amplify the tendencies we already possess – our innate ability to figure things out – feels too ephemeral. And CEOs aren't paid to be ephemeral; they're paid to *act* and to be *seen* to be acting. If the organisation needs to become more innovative, hire a consultant, send people on a course, set targets, *do something!*

To gain control, lose control

It may feel counter-intuitive, Zen almost, but the first step in making your organisation more innovative is to accept that, just as you can't *make* anyone learn something, **you can't *force* people to be ingenious. Fortunately, you don't need to. The *only* thing you need to do is to create the right growing conditions, the right organisational culture, and mass ingenuity will flourish, all by itself.**

Ingenuity blooms with the right growing conditions

The US leadership expert Warren G. Bennis once said: 'There are two ways of being creative. One can sing and dance. Or one can create an environment in which singers and dancers flourish.' You can, as a leader, try to be the lead singer, enjoying the accolades and praise of others. But it'll be far better for the organisation if you focus your energies on helping every other singer flourish. If that makes it sound easy, I need to apologise. Changing an organisational culture is one of the hardest tasks you can give yourself. Progress is measured in years, not days. Organisational inertia, once established, can take a great deal to shift.

While working for the culture-change consultancy We Do Things Differently, I was asked to help a British company that had a problem with its workforce. The company (whose blushes I will spare through anonymity) were a little like WD-40 – they only had one product, albeit a market leader. But there was an urgent need to diversify their product range. Could we make the employees more creative and help develop new products and services? After two days of intense workshops, their ideas were flowing thick and fast. Walls were filled with designs, tables laden with prototypes. How could the company's leadership not recognise what we were seeing?

At the wrap-up, we asked the inevitable question: 'What's holding you back?' After a protracted, awkward silence, the dam broke. How are we expected to come up with ideas when guys on the shop floor aren't even allowed internet access? Why were there different canteens according to workforce levels? Come to that, why hadn't anyone from the management team shown their faces during the past two days? It was blindingly obvious that they were trying to be innovative within a rigidly hierarchical, traditional culture. People-powered innovation was never going to become a reality unless the culture changed.

Feel the fear and do it anyway

At the end of my conversation with Garry Ridge, I asked the obvious question: 'Why don't more leaders build a culture that encourages ingenuity?'

> They're scared. Will this 'feelings' stuff work? I'll admit to you that, early on, I wasn't sure this was going to work. But we – not me – were brave and we believed that if you treat people with respect and dignity, and help them step into the best version of themselves every day, something marvellous might happen – and we started to see employee engagement rise, and we've now gone from a $300 million market cap company to a $2.3 billion company during that time and they both correlate.

So yes, establishing the kind of culture that cultivates mass ingenuity demands courage, sensitivity, patience and a clear vision. The purpose of this section is to give you a set of practical tools you can use along the way. Take inspiration from the organisations featured in this book and now distilled into realistic, culture-building actions.

Before we delve into the toolkit, however, let's just remind ourselves of three considerations in the external context, and why the time to foster people-powered innovation was yesterday.

It's all around us – you just need to look

Steve Flowers, from the University of Kent's Business School, aptly describes how people-powered innovation is 'the invisible industrial revolution, hiding in plain sight'. But, as he explains, 'once you see it, it totally changes the way you look at innovation today'. Just because it's not clearly visible, however, doesn't mean that you should either take it for granted or not invest in it.

It's disruptive – deal with it

Teenagers know more about climate change than politicians. They're creating coronavirus apps in a fraction of the time it takes governments to do it. They're inventing bio-markers for cancer (Jack Andraka – look him up). Patients know more about their conditions than the experts treating them. So what can you do? However disturbing the changes we're living through, we can be sure of only one thing: we're not about to return to linear, predict-able change, dispensed by authorities and matured through age. Ever. All you can do is develop a perspective that blends humility with curiosity. We *should* be curious, because the people we can learn from now were hitherto unimaginable: users, employees, investors, advocacy groups, social media, bloggers, citizen journal-ists, scientists… If it feels overwhelming at times, see the positives and build your own information filters.

It needn't be a threat but it's going to happen anyway

We have to see the locus of innovation as the people who use our products and services, as much as it is the people who collect a pay cheque. Even if you wanted to, you couldn't stop user-innovation. Just ask IKEA. In 2006, a young Malaysian woman, Jules Yap (not her real name), started 'IKEA Hackers' – a website which aggregated the innumerable ways in which IKEA products could be repurposed. The initiative grew like Topsy, and IKEA was not happy. What was the point of those carefully designed self-assembly instruction leaflets if people just ignored them? Citing breaches of intellectual property, they sent Yap a cease-and-desist order. The legion of IKEA hackers around the world came to Yap's rescue, threatening to find some other furniture maker's products to hack. They might have been creating their own innovations, but they did so by buying IKEA stuff to begin with. So common sense prevailed and IKEA acknowledged the stupidity of trying to prevent people-powered innovation. In 2018, they launched their first hackable products. They now have an IKEA Open Platform to house user ingenuity and actively support IKEA Hackers. A Damascene conversion or a cynical attempt at damage limitation? Whatever the motive, they avoided a potentially catastrophic PR disaster.

All of that is not meant to deter you from taking action – quite the reverse. And the rewards are abundant: your people feeling fulfilled; low churn rates; enhanced engagement; increased productivity; crew, not customers; a shared sense of purpose. As Sir Ken Robinson says: 'Human resources are like natural resources: they're buried deep underground. But if we find things that energise us, you can't keep us down.'

TEAM – the eight keys to people-powered innovation

Remember when I shared the system of *Hügelkultur*, used in raised bed gardening? That was about getting the design principles right so that you have a sustainable feed of nutrients coming from the bottom up. But you also need the right growing medium if your crops are going to flourish: the top soil, compost, bonemeal, fertiliser. That's what the remainder of this section deals with – how you can create the best possible culture for people to be their best ingenious selves. Based on the organisations I've studied, I've identified eight ingredients. To help you remember them, I've paired them around the acronym TEAM:

- Trust and Transparency.
- Engagement and Equity.
- Autonomy and Agency.
- Mastery and Meaning.

None of the organisations I visited would claim to have all eight of them down pat. But they are creating cultures that have most of them at their heart. At the end of each pairing, I'll suggest specific, practical actions that you can take.

TRUST & TRANSPARENCY

Trust is, in my view, the non-negotiable ingredient, rendering the other seven irrelevant if it's absent. In Chapter One, I described the trust deficit we're experiencing around the Western world. I make no apologies, however, for returning to the subject here, because it's foundational to making organisations more innovative, more productive and happier places to spend time in. Our attitude to building organisational trust will affect *everything* that follows: culture, mission, management policies and our user-relationships.

For Garry Ridge, in taking over at WD-40 Company, trust had to be his first priority:

> We had to build the trust first because most people come from organisations where they're gonna get 'em. They're looking for the opportunity to 'get' people instead of moving them on to their next place. Consistency of leadership is so important – tone at the top is so important. We have zero-tolerance towards not being who you are.

Writing in 2006, Robert Hurley demonstrated that only half of employees trusted their employer. In 2019, that number had risen to 75%. You have to hope that this is because a high-trust culture is now a proven asset in the race to attract talent. Hurley's study concluded that 99% of CEOs felt that trust was essential in building relationships, yet **95% admitted to not consciously doing anything to build trust**. It seems that little has changed in our perception of trust, encapsulated by the philosopher Annette Baier's observation that 'we notice trust as we notice air, only when it becomes scarce or polluted'.

The trust myths

It's as if we feel that trust is a kind of force of nature, and there's little we can do to affect it. Here are just some of the trust myths:

- Leadership trust is dependent upon personality.
- Trust is slowly built over time.
- Trust is inextricably linked to transformational leadership.
- Trust is absolute – you either have it or you don't.
- You have to 'earn' trust.
- Once broken, trust cannot be restored.

None of these is true. At all three layers of trust – organisational, relational and intrapersonal (self-trust) – there are many concrete steps that can help build it. Dr Paul Browning has made a lifetime study of leadership trust. His success in building trust has been gained the hard way. Paul became CEO of an independent school in Queensland that had suffered the most horrific betrayal of trust imaginable. It's hard to think of a more blighted culture of trust than Paul inherited, following the exposure of paedophilia in the school during the 1970s and 1980s. His predecessor at the school was accused of attempting to cover up accusations of the sexual abuse of students, which subsequently became the focus of a Royal Commission into Child Abuse. I've spoken to people who worked at the school before and after Paul's appointment – they rated trust in leadership then as 0/10, and 10/10 since Paul showed courage and sensitivity in lifting their battered morale. His approach was forged in the crucible of crisis management and academic analysis (he has a PhD in leadership, based around his experiences and research). His book, *Principled: 10 Leadership Practices for Building Trust*, shares the practices he adopted in turning around a low-trust culture. I'll summarise them at the end of this section.

Trust can be a tax or pay dividends

Stephen M. R. Covey has also researched cultures of low–high trust. In *The Speed of Trust* he sees low trust (evidenced by toxic cultures, micromanagement, bureaucracy and redundant hierarchies) as a tax on everything your organisation does – things take longer, productivity dips, engagement plummets, costs increase, customer relations suffer. On the other hand, when trust is high (evidenced through high levels of collaboration, easy communications, transparent relationships) talent is retained, productivity soars, people are inspired. I regularly use his tax/dividend rubric in organisational workshops. Depressingly, around 60–70% of people, on average, seem to have worked in organisations where trust is seen as a tax – and a punitive one at that. What a waste of potential. Like Browning, Covey lists leadership behaviours that help build trust, which I've also summarised later. As you'll see, there's some overlap, some differences, so use those that personally resonate.

Self-trust is contagious

The inescapable conclusion of my own research is that organisational trust reflects levels of relational trust within the organisation, which in turn is highly contingent upon intrapersonal trust. My consultancy work has frequently taken me into situations where attempts to uncover the 'innovation blockers' highlight dysfunctional and distrustful relationships between leaders and those (not) being led. These consultations often lead to quite painful conversations, because of the realisation that, in the words of Professor John Kotter, 'the core of the matter is always changing the behaviour of people', and that change often starts with ourselves. I recall one particularly difficult day I spent at an organisation where the CEO had asked me to find out why people seemed to be resistant to change. At the end of the day, she asked for the headline story.

'It's good news and bad news,' I began.

'What's the good news?' she asked.

'You've got really inventive people here. They're full of ideas.'

'So what's the bad news?'

'I'm afraid you are. They feel like you don't trust them, so they're terrified of putting ideas forward.'

The problem was that the CEO – a completely likeable, even inspiring, leader – didn't actually trust the one person she was dependent upon: herself. The leader she *thought* she was – always having new ideas, curious and not afraid of change – was being undermined by the part she didn't recognise – constantly switching between initiatives, projecting her own insecurity onto others. The staff knew that, even if their own initiatives gained support, another would be implemented before theirs had been properly evaluated. Our lack of trust in ourselves is the biggest innovation blocker of all. I've lost count of the times when a new innovation was abandoned *just* before it was about to make a positive difference. As Thomas Edison (a pretty handy lead learner himself) said: 'Many of life's failures are people who did not realise how close they were to success when they gave up.'

Protocols and symbols

A common feature in my case studies is the way in which organisations have used protocols and symbols to scaffold trust. XP schools (a visionary cluster of schools that we'll visit in Chapter Thirteen) swim in protocols – their most important are: 'If it's good enough for the kids (the end users), it's good enough for us.' Protocols come to the fore when difficult conversations need to be had. Protocols reinforce expectations and minimise game-playing and unexpected surprises. At sparks & honey, the open manifesto is how they hold themselves accountable. At Morning Star, the colleague letter of understanding performs the same function. Without protocols, trust can be here today, gone tomorrow.

It's the same with symbols. Perhaps the most famous symbol of all is the employee handbook at the super-swanky department store, Nordstrom, in the USA. With an enviable reputation for customer service and communications, you'd expect a fairly comprehensive list of do's and don'ts for employees to abide by. You'd be wrong. Here is Nordstrom's employee handbook, in its entirety:

'Use good judgment in all situations'

(Please feel free to ask your department manager, store manager or human resource office any question at any time)

Can you think of a more symbolic way of saying: 'We trust you – we hired you because you'll be great, so go and be great'? Garry Ridge's ever-present sofa puppet, Al (the soul-sucking CEO), serves as a potent symbol, to himself and everyone at WD-40, that their absolute priority is to find joy in their work, every day. Malinda and Yvon Chouinard's insistence that when the surf's up, tools go down, and Patagonia staff hit the water, means: 'We trust you – you work hard, and you'll get the job done, so let's enjoy ourselves.'

What all of these protocols and symbols confirm is that trust isn't earned; it's *given*. You have to give trust to gain trust. And that makes it infectious and scalable – trust grows as the organisation does. Micromanagement – the antithesis of trust – is neither trust-building nor scalable. And it's exhausting.

The user-producer trust dynamic

Up to now, we've really only detailed the internal trust dynamic in organisations. But the explosion in open innovation means that, increasingly, we have to think about borderless trust. Trusting user-innovators will become paramount. BrewDog has built a community that includes a large number of co-producers, as have Procter & Gamble. Organisations will increasingly rely upon the mass ingenuity of their users/clients – and how do you expect user-innovators to be creative if they don't trust you or your values?

Being transparent

While it's possible to have trust without transparency (and vice versa), there is usually a strong correlation between the two. The organisations I've visited, in general, 'default to open' – they start from the position that all information should be widely available and retain confidentiality only when circumstances deem it to be unavoidable. At sparks & honey, the open manifesto contains the following: 'Our fortunes and futures are inextricably linked, and the time of secrecy, guardedness and closed doors is past. We believe that walls are for sharing, not shielding.'

BrewDog's 'We believe' document declares:

> All 326 beer recipes, given away for free to the global home-brewing community. Our accounts and financial results freely available. Our profits and future plans shared. The future of business is to hide nothing. Involve everyone. We believe in radical transparency.

It's not that long ago when 'default to closed' was the organisational norm. This abrupt reversal is almost entirely an unexpected consequence of the internet. Organisations used to believe that the value of any information they held lay in it being proprietary: that's why it became known as 'intellectual property'. Then, a couple of things happened to change all that: first, everyone (including governments) became aware that the ubiquity of internet use means that it's virtually impossible to keep secrets. I'm not being naive here: Transparency International's claim that 6 billion of us still live in countries with serious corruption problems suggests we still have a long way to go. And it's also true that if you want to hide the truth, it's never been easier to distract and deflect through fake news. I still believe, however, that with billions of eyeballs searching for truth, deception becomes much harder to pull off.

The second shift, however, was the realisation, first articulated by Clay Shirky, that instead of withholding data until you know its value, the smart move is to make it open precisely so that the crowd will determine its value. Laszlo Bock, ex-Vice President of People Operations at Google, argues that 'one of the serendipitous benefits of transparency is that simply by sharing data, performance improves' and cites, by way of example, the decision by New York State to make hospitals publish death rates from coronary bypass surgeries. Within four years, deaths fell by 41%. It would be wrong to assume that surgeons previously didn't care whether their patients died as a result of their surgery. And, when you dig deeper, no single 'trigger point' emerges for the improved performance. This was not an exercise in 'naming and shaming' – airlines have also seen significant improvement in flight safety when they're transparent when things go disastrously wrong.

So, the civic push for open government, with users and customers insisting upon full disclosure, is compelling – it's nearly always better to turn transparency to your advantage than have it publicly embarrass you. The overwhelming experience for organisations embracing trust and transparency – and certainly for those featured in this book – is encapsulated by New York Senator Kirsten Gillibrand's belief that 'when you open the door towards openness and transparency, a lot of people will follow you through'.

Trust and transparency takeaways:

Paul Browning's 10 trust-building practices	Stephen Covey's 13 trust-building behaviours
1. Admit mistakes	1. Talk straight
2. Offer trust to staff members	2. Demonstrate respect
3. Actively listen	3. Create transparency
4. Provide affirmation	4. Right wrongs
5. Make informed and consultative decisions	5. Show loyalty
6. Be visible around the organisation	6. Deliver results
7. Remain calm and level-headed	7. Get better
8. Mentor and coach staff	8. Confront reality
9. Care for staff members	9. Clarify expectations
10. Keep confidences	10. Practise accountability
	11. Listen first
	12. Keep commitments
	13. Extend trust

- Model Edelman's Trust Barometer. Regularly measure trust at all levels: between user and organisation; employer and employee; manager and leader (except of course, in holacratic organisations, where auditing trust becomes simply person-to-person).
- Consider hosting monthly 'fuck-up' nights, where people share stories of failure and what they learned (join a public event in one of over 300 cities or host your own via fuckup. com).
- If you're looking to build fans and co-creators, make public your values, plans, financial data, management decisions and *especially* your mistakes (as BrewDog routinely do) – people buy what you believe in, as much as what you produce.
- Practising 'open by default' (e.g. town-hall meetings with no 'off-limits' subjects) will pay off in building employee engagement, staff retention and healthy communications. But sharing more sensitive information should be done by consent.
- Make lateral 'commitment statements' to peers (like Morning Star's Colleague Letter of Understanding) a mechanism for building trust *and* accountability.

ENGAGEMENT & EQUITY

As it is with trust, so it is with engagement. Organisations believe employee and user engagement matters – just not enough to do much about it. In a 2018 survey of HR directors, carried out by Achievers (employee engagement experts), almost 60% of those asked said that their organisation understood the importance of engagement. Yet only 28% said that their organisation was active in doing something about it – 20% said they didn't even measure it! Even more bewildering is the result of a *Harvard Business Review* survey, in 2014: 71% of CEOs admitted that employee engagement was critical to the success of their organisation. Yet only 24% of them said that their people were highly engaged. The cognitive dissonance is baffling: if you know engagement correlates to higher productivity, greater innovation, better retention and customer relations, why aren't you *doing* something to enhance it? Admittedly, at that time (2011/12) the world was picking itself up after the global financial crash, so the response I most frequently heard from HR directors was: 'In times of recession, CEOs don't think much about employee engagement – they think you should be grateful to even have a job.' But since then, we've had years of recovery and growth, so why hasn't engagement risen up the ladder?

I've written previously and extensively about engagement, so let me just reiterate the key message: you simply cannot expect people to be innovative, inventive or ingenious if they are not engaged. The financial cost of disengagement in the workplace is – in the USA alone – priced at $550 billion a year. In schools, disengagement is measured in exclusion, non-attendance and failure rates. And as for civic disengagement? The catastrophe of Brexit is a multi-billion-pound lesson in what happens when people feel left out or left behind. It may be easy to overlook, but disengagement is the poisonous viper that you don't see until it's too late. And if you still need reasons to take it seriously, consider the shameful waste of human potential associated with disengagement at work. The most *optimistic* global surveys estimate this to be 70% of workers; the most pessimistic calculate it to be 87%. Think about it: 7 out of every 10 people, hour after hour, feeling unfulfilled.

Why engagement matters

The organisations I've highlighted, unsurprisingly, enjoy exceptional employee engagement rates. WD-40 has 93% of workers feeling engaged. Patagonia has a 4% employee turnover rate, and 91% of employees say it's a great place in which to work. The other organisations I visited have similar rates of satisfaction and extremely low attrition rates. But what are the concrete benefits of high engagement? Well, there's productivity for a start: Gallup recently estimated that highly engaged teams are 21% more productive. Then there's absenteeism: highly engaged organisations have 41% lower rates of absentees and almost 60% lower rates of attrition than their less engaged equivalents. Customer service rates are much higher in engaged organisations (the joke about the waiter who, when asked by diners to make recommendations, said 'I recommend you go eat somewhere else' isn't apocryphal).

Too often when bosses *do* something to enhance engagement, they get it wrong, by pursuing extrinsic motivation, through higher salaries or performance bonuses. The return on that significant investment is relatively poor: only a marginal improvement in engagement, according to PayScale's report, *The Formula for a Winning Company Culture*. What matters more, according to PayScale, is salary *fairness* (one of the reasons why I've connected engagement to equity). We also know that salary, while an important factor in recruiting talent, matters less than recognition when it comes to retention. The Forbes Coaches Council concluded:

> In decades past, motivating employees was all about raises, promotions and bonuses. Those days are gone, and today's employers are quickly learning that engagement stems from different kinds of incentives – ones that impact an employee's emotional, rather than financial, health.

But does engagement = ingenuity? Absolutely, according to Glen Elliott and Debra Corey, authors of *Build It: The Rebel Playbook for World-Class Employee Engagement*. They assert that engaged workers demonstrate three common characteristics:

1. They make better decisions (because they understand the organisation and its clients better).
2. They're more productive (because they love what they're doing).
3. They innovate more (because they deeply want the organisation to succeed).

In other words, it's the intrinsic motivations that matter. But I believe that Elliott and Corey have missed an important element: they're right to point to the importance of how people feel in terms of being more innovative. But they become ingenious when CEOs invest in building a culture of learning within the organisation. If you're growing and learning, you'll be more confident and creative. Tech start-ups have grasped this extrinsic–intrinsic fallacy. They know that, to anyone under the age of 40, compensation isn't the driver – acquiring mastery through learning is what matters (we'll come to mastery in a moment). And because they usually can't afford to pay fat salaries and bonuses when they're starting up, they've had to study how to build engagement intrinsically. We all should look at how people are motivated - when they're acting voluntarily in expending discretionary effort - and learn from it.

User engagement – the new imperative

What's good for employees is also good for users and *especially* user-innovators. So in the coming era of mass ingenuity, it's going to be just as important to have deep engagement with *everyone* that has a stake in your organisation's success. As we saw in Chapter Six, in creating community energy projects, Repowering could easily have limited their operations to an investment scheme or simply raised the finance and then installed the solar panels on the tops of social development blocks. But their purpose is about learning and empowerment, so building deep user engagement is at the core of what they do. When that first kilowatt of energy, created from one block of flats on the estate, was traded by blockchain technology to a resident in another, it might not have seemed much. But Repowering are rewriting the rules of the domestic energy market – they're redistributing who owns the levers of energy. As co-founder Agamemnon Otero said to me: 'Repowering is not the Energy Garden or the solar power cooperative. It co-produces food and energy with local people because THEY are the project.'

Organisations that fail to see the potential of their users as co-producers will increasingly lose out to those that build deep user engagement. It's no longer about user experience; it's about user empowerment.

Equity and ingenuity

It should be obvious that equity is a key aspect of employee engagement. You can hardly expect anyone in an organisation to feel motivated if they're being treated unfairly. We've known about the damaging impact of inequity – on morale, motivation and discretionary effort – since workplace psychologist John Stacey Adams' seminal *Equity Theory* was published in 1963. Essentially, Adams argued that pay and benefits alone have relatively little impact on motivation. Far more important is whether workers feel that their input (effort, loyalty, knowledge, skills and experience) is in balance with the output (pay, yes, but also security, recognition, challenge and responsibility). People inevitably compare their situation with those around them, and, if they *feel* they are being treated unfairly – and perception probably matters more than reality – they will be disgruntled. It's hard to be creative if you're unhappy in your work (although Morrissey could be the exception that proves the rule).

Even allowing for the arc of the moral universe inevitably bending towards justice, it still feels insurmountably long when it comes to societal inequality. Take income and gender inequality, for instance. The World Economic Forum, in 2018, estimated that finally eliminating the gender pay gap would take a further *200 years*. Despite important legislation, the #BlackLivesMatter campaign shows racial inequality is as bad as we've seen for decades.

The reality is that people of privilege (and as a middle-class, straight white man I am firmly in that bracket) have to have uncomfortable conversations if we're to move forward. Recently joining the ranks of the invisibly disabled has only served to highlight just how equity-myopic people like me have been. In 2016, I organised a conference on education. Advertising the invited speakers on Twitter drew a response I hadn't envisaged. To my shame, I was reminded that I had invited no people of colour to speak. I could rectify the situation (which I did) but I should have seen it as a problem long before that point.

It's that same myopia that probably meant that when I was drawing up a shortlist of likely characteristics of my case-study organisations, I hadn't included equity. But it became obvious that, for them, making the world a more equal place wasn't a cosy addition on their corporate social responsibility checklist – it was what drove them. And therein lies the equity paradox: for innovative, socially conscious organisations, it's often seen as 'the right thing to do', yet my investigations underline that it is precisely *through* the pursuit of equity that most of the organisations featured in this book have succeeded and become innovative. Indeed, some only exist because of their belief in a fairer society:

- New Roads school (Chapter Thirteen) was founded on the principle of diversity in its student intake and staff who work there. They've also achieved outstanding academic results.
- Repowering exists to ensure that communities generate and control their own energy. Each member of the share ownership scheme has one vote, whether the investment

was £1 or £1 million. It has won awards for the effectiveness of its schemes.

- The Dignified Mobile Toilet group in Nigeria was set up to ensure that access to a public toilet wasn't only for the wealthy.
- Liger Leadership Academy's *raison d'être* is to create future change agents, irrespective of geographic location or access to schooling.
- Riders for Health was formed solely to address the disparity in access to healthcare in poorer African countries.
- Morning Star's self-management structure gives every employee a voice in how the company is run.
- BrewDog's insistence upon paying all of its hospitality employees at least the living – not minimum – wage may have an impact upon costs, but it minimises churn and turns customers into fans.
- Patagonia's mission is: 'We're in business to save our home planet. We appreciate that all life on earth is under threat of extinction. We aim to use the resources we have – our business, our investments, our voice and our imaginations – to do something about it.'

One of the most celebrated examples of this equity paradox was when the first international assessment tables of national education systems (PISA) shocked everyone by placing Finland at the top. Those who were most surprised by this revelation were the Finns themselves. They hadn't created a system in order to excel at international tests. Their driving force was, and still is, to ensure that *every* Finnish child had the same quality of education. Conversely, countries that overtly stated that they needed to be among the leading test-takers globally – like the UK and the USA – were, at best, found to be strictly average (and remain highly unequal).

All of the pioneer organisations featured in this book demonstrate that having equity as the central driver improves performance, inspires loyalty, engagement and innovation. It's also part of the reason why cooperatives are now one of the fastest-growing sectors in the world. Most organisations boast that they comply with legislative requirements. Too many will talk proudly of their external corporate social responsibilities but fail to live their beliefs in their own workplace. The new reality of user engagement will put even more pressure upon organisations to be equitable places to work.

The World Economic Forum's assertion, in 2016, that 'we don't need a crystal ball to predict that today's social unrest and growing social inequalities, in spite of the promises brought on by the Fourth Industrial Revolution, won't let up without a drastic improvement in opportunities' holds true whether you are looking at gun violence/poverty correlations or the global auction for talent. Organisations should no longer view equity as a lofty aspiration but, instead, as a central strategy for growth and innovation.

Engagement & equity takeaways:

- Before you can enhance engagement, you have to measure it. There are dozens of tools already out there and, while some measure compliance more than engagement, don't allow the perfect to become the enemy of the good.
- The new paradigm also requires you to think about user engagement. There are few reliable metrics out there, so you may have to create your own, but this is a useful process in itself. What kind of relationship do you want to have with your users? Enlightened sounding board? Co-producers? Partners in development?
- Don't fall into the trap of thinking engagement is a top-down responsibility. Look at how to co-create an ideal

organisational environment (try using the free Canvas tool, designed by organisational consultants Corporate Rebels, as a means to bring people in[1]).

- Consider how you reward your people – are your incentives likely to foster short- or longer-term engagement? Purely transactional incentives (performance-related pay increases are classic examples) will not make your people feel greater fondness towards the organisation. Memories build dedication, incentives foster competition.

- Dubai's Knowledge and Human Development Authority saw increased employee engagement when they adopted a self-determined, self-managed, co-created and highly visible commitment to well-being.

- Don't wait until the 'exit interview' to find out why your people are disengaged enough to leave – carry out periodic 'stay interviews' to find out what's keeping them with you and surface engagement issues before they become serious.

- Recognition schemes based upon tenure or long service are neither values-driven nor relevant. Ditch the 'employee of the month' awards and coach managers to say 'thank you' regularly and with conviction. According to Inc.com, 7 out of 10 employees who receive appreciation for their good work said they're happy with their jobs. When it comes to recognition, it really is the thought that counts.

- Learn from BrewDog and WD-40 Company: the single most effective way to reach >90% engagement levels, and <10% attrition rates, is to make a dynamic learning culture your #1 priority.

- There is no engagement without equity.

- Equity requires intentionality, high visibility and humility.

---

1 https://corporate-rebels.com/Blog/wp-content/uploads/2017/04/Corporate-Rebels-Canvas.pdf.

- Learn from sparks & honey – equity and diversity go hand in hand and start with your governance: an advisory board of 40 includes 23 women, 17 men; 11 LGBTQ people; 5 generations; 16 ethnic origins; 12 languages; 1 wheelchair-enabled.
- Ask yourself the hard questions: 'Do we genuinely pay equally?' 'What cultural blockers are in place that prevent equality of opportunity?' 'Are opportunities for progression even-handed and available to all?' 'How do the ways in which we mentor and coach young talent and young leaders foster equity?'
- Make equity a talking point: how often do we ask our people if they feel they are being treated fairly?

AUTONOMY & AGENCY

Let's start with a clarification: autonomy and agency are not the same. Autonomy implies self-direction, freedom to choose, being independent. Agency is usually defined as a capacity to act, the route through which something is achieved, change realised. As with the other ingredients of ingenuity's growing medium, you can have autonomy without agency and vice versa – having both is best.

If you're looking to make your organisation people-powered, autonomy becomes a prerequisite. Expecting people to be innovative in an environment of low autonomy is like asking someone to ride a bike with the brakes permanently on. That's not to say that your culture should be loose and unstructured. Your team will thrive when autonomy is defined by clear boundaries and expectations. As Nietzsche said: 'The artist is he who dances in chains.' Innovation needs discipline.

The triple-helix

We know, from Dan Pink's *Drive* and Amabile and Kramer's *The Progress Principle*, that autonomy is inextricably woven into two of the other ingredients: engagement and trust. There may be the *freedom* to act – but without trust (Covey's trust tax), there's no *incentive* to exercise autonomy. When autonomy accompanies trust, on the other hand, the engagement dividend soars.

So, given all that, why *wouldn't* more autonomy be a good idea? Well, it turns out that there's one application when complete autonomy isn't helpful. Micromanagement is one of the key reasons why people leave an organisation, but the opposite doesn't help either. The well-intentioned manager might be flattered to hear that 'he leaves me alone to get on with my work', but in such situations, according to author Tom Rath, 4 in 10 workers who see little of their boss, working in relative isolation, soon become disengaged.

'Let my people go (surfing)'

Despite the weight of evidence in support of self-direction, it would be misleading to suggest that we're all becoming as autonomous as the vehicles we'll soon be driving. In fact, this is one of the great ironies of twenty-first-century life: at a time when we're flooding the workplace with machines that make independent decisions, we're driving autonomy out. The Swiss–Swedish multinational corporation ABB raised eyebrows with a giant billboard ad saying 'Let's write the future together, with robots that have what it takes to collaborate'. At the same time, the late Stephen Hawking was warning us that 'the short-term impact of AI depends on who controls it; the long-term impact depends on whether it can be controlled at all.'

If we accept the conclusion of self-determination theory (that people need autonomy to fulfil their potential), then we should look at how exemplar organisations have created environments in which autonomy thrives. Yvon and Malinda Chouinard's book about Patagonia's practices was titled *Let My People Go Surfing* for a good reason: you will get better results and have happier employees when they can choose when they work. Explaining their flexible working environment, Chouinard says: 'A serious surfer doesn't plan to go surfing next Tuesday at two o'clock. You go surfing when there are waves and the tide and the wind are right.'

Sounds like a great place to work, doesn't it? One could reasonably expect some abuse of such freedoms, but this was not the case in the organisations I visited, for two good reasons: firstly, they put frameworks in place to prevent it; but secondly – and primarily – they believe that, given freedom, people will go above and beyond the level of commitment to be found in more constrained and suspicious organisations. Chouinard's strategy seems to be 'do what needs to be done, and you can work as you choose to work'.

A question of agency

At WD-40 Company, Garry Ridge's conviction is that if you are the leader who always has the answers, you'll have employees that never ask any questions. So those three favourite words ('I don't know') open the door to a sense of agency. Like Nordstrom's staff handbook, he is putting the onus on the person to act through their best judgement, so a culture where not knowing is fine, but with that freedom comes the responsibility to ask. And the question that every innovative culture should welcome is…

'*Why?*'

Is it all or nothing?

Agency naysayers have a well-rehearsed litany of excuses for giving control away. The most pernicious is the argument that 'it only works if you change everything'. Not so, argues Ricardo Semler:

> Start by creating freedom in a certain field [...] to see what works for your organisation. When you feel satisfied with the results, you can add more [...] Change is not something that happens overnight, and it only happens when you make a start somewhere.

For most organisations, that starting point is either structural or procedural. Few of the places I visited had the holacratic structure of Morning Star, but all of them instilled a form of agency (within clear boundaries) into their procedures. BrewDog subscribe to the notion of 'disciplined innovation'. For James Watt, it is about setting the overall vision and then freeing people up to act independently:

> We hand our teams a high level of autonomy. Our teams are inspired to set their own objectives, working with their line managers to identify how they can set realistic targets relevant to their ambitions and progression plans. Budgets are developed by teams independently and signed off by our mission control.

Innovation theorists often cite a couple of models that organisations can adopt in building a culture where people gain agency but do so progressively. One is the concept of three communities: interest, engagement and practice. The idea is that no one should feel pressured to engage in an innovation if feeling unsure or insecure. They can simply observe the process and be kept informed about its implementation (community of interest). Gradually, they may wish to engage with the innovation, but without a commitment to act – taking part in team meetings or being a critical friend (community of engagement). Once they feel confident, they join a community of practice – the people who are making the change happen. Each organisation will have team members who feel comfortable being in the community of practice for innovation X, but would prefer to be in the community of interest, or engagement, for innovation Y.

The other model is the 'sigmoid curve' of innovation. This mathematical concept was adapted by author and management consultant Charles Handy. He reasons that with almost any initiative, or human endeavour, there are phases of development, introduction, growth and maturity, where levels of activity rise alongside enthusiasm and confidence in the initiative. Eventually, however, the idea starts to run out of steam and performance declines (giving rise to the S-shaped sigmoid curve). The trick, for any organisation, is to have a variant, or new refinement ready to kick in, just before the curve starts its downward trajectory.

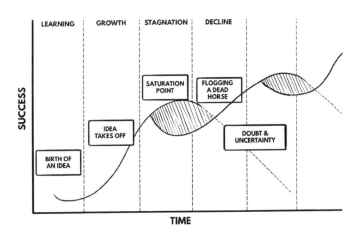

Too often, committing to a culture of agency is equated with a free-for-all, letting a thousand flowers bloom. The net result of undisciplined innovation is fear and paralysis – there's simply too much being tried out for people to feel secure in knowing what works. Innovations come and go and eventually 'initiativitis' creates cynicism and exhaustion.

But just because you can't do it all is no reason not to do anything.

The Repowering case study also highlights the interplay between learning and agency. The thousands of young people who have been trained by Repowering (with many now earning a living in the renewable energy industry) were probably less excited about putting up solar panels on the roof of their flats than in the ability to take control of their energy needs. Learning and agency make transformative bedfellows, with each feeding the other. Once you have greater control of anything – your energy, your finances, your life – you become motivated to learn more.

Autonomy and agency takeaways:

- Look critically at your structure – hierarchical organisations are autonomy-killers.
- If holacracy is too risky, there are simple steps towards self-management that can be taken: for example, redefine jobs/roles so that accountabilities are more lateral, less vertical; think about tasks in overlapping circles, rather than person-specific responsibilities.
- Autonomy is hard in large teams – think about how to restructure so that teams are smaller.
- Undertake audits to find 'autonomy blockers' – ask your people to tell you the processes and procedures that exasperate them. Then ask them to collectively figure out a solution.
- Democracy drives autonomy – you can't delegate autonomy only to the chosen few who are trusted with it. Additionally, your user-innovators will insist upon equality of opportunity and choice, so eliminate 'selective' freedoms.

- Symbols matter – you can't claim to run an autonomous organisation if you have reserved senior managers' parking spots or perks for leaders.
- Agency needs security and humility. As Gwyn ap Harri (Chapter Thirteen) tells his people, 'Don't *not* do anything because of your fear; don't *just* do something because of your ego.'
- The more rules you have in your staff handbook, the less agency you will have in your people. Remember Nordstrom? If you're looking for inspiration, download the staff handbook at the world's most successful video gaming company, Valve – it's an agency charter.
- Agency happens when leaders ask the right questions ('Why do we do X, Y, Z?') and when they stop providing all the answers. Take inspiration from Patagonia's Yvon Chouinard's 'management by absence' strategy.
- Sharing information (practising transparency) is a critical contributor. People will not take actions or make decisions if they suspect that they have less information than others.
- Eliminate fear of mistakes. Remember Garry Ridge's insistence upon replacing the language of failure with the 'learning moment'? When it's OK to talk about getting things wrong, your sense of agency is protected.

MASTERY & MEANING

Whilst none of the organisations I visited had all eight ingredients in place, they had all built caring, curious environments, so a virtuous circle exists. Trust triggers engagement. Transparency supports equity. Autonomy leads to agency. You get the idea.

It should be no surprise, therefore, to see that autonomy can also lead to mastery. I don't need to explore the symbiosis involved

– Daniel Pink explored this artfully in the aforementioned *Drive*. What interests me here is looking at what we can learn about mastery by looking beyond the workplace to see how it fosters ingenuity, and what we can practically do to build mastery.

First, let's try to define it – though that's not particularly easy. Too often mastery is seen as an end and not the means. Dictionary definitions associate it with command and superiority, having arrived at a state of expertise. Pink's version – the desire to get better and better at something that matters – gets us closer to the sense of a journey and not the destination. The definition that nails 'mastery as progression', however, comes from management expert Peter Senge:

> People with a high level of personal mastery live in a continual learning mode. They never 'arrive' […] personal mastery is not something you possess. It is a process. People with a high level of personal mastery are acutely aware of their ignorance, their incompetence, their growth areas. And they are deeply self-confident. Paradoxical? Only for those who do not see the journey is the reward.

Mastery, therefore, can be seen as a motivation, but it's also a *learning process* central to one's personal development. Instead of believing you have a fixed mindset, mastery helps build what's now popularly known (thanks to the work of Stanford Professor Carol Dweck) as a 'growth mindset'.

Mastery and self-determination

Having a growth mindset is a critical part in the three components of self-determination we looked at in Chapter Two (competence, relatedness and autonomy), and the need for self-determination is bolstered by the pursuit of mastery. Put simply, we need to know that we're *good* at something and, knowing that, we feel more in control of our lives. For a bonus point, gaining mastery also makes us want to learn more.

Why does this matter? Well, if your organisation is a business, consider this: a report commissioned by LinkedIn found that 44% of people said that personal development and career advancement opportunities were the reason why they chose their current jobs. This is especially true of younger employees who aren't lured by money, preferring instead more freedom and a career where they make daily progress through a culture of learning. Can you say, hand on heart, that all your people fall into that category?

Tree-climbing fishes can spontaneously innovate

Mastery is one of those concepts where it's hard to imagine an antonym that would suffice. If the process indicates a desire to get better at something, can you imagine people wanting to get worse? Ultimately, it's a question of belief. I don't believe anyone invests time and energy into something to do it badly. It seems more likely that they're in the wrong role – the square peg in a round hole. That doesn't mean they're incapable of pursuing mastery though. Among the many quotes wrongly attributed to Albert Einstein is a particularly apt one: 'Everyone is a genius. But if you judge a fish by its ability to climb a tree, it will live its whole life believing it is stupid.'

I started my working life as a civil servant. I often joke that I was the most incompetent civil servant in the history of the service. But I was that fish and I felt stupid for two years. In a 10,000-strong workforce, there was no one to talk to regarding a role that might better allow me to shine; so, for the sake of my self-respect, I quit. I hasten to add that I'm not looking for sympathy: it was a soulless, mind-numbing job. And I went off to be a professional musician instead – so no regrets. I mention it by way of introducing a powerful approach to building mastery.

Playing to our strengths

I speak of what is frequently described as the 'strengths-based approach' to management. In siloed organisations with rigid role descriptions (and it doesn't get more rigid than the benefits department of the civil service), many people never get the opportunity to demonstrate ingenuity, simply because they're in the wrong job. In flatter, more fluid teams, fish get more of an opportunity to find water. Strengths-based organisations, like Morning Star, have understood the benefit of having people play to their strengths:

> We believe you should do what you're good at, so we don't try to fit people into a job. As a result, our people have broader and more complicated roles than elsewhere [...] Since we believe you have a right to get involved anywhere you think your skills can add value, people will often drive change outside their narrow area. We have a lot of spontaneous innovation, and ideas for change come from unusual places.

The great management thinker Peter Drucker was advocating a strengths-based approach back in the 1950s, so these are hardly new ideas. In 1989, he wrote: 'Management is about human beings. Its task is to make people capable of joint performance, to make their strengths effective and their weaknesses irrelevant.' In other words, this is not an approach that disregards weaknesses; it's simply about focusing on building on strengths and using the collective strengths of teams to minimise any weaknesses.

The Gallup organisation, in 2016, conducted a huge study of almost 50,000 business in 45 countries employing 1.2 million people. Companies that use strengths-based approaches see improved sales, increased profit, higher user engagement, lower turnover of staff, increased employee engagement and fewer safety incidents. In 2015, the Corporate Leadership Council found that:

- Around half of all organisations surveyed were committed to strengths-based management.
- Organisations that focus on building from strengths see a >36% improvement in performance.
- Organisations that focus on improving weaknesses, by contrast, see a 27% drop in performance.
- People who use their strengths every day are six times more likely to be engaged.

This focus on strengths has significantly grown in the past decade, with applications in education, healthcare, social care and community development. With its critical shift – the problem is the problem, not the person; emphasising potential, not deficiencies – it's easy to see why human-centred occupations are realising the power of strengths-based approaches. There is, however, a significant obstacle to be overcome. When asked, only 1 in 3 people would claim to know what their strengths are!

Despite the evidence supporting it, acceptance of strength-building has been slow and is far from universally accepted. One reason lies in our model of formal training. As Marcus Buckingham of the Gallup Organization discovered through thousands of interviews with managers, most training has the goal of making people better at something they were weak in. Furthermore, he argues that two long-established beliefs hinder the acceptance of strengths-based approaches: (a) anyone can be competent in anything if they work hard enough at it, and (b) the greatest room for individual growth lies in areas of weaknesses.

As a manager, I spent far too much time working on people's weaknesses. This was, largely, down to two factors: first, I thought that was what managers did (i.e. improve the things people weren't experienced or confident in doing); and, secondly, because nobody told me about strengths-based approaches. In the male-dominated culture I found myself in, it was a sign of weakness to be seen as 'going easy' on people who were not performing well. It was hard work, and had I known the benefits of strengths-based leadership, I would have managed people completely differently. Drucker's wisdom rings true: 'One should waste as little effort as possible on improving areas of low competence. It takes far more energy and work to improve from incompetence to mediocrity than it takes to improve from first-rate performance to excellence.'

Few of the organisations I visited would describe themselves as strengths-based but most displayed aspects of it. For organisations that are committed to innovation and personal mastery, a strengths-based approach is an obvious strategy to implement, and there are a plethora of guides and consultancies available to help you do it.

Work in search of meaning

The final ingredient – meaning – is often conflated with 'organisational purpose'. I'm not saying that what your organisation stands for isn't important (I've already noted the need for millennials to work for organisations that share their values). It's just that what perhaps matters more, in a people-powered organisation, is the way a sense of meaning fuels innovation, on three levels:

1. **The personal – who I am, what I aspire to.**
2. **The inter-personal – my relationship with those I engage with.**
3. **The societal – being involved in something bigger than yourself.**

And a reminder: we're talking about 'occupation' (i.e. what occupies us) here, not just employment (the stuff that pays a wage).

Being alive

We don't become part of organisations (whether political, social or employment) for the prime purpose of knowing ourselves better – but it *is* a factor. The appearance of life coaches in organisations underlines this. In 1974, the author Studs Terkel documented the lives of over 100 Americans working in an unglamorous search for meaning: housewives, prostitutes, production-line workers, grave-diggers. *Working* is a wonderful book and, although it speaks of a different time, some things are immutable. His conclusion? Work is a search for 'daily meaning as well as daily bread, for recognition as well as cash, for astonishment rather than torpor'. Some of the interviewees find pleasure and pride in their work ('When I put the plate down, you don't hear a sound,' says Dolores, a waitress. 'When someone says, "How come you're just a waitress?" I say, "Don't you think you deserve to be served by me?"'). For others, work is something to be endured (Mike, a steelworker, says, 'The day I get excited about my job is the day I go to a headshrinker. How are you gonna get excited about pulling steel?').

How is it that Dolores finds fulfilment in a task considered menial, while Mike doesn't? Abe Maslow revised his famous motivational 'hierarchy of needs' in 1970. His initial model suggested that, after our basic needs were met (food, warmth, security, relationships), we are motivated to meet psychological and self-fulfilment needs (achieving one's potential; being creative). The expanded hierarchy adds a further layer on top: self-transcendence (the need for meaning beyond the self). Psychologists Bryan Dik and Ryan Duffy, authors of *Make Your Job a Calling*, found that 68% of college students surveyed considered a spiritual calling and sense of higher purpose essential to them when choosing a career. We may not have all the answers, but if we want people to be creative, we have to ask them questions about *meaningful 'occupations'*. What aspects of their work provide a sense of fulfilment? What doesn't?

How does their work help them to understand themselves better? What *occupies* them when they're not at work? How might their role be adjusted so that they can grow a sense of personal mastery?

Being with you

We met Teresa Amabile in Chapter Seven. Her inner work-life theory ('making daily progress in meaningful work') has serious implications for how people are led. She concludes: 'Management should enrich the lives of the people working inside the organization – by enabling them to succeed at work that has real value to their customers, the community and themselves.' How can we understand that enrichment if our relationship to customers is constrained by a script or our dealings with colleagues are not self-directed? And the new paradigm offers great opportunities to establish relations with the legions of user-innovators, as co-producers, not just customers. So how can the people who work in our organisations establish meaning through respectful and humble dialogue with us as peer producers? Ricardo Semler decided to scrap SEMCO's HR department because it got in the way of people, associates and peer producers resolving conflicts themselves. Ironically, it led to SEMCO creating a consultancy to advise some of the world's biggest corporations on HR strategies. There's a lesson in there somewhere…

Being a part of something bigger than yourself

There isn't anything inherently special about those young people I met at the Liger Leadership Academy in Phnom Penh. They are not equipped with special talents that kids in, say, inner-city New York have missed out on. The difference, it seems to me, is that Jeff Holte and Dom Sharpe have worked tirelessly to give them a range of authentic experiences that other young people don't get. Every year, every student has to write an essay around the question: 'How have I changed Cambodia this year?' These students display extraordinary problem-solving ingenuity simply because they know that the future of their country depends upon it. That's what social purpose looks like.

We're blessed to have the most ethically and morally conscious generation of young people about to run the world. If we want them to join our organisations, instead of bland social corporate responsibility statements, we need to find ways of devising people-powered social impact. In successive Deloitte surveys, millennials have made their intentions clear: 60% said they chose an employer with a sense of purpose; 71% said companies should do more to address global issues, resource scarcity (68%), climate change (65%) and income inequality (64%).

Having a strong stance on social issues, however, is only the start. Organisations need to ask themselves how they can turn that commitment into people-powered agency. They only have to look at Patagonia, Repowering and all of the schools featured in this book for inspiration. Their socially driven inventions (and interventions) have originated with their workers, their user-innovators and their customers, *ahead of* their leadership teams.

Paul Sinton-Hewitt is the founder of the global running phenomenon Parkrun (300,000 runners, every weekend in over 1,500 locations). As he put it, in a *Guardian* interview:

> I know what it means to have targets and to sell. I get all that. But there's another economy here. An economy of helping people to be the best they can be, to change their lives and grow as individuals.

That's a powerful description of true occupational meaning: who we are, who we engage with and who we want to be.

Mastery and meaning takeaways:

- Large departments are antithetical to finding mastery and meaning. Can they be broken down into smaller, more autonomous teams?
- Rewrite job descriptions so that reporting and accountabilities can be more lateral/peer-based instead of vertical.
- Rethink performance evaluation. Does it develop strengths or focus upon deficits? Is it even necessary – could peer ranking/evaluation replace it?
- Encourage goals that are set by your people (not imposed by managers) and peer-reviewed.
- Is your organisational structure supporting – or hindering – strengths and mastery?
- Conduct audits to identify to what extent people are in 'continual learning mode'. Are they gaining confidence?
- Replace 'tasks' with self-designed commitments.
- Do you recruit for strengths or for rigid person specifications?
- Consider how internal communications can make others aware of member strengths.
- Turn managers into learning coaches.
- How can you reinforce a strengths-based approach by connecting it to your 'brand'?
- Examine your learning and development programmes – how do they support your people in finding personal meaning?
- How do you make your social purpose known to user-innovators in your community? How is it 'lived' beyond a commitment?
- How are your people able to be directly involved in activities that support your social purpose?

PART SIX

The Power of Us in a Post-Covid World

The After Corona world must be fundamentally changed from the world Before Corona. How are we preparing the generation who will have to figure it out?

CHAPTER TWELVE

Taking It to the Streets – A New Era of Activism?

My three-year discovery of people-powered innovation began in the USA at the South by Southwest festival, where former Vice-President Joe Biden spoke passionately of the need to bring together the collective intelligence of the global medical community (including informed citizens) to bring an end to the scourge of cancer. Along the way, I'd personally faced an unwelcome recurrence of the disease. And my research ended in Australia, when a training tour I was running was cut short as the During Corona world became a little clearer. International travel – and organisations – had begun shutting down, and my immediate challenge was simply getting home while I still could. The journey back took me through the normally bustling cities of Melbourne and Sydney, through Abu Dhabi's emptying airport and ended in an eerily desolate Manchester Airport baggage hall. By the time I turned the key to my home in North Yorkshire – a day before the UK belatedly locked down – it occurred to me that Biden's intimate knowledge of medical research was about to become a really significant strength in his presidential job application.

Towards the end of my travels, however, a further realisation slowly dawned on me. I had visited deeply impressive organisations, talked with leaders who had real vision and was inspired by the young people who will be tomorrow's innovators, fixing our planet. Maybe I should have spotted it sooner, but there it was, sitting waiting for me when I returned home: the eight qualities that define innovative organisational cultures (trust, transparency, engagement, equity, autonomy, agency, mastery, meaning) have either been in decline, or lost, from civic society in recent years. Put another way: many of us are drawn towards them in the organisations we work for, precisely *because* they're missing in our daily lives.

Consider the evidence. The loss of trust in our media and institutions. The crisis of disengagement in our schools and workplaces. The ever-widening social inequality. The de-skilling of labour. The quest to 'take back control'. And – the most sobering – a plaintive search for identity and meaning experienced by our children and young people. Sociologists and psychologists will probably maintain that this has been happening for a very long time. Or even that it was ever thus. Nevertheless, in the three years I'd spent seeking out mass ingenuity, the events I'd see on TV screens, wherever I happened to be, suggested that our long-established social contracts – policing by consent, the rule of law, free speech and legislative supremacy – were close to breaking point.

'No justice, no peace'

After the murder of George Floyd, a prolonged wave of street protests flared up all over the world. Coinciding with the coronavirus lockdowns, these large-scale protests provoked alarm and admiration in equal measure. How strongly were people of all ages feeling that they'd risk their health, and that of their family, to make their voices heard? And although the initial focus was justice for the Floyd family, in the three weeks following the tragedy, the direction of the anger widened. Statues of slave traders were pulled down, celebrities and politicians publicly condemned police brutality and institutionalised racism, cities changed street names to 'Black Lives Matter', Netflix removed comedies that contained culturally insensitive portrayals of discriminated-against minorities. It was as if the world had woken from a self-induced coma in the 1950s. Because of citizen journalism, if protesters were attacked by police, it was instantly shared around the world, thus confirming the underlying cause of the protest. Even in the bombed-out ruins of Idlib in Syria, young graffiti artists painted a tribute to George Floyd. There was a whiff of the summer of '68 about it.

The #BlackLivesMatter campaign hit a raw nerve for black and ethnic minorities. Not only had police brutality been seen to target their community, coronavirus deaths were significantly higher in those communities. The early affirmations that we were 'all in this together' had been exposed – case numbers and mortality rates were unevenly distributed. If you came from a rural, middle-class white community, you were far less likely to be subject to police brutality *and* severe effects of Covid-19 than if you had darker skin, lived in a densely populated city or were poor.

George Floyd's death at the hands of the Minneapolis police takes its place in a long line of black people being murdered by police officials. Previous injustices also sparked protests and calls for change. However, there was something different about this moment – things actually began to change. Speaking at a protest in Minneapolis, city council president Lisa Bender said:

> In Minneapolis and in cities across the US, it is clear that our system of policing is not keeping our communities safe. Our efforts at incremental reform have failed, period. […] Our commitment is to end policing as we know it and to recreate systems of public safety that actually keep us safe […] We recognise that we don't have all the answers about what a police-free future looks like, but our community does. We're committing to engaging with every willing community member in the City of Minneapolis over the next year to identify what safety looks like for everyone.

State governors, after decades of avoiding the issue, vowed to remove confederate monuments and statues of controversial figures. Cities all over the world followed suit.

Learning the lessons of the past

Even before the global howl of protest at racial inequality, the recent past had seen not just more but *more effective* social movements seemingly springing up everywhere. If it feels to you as though people are becoming more active, then you're right. Erica Chenoweth of the Crowd Counting Consortium says:

> What we're seeing in the United States is symptomatic of what we see around the world […] [Between] resistance against authoritarianism, colonial and foreign and military occupation […] we've had more mass movements in this decade than in any decade since 1900.

Four of the five largest demonstrations in US history took place during 2017/18, including the March for Science and the Women's March (2017 and 2018). This latter came about in protest at Donald Trump's treatment of women (made graphic by the Access Hollywood tapes). Between 3 and 4 million women, not just in the USA but around the world, demonstrated on the day after Trump's inauguration. Together with the #MeToo movement – a global response to the abuse revelations involving Hollywood mogul Harvey Weinstein (and others) – the impact upon social norms has been revelatory. There are few countries where women have not spoken out on sexual harassment. Corporations have been shaken, celebrities previously thought of as 'untouchable' have been exposed and legislation introduced. It may be that we'll look back on the power of these two movements as the moment when half the planet's population began to be treated equally, and people of colour were given hope that change could indeed come.

March for Life and #MeToo will also be viewed as models for future social movements, so expertly have they been organised. Rather than protest movements operating on a kind of Groundhog Day principle, whereby the mistakes of the past are recreated through a failure of collective memory, the increasing sophistication of networking, and the factors discussed throughout this book, have led to activism that works.

Take the biggest of global issues: the looming environmental catastrophe. No one would have predicted that a shy, 15-year-old Swedish schoolkid with Asperger's syndrome would spark a global movement of young people striking from school in protest at governmental complacency in response to the existential threat of climate change. But that's exactly what Greta Thunberg achieved. In August 2018, no one took much notice of the somewhat lonely teenager sitting outside the Swedish parliament, every Friday. But within a few months, she had inspired schoolchildren in major cities all over the world and become *Time* magazine's 2019 Person of the Year. Her ability to capture the zeitgeist was impressively shown in June 2020, in an interview with the BBC:

> Society has passed a social tipping point. We can no longer look away from what our society has been ignoring for so long whether it is equality, justice or sustainability […] People are starting to find their voice, to understand that they can actually have an impact […] Doing our best is no longer good enough. We must now do the seemingly impossible. And that is up to you and me. Because no one else will do it for us.

For a good example of what Greta is describing – activism with impact – you need look no further than Extinction Rebellion. Formed by about 100 senior academics in May 2018, sporadic protests were followed by 10 days of civil disobedience that brought London to a standstill in April 2019. Media images of elderly, articulate, middle-class protesters glued to buildings, stripping off in the public gallery of the House of Commons or sitting on top of trains clearly flummoxed the government. The UK's environmental minister, Michael Gove, was forced to admit that he needed to do much more.

Eco-warriors are too often dismissed as the coordinators of short-lived, and ultimately doomed, stunts. This was exactly the characterisation of the Occupy movement that took over parts of major cities around the world during 2011. Although much smaller now, it's wrong to suggest the Occupy movement fizzled out, leaving no discernible legacy. For one thing, Extinction Rebellion's 2019 protests learned from Occupy's mistakes in two critical areas. First, they didn't 'dig in' for a long-haul encampment in one chosen location, as Occupy had done. Their agility in moving around London may have irritated London commuters, but it also made them elusive and therefore hard to stop. Second, whereas Occupy often stubbornly refused to articulate specific aims, Extinction Rebellion could not have been clearer in their demands of governments globally:

- Tell the truth – by declaring a climate and ecological emergency.
- Act now – to halt biodiversity loss and reduce greenhouse gas emissions to net zero by 2025.
- Beyond politics – commission and be led by the decision of a citizens' assembly on climate and ecological justice.

And it worked. From 15 April 2019, 10 days of non-violent resistance resulted in over 1,000 arrests, blanket media coverage and synchronised protests around the world. Within 10 days, 27 countries had seen copycat protests. The movement was even endorsed by the appearance of a Banksy mural (a child tending a plant next to the message 'From this moment despair ends and tactics begin'). Just days after the 'closing ceremony' in Hyde Park, London, the UK government had passed a motion declaring a 'climate emergency' – an action consistently demanded for years but considered unrealistic – and governments around the world were revising targets and promising urgent actions.

Remember that the three forms of people-powered innovation mentioned in Section One include advocating for new products or services (like a new model of policing or public consultation), so it's to be expected that the strategies and organisational techniques deployed by user-innovators and peer producers would also be adopted by social movements. In short, they just got a lot smarter.

Facilitate, don't assimilate

Just as the tools of people-powered innovation apply to social activism, the choices for 'producers' (in this case governments and industry alliances) are the same: work with them, ignore them or try to eradicate them. When the Organization of the Petroleum Exporting Countries (OPEC – the powerful group of oil-producing nations) said, in July 2019, that climate activists like

Greta Thunberg were 'perhaps the greatest threat to our industry going forward', it seemed to be a recognition that this generation of young people were not going to be seen and not heard. OPEC's Secretary General, Mohammed Barkindo, said that children of some colleagues at OPEC's headquarters 'are asking us about their future because […] they see their peers on the streets campaigning against our industry', and that the mobilisation against oil was beginning to 'dictate policies and corporate decisions, including investment in the industry'. Thunberg tweeted her thanks to OPEC, describing it as 'our biggest compliment yet'. And then, along with a growing phalanx of young activist groups, set about organising the Global Climate Strike. On 20 September 2019, over 6 million people, in 150 countries around the world, turned out in protest at the growing climate crisis – the largest public protest in history. Organised by a bunch of schoolchildren. Set aside the eloquence and power of the message these young people demonstrated. This was a hell of a feat of organisation.

It's hard to dismiss these campaigners as exceptions, not least because there are so many of them. I'm very fortunate in my working life to be able to meet students who are intent on making an impact. Remembering my adolescent self is embarrassing by comparison. My generation – the baby-boomers – is largely misled by the 'Gen Z' stereotype of narcissistic, screen-addicted, self-serving young people. More and more, however, we seem to be getting the wake-up call that Mohammed Barkindo got. And it should be a cause for great celebration. Their ability to organise through globally connected networks, their savvy use of social media to wrong-foot opponents and their extensive depth of subject knowledge are all going to come in handy when we finally accept that we've screwed up the environment, the economy, democracy, social care, healthcare, education, public housing… I could go on. At a time when parliamentary democracy in the UK is a laughing stock, I honestly believe we could do less harm if we simply handed over the keys to the House of Commons and said 'It's all yours.' We will see more reasons to be thankful for the current crop of young people in Chapter Thirteen.

While there will always be a place for high-profile mass public demonstrations, the lessons learned from Occupy and others is that, increasingly, it's grassroots actions that will win hearts and minds. In a sense, it's activism made active. And the response to Covid-19 has given us a million illustrations.

Living with ambiguity

For all its horror, the Covid-19 pandemic has given us a much-needed sense of perspective. In the UK, the political discourse had been consumed for three years by Brexit. Now, it didn't seem to matter anymore. Suddenly, we wanted to hear from experts. No more simplistic slogans – we looked to our politicians to give us the plain, unadorned truth. We all came to terms with the sense of existential ambiguity normally only felt during periods of global warfare. Alongside that, however, was an introspection on some of the fundamental questions we now find ourselves asking ourselves: how do we wish to be governed? What does nationalism mean when our entire species is under attack? Where do we find the balance between personal liberty and our responsibility to look after each other?

Above all, during the early, darkest days of the pandemic, we desperately sought hope and compassion. I was no different to anyone else. Since I'd consciously chosen to understand organisations that commit to something bigger than themselves and are places where ingenuity flourishes, I wanted reassurance that their actions at the outset of the pandemic would exemplify both hope and compassion. I needn't have worried:

- BrewDog saw their revenue drop, overnight, by 70%, as pubs around the world were ordered to close. During the first week of lockdown, someone stole a huge truck filled with almost the entire stock of their most popular beer, Punk IPA. Alongside the other 130,000 Equity Punks, I received an email saying they were fighting for their survival. Despite that, they kept their workforce intact. The co-founders, Martin Dickie and James Watt, took no salary for 2020, and the leadership team took a significant pay cut. BrewDog switched part of their distillery from gin and whisky to producing hand sanitisers, which they gave away to hospitals and care homes throughout Scotland. Their delivery vans switched from dropping off beers to dropping off free school meals for children from disadvantaged communities. They created over 100 virtual pubs where people could meet, play online pub quizzes, be inspired by Martin to brew their own beer, and enjoy live music and comedy. Their bars became 'BrewDog Drive-Thru', ensuring customers could make contactless purchases. Their online sales soared as their community rallied to support them.

- sparks & honey refocused their culture briefings to alert businesses, clients and the general public to the cultural implications of the pandemic. Remote daily briefings shared global insights around the virus and consumerism, the economy, the environment, education and technology.

- XP school – in keeping with schools all over the world – had only days to switch their entire curriculum to a virtual school, while also being required to look after vulnerable children and children of key workers in the school.

- Pan Pantziarka's ReDo initiative suddenly found itself the centre of global interest in repurposing drugs, as more countries tested hydroxychloroquine as a preventative and treatment option. Pan urged for a balance between hope and caution. Caution, because so many, including the US president, rushed to declare 'a winner' before there was proof of efficacy. But also hope: 'Pretty much all of the advantages that we have proposed for repurposing in oncology are coming to the fore in this pandemic. The case for repurposing is suddenly clear to many more people.'

- As the pandemic began to sweep over Africa, Riders For Health became contact tracers and test-sample couriers in remote areas of Lesotho and Nigeria.
- Repowering opened more Energy Gardens in London, to meet the increased need for, and uncertainty over, fresh food availability.
- In early March 2020, as soon as the spread of the virus became clear, Patagonia closed its offices, stores, even its website, while committing to paying all of its employees in full. Unsurprisingly, it was one of the first global brands to do so.

A twenty-first century Renaissance?

These are just some of the inventive responses from organisations featured in this book, but they offer only the briefest of glimpses of a global outpouring of acts of ingenuity, compassion and activism. Even the most cynical of social observers couldn't help but be impressed. Inevitably perhaps, the panic-stricken requests for intensive care equipment weren't always well thought out. The UK ventilator consortium of Siemens, Rolls Royce, Ford and Airbus was formed to produce 10,000 ventilators for intensive care units. Within a few weeks, they stood down as it was realised that putting patients on last-ditch ventilation was less effective than preventing the need for such ventilation. So attention switched to continuous positive airways pressure (CPAP) machines that could help people breathe before their condition worsened. The Mercedes Formula One team worked with University College London to produce a more effective CPAP solution. Working flat out, *in fewer than 100 hours*, they had gone from initial meeting to supplying the first of 10,000 machines commissioned by the UK government. All over the world, design and development processes that had hitherto been measured in years were being truncated to days. In France, for example, Just One Giant Lab quickly became an international alliance of over 4,000 members (encompassing healthcare workers, designers, engineers, makers and technologists) working on dozens of Covid-related challenges.

As impressive as these gestures are, the role of citizen scientists around the world played a vital role in creating data platforms that tracked the virus spread. They helped 'flatten the curve' of the initial outbreak and will minimise the pandemic's mortality rate in the months and years to come. The UpCode Academy, in Singapore, tapped into the government's desire for data transparency by making a wealth of data available to all. Covid-19 SG tracks every known coronavirus case, where the infection originated, recovery times and clusters of infections, thus enabling residents to make informed decisions. Similarly, Foldit is a simulation that enables gamers to identify proteins by playing video games. When the coronavirus outbreak occurred, almost 3,000 people patterned how the virus's proteins could be affected by new drug therapies.

These are impressive statements of what can be achieved through the power of us. The outpouring of ingenuity, all over the globe, was often seen in sharp contrast to some governments' faltering attempts to gain control of the coronavirus. The US and UK administrations became overwhelmed as their initial complacency – in not taking the pandemic seriously during January/February 2020 – turned to barely disguised panic following the exponential spread of the virus. There were moments when it seemed as though there had been a shift in power: from ministers and spokespersons, to the private sector, researchers and grassroots groups mentioned here. When the pandemic is finally brought under control, it will be seen as a landmark achievement, not in inter-governmental coordination (generally judged to be poor or non-existent) but in harnessing people-powered innovation to solve the biggest of crises. Who knew we were capable of such a coordinated, urgent deployment of the cognitive surplus that had been lying dormant for years, just waiting for a chance to save the world? Well, we did. We knew, deep down, that we could determine our own futures, steered by our best selves. But that quiet internal voice had been drowned out among a cacophony of individualism, invective and self-interest. The big question remains, however: can we sustain this compassionate creativity once the field hospitals are closed down?

The economic and social consequences of Covid-19 will be with us for decades. Once we're through this, the world we knew will have gone and we will have to rethink and redesign the world to come. It will be a task for the current generation, currently in high school and college, to figure out. The baby boomer's responsibility is to ensure that they have the power of us behind them.

Key points:

- We are witnessing new and more effective social movements redefining social, environmental and cultural norms, deploying the tools and techniques of mass ingenuity.
- During the coronavirus pandemic, these grassroots actions often outperformed governmental responses that were slow and unwieldy.
- Grassroots groups, citizen scientists and peer producers are now better connected and have learned from previous attempts to leverage social reform. They are willing to lead communities in a post-Covid world. Given the scale of the anticipated economic depression, we may have no option but to work closely with them.

CHAPTER THIRTEEN

The Future Is Theirs – Meet the Problem-Solvers

Before we close, let's address the question that every parent grapples with, that politicians neglect and that some of the people I interviewed are already finding answers to: how do we help young people become fearless agents of their own destinies? I confess that in my darker moments I find another way of putting it: how on earth can they *fix* the earth, so that they can even *have* a future on it? One of the reasons why Greta Thunberg attracted so much attention is her refusal to sugar-coat the pill. When she addressed the United Nations in October 2019, she got straight to the point:

> I should be back in school on the other side of the ocean. Yet you all come to me for hope? How dare you! You have stolen

my dreams and my childhood with your empty words. And
yet I'm one of the lucky ones. People are suffering. People are
dying. Entire ecosystems are collapsing. We are in the beginning
of a mass extinction. And all you can talk about is money and
fairy tales of eternal economic growth. How dare you!

Greta Thunberg spoke an inconvenient truth. We are leaving
young people with the stiffest of tasks, in the harshest of circumstances and with the least available support. Despite all that, I
have never been more hopeful for the future. Why? Because I
have spent much of the past 10 years in the company of this
generation, and I never fail to be impressed, and moved, by the
way they think, feel and act. It's the responsibility of any society
to provide mentors and role models for them, and to give them
the chance to develop the skills and experiences they'll need to
remake the world beyond Covid.

So this chapter will take you to schools from the two societies I
know best (the USA and the UK). We'll meet the problem-solvers
and their mentors and try to understand the context that has
allowed them to flourish. We'll also look at how young people
around the world have responded During Corona. For young
people, the pandemic has essentially been a rehearsal for the slew of
challenges coming their way. The great educator Seymour Sarason
used to say that the best way to prepare young people for the life
beyond school is to put them in the life beyond school as often
as possible. So let's start there.

School: New Roads School, Santa Monica, USA
Mentor: Luthern Williams
Mission: A private school with a public heart

Situated in affluent Santa Monica, California – an ocean-front city
being swallowed up by Los Angeles' urban sprawl – it could be

forgiven for playing safe and providing a cocooned environment where privileged children could get a traditional education. But New Roads was never intended to be 'safe'. Although it was born in 1995, it had, in the words of Head of School, Luthern Williams

> grown out of a 60s consciousness – a moral imperative for kids to be able to live and learn together, and hopefully this experience would also transform their parents, and would become a means of transforming society and free us from the crippling influence of racism and class.

To do this, the school had to mirror the world it wished to see and reflect the metropolitan region it serves, so although it's an independent school (and therefore a business) New Roads forgoes 28% of its total revenue to enable 40% of its families from the greater Los Angeles area to receive financial aid. This enables New Roads to recruit students 'regardless of financial wherewithal'. That policy alone makes New Roads pretty unique. But diversity doesn't end with student recruitment. The school has the most diverse teaching and administrative staff that I've ever encountered and sends a powerful message to students: 'Be proud of who you are (and if you don't yet know who you are, you'll find it here). You can succeed, regardless of race, sexual orientation, ethnicity, ability or class.' It's a message that makes the entertainment industry's super-rich send their kids to New Roads, alongside parents from economically disadvantaged districts like Compton, once labelled 'America's most dangerous city'. The school also has a high proportion of students on the autism spectrum, with almost all of them gaining acceptance to college, including prestigious Ivy League colleges.

All of this might make New Roads sound like a utopian community – and it is unashamedly idealistic – but it achieves great academic outcomes precisely *because* of its commitment to diversity.

As Luthern puts it: 'Diversity drives the curriculum.' On the day I visited, Donald Trump had just quashed the Deferred Action for Childhood Arrivals (DACA) programme. Some students, clearly angry, wanted to see teaching suspended so they could march in protest, while others were uneasy about the idea. The entire school stopped and had a discussion, which resulted in a compromise being reached. To hear students talk so eloquently about politics, race and culture, in an atmosphere infused with respect for others' opinions, is deeply impressive. It was also clear that with great freedom comes great responsibility. Luthern sets high expectations:

> We assume from the time they're in kindergarten that they are not empty vessels – they have thoughts, they have feelings and they're to be taken seriously […] as intellectual and social beings throughout their time here. We want our students to be global bridge-builders. So we have to teach them to be mindful of their words and their actions.

It's too easy to see diversity through the lens of race or class. At New Roads, it's all-encompassing, including the curriculum and parents, in shaping the business of learning:

> We call ourselves 'an educational village'; our parents' association is now called 'the Parent Village' because the perception was that parents would think: 'I'm responsible for my child, I'm not responsible for all these children.' I've tried to shift that – that we're all responsible for ALL these children, and it was always in the mission that parents as well as the children would learn.

One of very few African American principals in the independent school sector, Luthern himself is a living, breathing exemplification of 'practise what you preach'. The first time I visited New Roads, the students presented a 'Dance in Action' project, portraying the early life of Malala Yousafzai as she faced down the Taliban in pursuit of an equal right to education. It was intensely moving and illustrative of the school's philosophy: if you want students to change the world, they have to understand themselves and how we are all connected.

School: Matthew Moss High School, Rochdale, UK
Mentor: Mark Moorhouse
Mission: Learning for life

It's fitting that Matthew Moss High School is located in Rochdale, because 180 years after the birth of the cooperative movement, it is keeping alive their principles of care for community, autonomy and independence, and a belief in education as a route to social equality. In 2014, the school leader, Mark Moorhouse, began an experiment that should have revolutionised formal learning. That it hasn't is due partly to Mark's modesty and partly to education's innate conservatism.

D6 is an experiment in self-determinism. What would happen if, for one day a week, you handed over the keys of a school to its students? What if they were learning not from teachers but from each other and from recently graduated students? Instead of students from the local community college being paid minimum wage to flip burgers on a Saturday, what if they were paid by Matthew Moss High School to be informal learning coaches? What if, instead of assigning coaches, specialities and classrooms to students, you just put them together to figure it out for themselves? Would it be like a scene from *Lord of the Flies*? Would anybody even show up (D6 is completely voluntary)?

After the first Saturday, Mark sent me an email, simply saying: 'You've got to see this.' So I did. I was expecting to witness a scattering of students kicking a football around or playing video games.

What I saw was a river of learning. Young people were excitedly clustered around whiteboards, marker pens in hand, working on math equations or moving fluidly between rooms as their learning needs changed and different coaches were sought for physics problems, or Spanish translations, or textual analysis. No one seemed to be sitting quietly. No one was giving a lecture. No one was kicking a football around.

Wait a minute – what's going on here? When given a completely free rein, almost every student was working on *exam prep*! Didn't they get the text message about having a laugh with your mates? I was struggling to compute, so I asked Mark if I could speak to them. Hadn't the coaches felt the need to prepare some lectures? Oh sure, they said. Some even launched into teacher mode. But the students cut them off, saying: 'We're OK with that, thanks, but what do you know about polynomials, because they're driving us mad?' But what if they asked you something outside your subject of expertise? 'We don't really have specialist knowledge, so that doesn't come up. But we know how to do exams – we've spent the past two years doing them. Besides, if we can't help, we've got friends down the hall who can.'

And that's how it came to resemble a river. The perpetual motion of just-in-time learning. The 'law of two feet' made real – if you're not getting anything out of it, move to another group. I was tearing up just watching it.

Over a coffee, I asked Mark to explain how D6 works. Mark's blunt Yorkshire speaking patterns shouldn't fool you – this is a very deep thinker. He's a leader who knows that learners – he makes no distinction between staff and students – cannot be at their creative best when behaviour and relationships are dysfunctional. It was interesting to see that he also used the liquid metaphor. Explaining what made D6 special, his arm formed a 45-degree angle:

> Water can't flow uphill. When you ain't got a power gradient
> – a critical parent/adaptive child relationship – you open the

door: between communities, between social strata, between weekends and weekdays, things that have been siloed in the workplace – what can't happen? When you go like that [lowers his arm to the horizontal], it becomes *your* place. You choose where you want to go to learn and connect with people who have no gradient, where peer-learning is the norm. The flow is just magnificent. It's like water.

In a performance-obsessed culture, D6 would count for nothing if it weren't for the remarkable outcomes it gets. Having been evaluated over a number of years by researchers, the conclusions are consistent. Students regularly attending D6 will attain one grade higher, in every subject, in their terminal exams (GCSE and A levels in the UK), than those who don't. Attend 17 or more sessions and that rises to a grade and a half, in every subject. And the picture is even more dramatic when it comes to students from poorer backgrounds. Using those in receipt of free school meals as the yardstick, Mark shared the impact:

> Globally, poorer students don't do as well as their better-off peers. That's how it's always been. Poorer students attending D6 for seven or more sessions will eliminate that gap. Learners attending 17 or more sessions *double* the progress of their more advantaged peers. It's remarkable – all those inequalities of a quiet home to study in, trips to the museum, private tutoring, all those inequalities can be wiped out through a trusting and open initiative which costs this school £1 per learner per hour to run. That's the best £1 per hour per learner we've EVER spent!

Self-determined learning usually leads to student agency, and that sense of agency came to the fore during the early days of the pandemic. Matthew Moss students designed and 3D-printed face shields for local surgeries when the UK was experiencing a desperate shortage of personal protective equipment. They began delivering them to grateful general practitioners, and soon orders were coming in from all over the UK.

D6 demonstrates that groups of young people, with minimal adult intervention, can do remarkable things. Sometimes all that is really needed is just to get out of their way.

School: Tri-County Early College (TCEC), Murphy, North Carolina, USA
Mentors: Alissa Cheek, Adam Haigler, Ben Owens
Mission: An open-source learning school

Murphy is a pretty, if sleepy, little town deep in the heart of Trumpland. As I drove in, I passed a huge billboard advertising 'Guns and drugs'. What could possibly go wrong with that combination? Social deprivation is high, aspirations low. Yet, when students graduate from this high school, they get two certificates. One is their high school diploma. But 75% of them also get an associate degree. Under the 'Early College' scheme, established by Bill and Melinda Gates, TCEC students are able to part-complete their degree by spending half their time at the community college next door. Most of these students are the first-in-family to attend college, and because they've already gained around two years of undergraduate credit, they'll complete their degree without a mountain of student debt. And let me just stress: this is *not* a school for 'gifted' students. Like the students at Matthew Moss High School, they arrive with slightly below-average test scores. And yet they leave not just well on the way to completing their degree studies but as really good, empathetic humans.

They're people like A.C., who set up a social enterprise to make senior citizens aware of the need for smoke alarms. The son of a firefighter, he'd seen how devastating a house fire could be so went around the community fitting alarms for free. A week after he installed one in an elderly lady's house, she suffered a catastrophic fire – but, thanks to A.C.'s alarm, she managed to escape before inhaling the deadly smoke. A.C. literally saved her life. Another student had created a version of Lego with Braille lettering on the pegs, as a learning toy for visually impaired kids.

And then I met a truly remarkable student, Erin Manuel. At the age of eight, Erin watched with horror as the Haitian earthquake hit that impoverished country. She felt compelled to help so started selling her artwork at farmers' markets, raising $17,000 in the process. In the intervening years, she's made several trips to Haiti and established a partnership between TCEC and a Haitian high school. But this still wasn't enough. TCEC were able to assess her social enterprise as a valid component of learning, and she helped to install solar panels in Haiti through prototyping them at TCEC. Erin soon realised she could make more money by fundraising than by purely selling her artwork, so she legally established a foundation and set about writing grant applications. When I interviewed her, she'd just secured a $25,000 grant to assist her adopted school. Now ask yourself: 'What was I doing when I was 17?'

Like so many other organisations I'd visited, TCEC models the attributes it wishes to see in its users. It's part of the teacher-powered network in the USA, so decision-making is distributed. As part of this process, Principal Alissa Cheek has devolved a lot of decisions For instance, teachers decide upon curriculum and budgets. Alissa even handed over the marketing of the school to the students, because they were tech-savvy and were also the best advocates of the learning. A typical day doesn't follow the normal path either. Students spend their time either in fairly conventional lectures at the community college or engaged in community-based projects, with each student having an adult mentor to work with.

Two of TCEC's senior teachers, Ben Owens and Adam Haigler, charted the school's development in their highly recommended book *Open Up, Education!* On the day I visited, Ben Owens was completing his final day as a teacher at TCEC (he now works as a consultant) – it was like a scene from *Goodbye, Mr Chips* or *Mr Holland's Opus*. By the time Ben's farewell speech concluded with the line 'Y'all change the world – because I know you will', there was not a dry eye in the house. This school is the real deal. Although North Carolina's high school graduation rates are improving, 14% of students still fail to complete their high school education. At TCEC, the failure rate is only 3%. With temporary portable boxes that pass for classrooms, what they've achieved here has been done on the smell of an oily rag. How have they done it?

As Ben dispensed celebratory cake, Adam explained a key element of their success: expert application of a 'competency-based approach'. With competency/mastery, students aren't able to move to the next level until they have demonstrated mastery. At TCEC, this is almost entirely demonstrated through projects that help the local community. Under this 'assessed when ready' scheme, students mirror the workplace by striving for mastery of particular concepts or skill sets. There are three levels:

1. In progress (mastery not yet demonstrated).
2. Mastery achieved.
3. High mastery (the student has taught another how to achieve mastery).

This 'everyone a teacher, everyone a student' ethos echoed what I'd heard at WD-40 Company and Matthew Moss. Ben explained how his previous career as an engineer at chemicals conglomerate DuPont shaped his approach to teaching: 'At DuPont, we consistently had difficulty finding the talent we needed in our manufacturing facilities all over the country. This told me that there was something fundamentally wrong with how we were educating young people.'

I asked to meet with a group of students. I suspected their success could be attributed to being given excessive amounts of homework. Not so, one student cheerfully explained – the school doesn't give out any homework: 'No, we give ourselves homework. If you need to prove mastery, you do what needs to be done. I give myself a lot of homework because of the goals I've set myself.'

I asked another student to describe how this might be a more effective way of learning:

> If you just learn stuff but don't have to do anything with it, you lose the knowledge. If mastery is on the line, you have to work much harder yourself to get a deeper understanding. To get high mastery, I have to figure out a way to explain it that's going to make sense to others, so I have to step outside of my own way of thinking and put myself in their shoes.

'You share your work with the local community. What does that give you?' I asked. Erin Manuel spoke for the group, saying:

> It gives you more confidence. I don't know if you'd noticed, but we don't say 'like' or 'um' much. Students from more traditional schools can't do that so much. Most of us students like to have the feedback of our community more. Because you get to see what they think of you and you get to see how you can achieve a bigger goal.

It's that 'bigger goal' that we keep losing sight of in education. A.C. had to learn a ton of physics and chemistry in order to save that woman's life. Erin had to learn how to apply for funds in order to create her foundation. After having met them both, I came away with one overriding conviction that if you can build these curious, empathetic, creative and brilliant communicators here, you can do it anywhere.

School: High Tech High Middle School, Chula Vista, USA
Mentors: Melissa Daniels, Larry Rosenstock
Mission: Equity, personalisation, authentic work, collaborative design

More traditional versions of school seem to cling to the 'seen but not heard' credo – no talking in class, so-called 'silent corridors'. I'm absolutely convinced that we do our young people a disservice by tolerating this invisibility. And if you still need convincing, you need to talk to Life California.

That isn't an American tourism initiative – it's the name of an eighth-grade student at the High Tech High school in Chula Vista. I know it sounds like the kind of name dreamed up by central casting, but it was actually chosen for this bright, articulate charming African American adolescent by her parents. The 'Life' part is obvious when you meet her, and the family name isn't because her parents are Mr and Mrs California, but because 'My dad heard you could choose any name you liked, and he liked that one'.

Life's school is almost in Tijuana, Mexico, home to the busiest border crossing in the world. High Tech High famously believes in students doing real-world projects and in maximising opportunities for students to speak. I first met Life when she was a student ambassador. As a 10-year old school tour guide, she told me about the school's ethos and why she chose to attend. I have rarely heard *any* human present ideas with such perception, warmth and humility, though she's by no means exceptional at the cluster of High Tech High schools, founded and led by the CEO, Larry Rosenstock. High Tech High students have multiple opportunities to interact with adults (all 16 schools have an open-door policy) and they regularly give talks and presentations. The then middle-school director, Melissa Daniels, made a point of making sure I heard from a number of students to allay any reservations that Life had been hand-picked to present. Nevertheless, I suspected that Life was articulate from the day she arrived in the maternity ward, so when I met up with her three years after our first meeting, I asked if she was just naturally gifted at speaking or was there something about the education she was getting?

> Before coming to this school, I don't know if I'd have had that opportunity to prove to myself that I had leadership potential. This school really cared about me. At other schools, it's just the goal to get students to pass exams. Here, they wanted to make sure that I grew and developed as a person, as well as a member of society.

Like all of you, I'm no different when it comes to talking to young people. The obvious question is: 'What do you want to be when you grow up?' In Life's case, it has been the same ambition for as long as she can remember:

'I want to be president.'

'President of what, Life?'

'The United States.'

'Great – how will you do that?'

She had it all figured out:

> My preferred school is UCLA, for four years of political science, then to Harvard Law School – I'd like to become President of the Harvard Law Review. This is something that Barack Obama did. After I've been a lawyer, I'd like to run for political office. Originally, I wanted to become a senator, but then I looked at the numbers who became president, and it was much smaller than the governors who became president, So my big step

would be to become Governor of California and then run for president.'

That this statement was made without a trace of arrogance tells you all you need to know about this remarkable person, as well as the remarkable mentors who have encouraged her to shoot for the moon. If you're reading this in 2040, and the Governor of California *isn't* called Life California, I owe you a beer.

School: XP School, Doncaster, UK
Mentors: Andy Sprakes, Gwyn ap Harri
Mission: Above all, compassion

The town of Doncaster lies in South Yorkshire. It forms part of the mining triangle of Barnsley, Doncaster and Rotherham – an area that, following the systematic dereliction of the mining industry by the Margaret Thatcher government in the 1980s, was 'forgotten'. If you've seen the films *Brassed Off* or *The Full Monty*, you'll have a pretty accurate picture. In 2016, Doncaster was judged to have some of the worst-performing schools in the UK.

Proud Doncaster resident Gwyn ap Harri created an education technology company, based in the town, then restored the old cinema to be his family home. Faced with the prospect of not finding a decent school for his kids to attend, he set about starting up a new school. He is the epitome of a start-up entrepreneur, and one whose journey touches on some familiar innovative environments. He was inspired to start up XP School after visiting High Tech High and speaking to students not unlike Life California. His model for establishing a new kind of school was found, not in education books, but in James Watt's guide to setting up BrewDog, *Business for Punks*.

On one of several visits to XP, I talked to Gwyn about how he came to establish the school. He talks as he leads – sentences start, but often don't end. A new idea is impatiently pushing the previous one aside. My question 'So, Gwyn, how does XP resemble a start-up?' results in a typical exchange:

> I founded a software company. As it grew, I was advised to hire a project manager. One consultant arrived on his motorbike and threatened to ruin the company […] So he didn't get hired […] I just googled 'project management' […] Researched agile project management. Scrums and all that rubbish […] Just build stuff. Prototype, iterate. Plan for six weeks, not six years. When I started this school, there was no reason to do it any other way. Spend an hour on something, you'll get it 80% right. To get it 90% right, you might have to spend 20 hours on it. Get the next two weeks really sharp, details, the longer you go beyond that, the fuzzier you should be planning. People think we're a cult, hippies. We're not; we're punks.

XP is what a BrewDog school might look like. For example, following the BrewDog mantra 'Cash is King', Gwyn knew that they would need to factor in the 'extras' for XP students – like the compulsory outward-bound trip up a mountain in Wales that marks the start of every student's career at XP – and made sure every other penny counted:

> We've not spent a penny on cover teachers (deputising for staff who are on leave). We're a crew, so we look after each other […] We spend zero on recruitment […] For the first two years, our accounts were done on a single Google spreadsheet. Our teachers control their own schedules, because we want fewer teachers, teaching fewer numbers of kids, more of the time. If you base a decision on values and purpose, it's never wrong. It might not be the best way to do something, but it's never wrong. So let's review, iterate, do it again. The hardest thing about this school is that there's nowhere to hide. Because

everything is shared with each other. Don't do things for ego, but don't not do things out of fear. Everything can be fixed.

Because he'd never set up a school before, and it's a weighty responsibility, the safe thing for Gwyn and Andy Sprakes, his co-founder and executive principal, to have done, would have been to follow the template all schools essentially follow. But Gwyn firmly believes that if you do what you've always done, you'll get what you always got. So the school behaves like a start-up. But does the radical way in which the school operates feed through to its core business: the students? I had an opportunity to see for myself when I was invited to take part in one of their 'coming-of-age' rituals – the 'passage presentations'.

When students at XP move from one phase of their education to another, they are required to present to their parents, friends and invited guests. Their presentation is meant to summarise what they have learned so far, to share their most challenging and rewarding moments, and to speculate on their future aspirations. For white working-class boys especially, it can be a daunting experience. Boys like Bobby. Bobby is a 13-year-old boy on the autism spectrum. He's extremely bright but has difficulties focusing on prolonged tasks. He was brutally honest in his self-assessment ('To be honest, I don't have a hobby, nor many interests'). His first exposure to the concept of 'crew' was that compulsory outward-bound week in Wales:

> When we went camping and were told we'd have to walk for six hours that day, I had a mental breakdown. [He wasn't being over-dramatic here. It was a traumatic experience for him.] However, my crew helped me and I calmed down. Outward bound made me bond with my crew and understand how crew works.

It was when he turned to his overall reflections that his watching mother seemed to be visibly moved:

> My teachers here have not only taught us STEM and humanities, but how to be more compassionate to people. We've also learned how to respect our community such as miners and how they helped the country run. When I first came to XP, I struggled to work in groups. Throughout my time at XP I have gotten better at dealing with people annoying me. I have an interest in science and IT, so I may make video games as a career in my later life – XP has helped me grow as a learner and a person.

When Bobby had left the room, I asked his mother why she'd been so moved by his self-assessment. She spoke about the previous schools he'd attended, then subsequently left, due to the school's inability to adapt to his autism:

> Bobby is how Bobby is because of people forcing him to do things he doesn't want to do. He did suffer a proper breakdown on the camping trip and I worried that XP would be another one to add to the list. But to see him stand up and do what he's just done… Well, this school is my lottery win.

It's impossible to meet young people like Bobby, and Erin, and Life, and A.C. and *not* believe that we'll be OK in their hands. Not least because they represent an ingenuity, driven by social purpose, and a deep familiarity with technology that I can only marvel at. People like Will Stamp, a 17-year-old I met at John Monash Science School in Melbourne, who'd hacked into NASA's telescopes so that he could find not one but three previously undiscovered stars, one of which – I'm not making this up – was 300 times the size of the earth. Or Shubham Jaglan, the young boy I played golf with in New Delhi (he was 12 at the time and beat me by 15 shots). Shubham grew up in rural India, with nothing more than an old golf club and an internet connection. With just this, entirely self-taught until he moved to Delhi, he modelled his swing on Tiger Woods and became junior World Champion.

All of these encounters, however, happened in the Before Corona world. How, I wondered, would the so-called 'snowflake generation' cope with the psychological impact of a global pandemic? During World War Two, we were grateful to have this generation to pull us through (my father was an outstanding example of the selfless service we relied upon). Before the challenge of that war, however, no one of my father's age was laying any claim to greatness. They just needed the challenge to prove themselves. In the same way, might not the current generation also prove greatness through their response to the pandemic? I believe they will. And here are more reasons why.

The problem-solvers take centre stage

The examples I'm about to give are not 'beautiful exceptions'. Every town has a bunch of young people like the ones I've featured, and every house has the potential to have one.

At the source of the pandemic in Wuhan, the Chinese government stopped all public transport. A group of young volunteer drivers self-organised a community fleet of vehicles to get medical workers from their home to work. In India, young people organised survival packages for 'daily wage workers' (the basics of rice, wheat, tea, soap), so that people literally existing from one day to the next would be supported. Two New York City students set up 'Invisible Hands', a service to provide groceries, medicines and a friendly word (at a distance) to the elderly and vulnerable. They signed up over 5,000 volunteers in a matter of days. In Kenya, Stephen Wamukota, from Bungoma County in Western Kenya, received a Presidential Order of Service Award for inventing a pedal-operated hand-washing machine. The machine makes communal use of soap and water possible without touching surfaces and therefore safe. Stephen was nine years old.

Or there's Avi Schiffmann, a 17-year-old who 'struggled' at high school in Washington State. In 2020, Avi won the much-coveted 'Webby Person of the Year' award for best website, for his Covid-tracker site.[1] The site constantly updates in real time and was considered so reliable that it became the epidemiologists' go-to reference point when identifying spikes or patterns. Not content with that, Avi built a 'protest tracker' site,[2] which monitored global protests in the wake of the George Floyd protests. In an interview for the *MIT Technology Review*, Avi, describing his 'normal' life said:

> I'm not a really good student. No, really – I was a really bad student. I had a 1.7 GPA [grade point average]. I focused my time on programming-related stuff. In ceramics class the teacher would turn around and I was just working on my coronavirus site, which is what I was passionate about. I couldn't focus in any class. I'd stay up late working on programming – my attendance rate was 60%.

Avi was no more a terrible student than fishes are terrible tree-climbers. It's a condemnation of our education system that a young man like Avi has to go without sleep so that he can build the most-used Covid-tracker on the entire worldwide web, and the exam system can't recognise his talent. In the same interview, Avi revealed his motivation and aspirations:

> A lot of adults have asked me why I haven't taken any deals for selling the site. And honestly I don't want to. I can see why adults are against my decision. I just want to make really high-impact stuff. I could have made something really big and lived the rest of my life in the Bahamas […] I sort of plan to

1 nCov2019.live

2 2020protest.com

go to college eventually, maybe? [Pause] I probably won't go to college. I'm working on more interesting things.

It's not about the money

We find it hard to believe that young people wouldn't want to make a ton of money from their labour, but that's our inadequacy, not theirs. Remember Ryan Jun-seo Hong, the young Korean man who built a similar tracker to Avi's? I contacted him to ask how the pandemic had affected his generation and to ask about his plans for a very uncertain future. In impeccable English he replied:

> I think this Covid outbreak gave us an important lesson on how seriously we can be impacted by these disasters. For teenagers like me, I guess this Covid outbreak was the scariest thing we have ever witnessed with our eyes so far […] I'm pretty sure it led us to think about these disasters more seriously and it will definitely change our perspective on these disasters. And our generation should really take advantage of this to deal with bigger challenges ahead. I would love to build a charitable organisation to serve people, because throughout this journey of coronamap.live I found out that I was never happier than this in my entire life. I started helping people without expecting anything. I wouldn't have had the same feeling if I decided to monetise it. I learned that it was way more powerful than money.

Give them the keys and get out of their way.

Key points:

I've met so many of these future entrepreneurs and innovators to be convinced that, whether adults or adolescents, if we want to nurture ingenuity in people, we have to focus upon certain 'must-haves':

- Self-determined learning (within clear limits).
- Making a culture of collaboration (teachers and students) a 'non-negotiable'.
- Recasting students (and their parents) as user-innovators who will redesign learning.
- Clear and consistent protocols.
- Crews/tribes, not departments (to develop a common language).
- A focus on personal mastery, finding strengths, not rectifying weaknesses.
- A belief in entrepreneurship as a way of making the world a better place.
- Self-advocacy: curiosity is a means in itself; it has its own reason for being. We cannot be curious if we do not know each other and – especially – ourselves.

CHAPTER FOURTEEN

How Shall We Live?

Amid the anguish of watching exhausted health workers on TV, witnessing the epidemic ravage its way through elderly care homes or seeing the disproportionate death rates among black and ethnic minorities, the majority of us have also been provided with a unique opportunity. The lockdown pressed pause on 'normal' life, leaving us all to question what normal might actually mean After Corona.

The importance of this global moment of reflection was memorably, and plaintively, captured on BBC radio by Rabbi Jonathan Sacks:

> When war or disease affects all of us, you learn to care for all of us. I hope that's what happens now, that we build a fairer society, where human values count as much as economic ones. We've been through too much simply to go back to where we were. We have to rescue some blessing from the curse, some hope from the pain.

People spoke of the chance to think, to help teach their children, to slow down, to acquire new skills. We noticed birdsong, took regular walks (when allowed) and more than anything, we *made* things. The surge in sourdough bread-making could only have happened when people had too much time on their hands – three days to make a loaf of bread? There was an explosion of creativity. Composite music videos, personal memoirs, craft beer… Freed from the requirement to go to work, people got to work on the things they loved, whether that was quilting or writing short stories.

The mental health of citizens was a battle between the depression felt upon watching the nightly news and the new-found freedoms – free from the 'fear of missing out', free from the need to prove oneself at work and free to express oneself or learn a new language. And during this rare time to think, two compelling questions emerged.

The first was encapsulated in the pausing of the economy. Although the spectre of a global recession is still in the shadows, the metrics we have used to measure the economic health of nations are now being openly challenged. What really matters when it comes to a nation's prosperity? The pandemic reduced the notion of gross domestic product to an irrelevance: having access to healthcare, food, shelter and the support of one's community became paramount. The anti-lockdown protesters in Milwaukee, with signs saying 'I need a haircut!', or the far-right hooligans, citing their duty to 'protect' statues and monuments, having pitched battles with police in London, seemed to belong to the world Before Corona.

As leaders grappled with the balance between containing the virus and starving an emaciated economy, a consensus emerged: we *are* the economy. Not the purchases we make but rather the way we reward our newly appreciated key workers. Not the number of journeys we make but rather the number of vulnerable citizens we protect. And despite all the ambiguity that Covid provoked, on this issue at least, there appeared to be unanimity. When Brits were asked in a YouGov poll at the beginning of May 2020, when the 'peak' of coronavirus had passed, where the government's priority should be, 80% chose health and well-being over the economy. Even when asked to choose in the event of the virus ending, 60% still put health ahead of the economy. In the USA, despite the bleakest employment and growth forecasts, the response was very similar: 70% of Americans wanted the government to safeguard health, with 30% favouring restarting the economy.

There was a delicious irony in seeing administrations that had hitherto urged us all to 'let the market' decide now intervening in the economy in ways that would have had Karl Marx cheering. The state was being asked to buy a stake in all sorts of industrial sectors and services. At the same time, British Prime Minister Boris Johnson almost died of Covid-19, and the experience in an intensive care unit clearly shook him. In a video message while in self-isolation he said, 'There really is such a thing as society,' thus contradicting Margaret Thatcher's infamous assertion from 1987: 'There is no such thing as society; there are individual men and women, and there are families.'

The second question also arose from the pausing of the economy. During the lockdown, the skies above Beijing and New Delhi cleared, fish were seen in the canals of Venice and deserted inner-city streets could breathe again. It took a global pandemic to do what decades of climate change campaigning had failed to do: substantially reduce carbon emissions. Did we really want to go back to heavily polluted skies and seas? After all, it's estimated that around 7 million people a year die from the results of air pollution. Surely that's higher than even the most pessimistic of Covid death-toll forecasts would predict?

If it worked for Covid...

Something truly remarkable happened on 13 June 2020. A televised event from Dunedin, New Zealand, made us feel like we were watching aliens functioning on their planet, while we watched from ours. With almost all of the world still in various stages of lockdown, the Kiwis played a game of rugby. In front of 20,000 people. With no social distancing and fans drinking beer, shaking hands and hugging each other. They were able to do that because the New Zealand Premier, Jacinda Ardern, had declared the coronavirus eradicated from New Zealand. No cases had been reported for over three weeks, so, with borders still closed, it seemed pointless to socially distance anymore. The leaders who got on the front foot to attack the virus spread had seen the best initial results (time alone will tell if it worked in the long run).

The difference between the handling of the two crises had become all too obvious – why can't the same sense of urgency, seen in the Covid response, be applied to the climate emergency? Why has the same decisive action not been taken to mitigate a threat that has the potential to make coronavirus seem like a summer sniffle? The biggest lesson from Covid-19 seems to be that if you wait until you understand the true significance of the crisis, you've already lost control of it. But the coronavirus is personal – the climate emergency anonymous. Unless you live on an island facing an imminent threat from rising sea levels, it's hard to see how you're going to be directly affected for at least a couple of decades. But a killer virus? That's a clear and present danger now.

Nevertheless, the connections between the crises of the now and soon-to-be was eloquently summed up by Prithwiraj Choudhury, an associate professor at Harvard Business School. Speaking of the Covid lessons that could be applied to the climate emergency, she said:

> If we can tell that story of what we just went through and help people understand that this is an accelerated version of another story we're going through that has the same plot structure but a different timeline, that could be transformative.

Aside from the existential economic and environmental threats, pressing pause allowed us a glimpse into the near future, especially in how we organise ourselves as a society. In the medium-term, it's reasonable to assume that international trade and supply chains will be severely curtailed in the imperative to be more self-sufficient. Levels of pandemic preparedness differed sharply between administrations, with some clearly shamed by their inability to stockpile supplies (some UK PPE was found to be 10 years past its use-by date). An angry public will demand that future crises are minimised by increasing domestic supply and production of essential food and medical stocks. Ultimately, 'just-in-time' chains will likely reassert themselves but not before there's been a prolonged period of 'just-in-case'.

'You need to unmute!'

During Corona, sacred cows had become target practice. The biggest deviation from the 'old normal' was the disruption to the world of work. Perhaps buoyed by her spectacular success in eliminating the virus, Jacinda Ardern convincingly argued that, in order to spread the pain of the inevitable recession *and* achieve a better work/life balance, employers should instigate four-day weeks for all employees. In doing so, she was surely influenced by fellow Kiwi thinkers, the 4 Day Week Global Foundation, who have impressive evidence on the benefits of four- not five-day weeks: better productivity, happier employees, lower staff turnover. Predictably, such radical proposals triggered an equal and opposite reaction, with many researchers and policy makers demanding a six-day working week to 'make up for lost time'. The 'old normal' will be difficult to dislodge.

The length of the working week wasn't the only sacred cow being taken down. Despite decades of hesitancy about trusting workers to work from home, the coronavirus forced everyone to stay home. *And the sky didn't fall in.* Jack Dorsey was the first to break ranks. The Twitter CEO told all his staff that they need never have to come into the office again – even After Corona – unless they wanted to. Indeed, the exponential use of video-conferencing platforms has surely permanently transformed not just how and where we work, but also how and where we live. If teleconferencing becomes normalised, then why do we need to live in an expensive apartment in a major city? Or why spend two hours on the daily commute when you can live anywhere in the world and be hired by a business anywhere in the world? The global auction for skills was already upon us – the normalisation of teleworking should further accelerate a diaspora of employability. This will have profound implications for housing. The absurd property inflation seen in our capital cities Before Corona will come to a crashing halt During Corona. The After Corona world will surely see fewer people living in major conurbations and more of our populations becoming more evenly distributed.

Essentially, the global pandemic simply amplified the question that had been growing in volume for the past few decades: how do we reinvent our cities to make them ingenious, compassionate and *humane* places to live?

Smarter people make smart cities

That's probably the question that the citizens of Medellin, Colombia, asked themselves at the start of the twenty-first century. By the end of the 1990s, Medellin was known as the most dangerous city in the world. It was home to Pablo Escobar's drug cartel and, in 1991, 6,349 people were murdered there. In a single year. Since the early 1990s (Escobar was killed in 1993 and the drug cartel disbanded soon after), the homicide rate in Medellin has declined by 95%. Extreme poverty rates have fallen by 66%. In 2013, it was awarded the title of 'world's most innovative city' by the Urban Land Institute, and it's now a major tourist destination. How has this transformation happened in little more than a decade?

A succession of talented mayors undoubtedly helped. The most significant was probably Sergio Fajardo (2004–7). In just three years, he established the principles for Medellin's recovery (transparency, zero corruption, building the most beautiful buildings in the poorest areas) and set two key priorities: education and 'co-creation'. Fajardo insisted that people had to be centrally involved in rejuvenation efforts. He created a series of 'integral urban projects' where the worst slums would be transformed, in partnership with the people who lived there.

The mayor's application of people-powered innovation to urban planning was a stroke of genius. Groups of peer producers quickly formed and ideas flooded in. An online platform, MiMedellin, was created to enable citizens to suggest, test and implement initiatives. One of its leading figures, Laura González states her belief: 'It's about us, the people, redefining democracy through social innovation. At the center of this idea, citizens are considered experts when it comes to the solution to our own obstacles.' At the time of writing, MiMedellin had hosted 18,826 ideas, most of them from the young graduates who are making Medellin one of the most desirable enterprise hubs in South America. Their ideas cover a wide range of development areas: education, enterprise, architecture, pollution and more. One of the most poignant challenges is how to turn the Monaco building – where Escobar lived and tortured people caught up in drug trafficking – into a memorial to the murder victims of that era. It's an initiative that would have been unthinkable 10 years ago.

When it comes to co-created cities, Medellin was just a foretaste. 'Nexthamburg' has been operating as the city's 'Open Civic Innovation' lab since 2009. Its goal is to bring citizens and professionals together to find new approaches in urban development. It has inspired similar initiatives in Lisbon, Barcelona, Dublin, Istanbul, Bangalore, Reykjavik, Belgrade, Taiwan… The list of 'smart cities' keeps growing.

People first, technology second

People coming together to bring about community cohesion is also enjoying something of a renaissance. Citizens' assemblies are rapidly gaining in popularity. Made up of randomly chosen citizens, they played a key role in Ireland in the abortion debate and amending the constitution. In Scotland, a citizen assembly advised on the fallout from Brexit and a possible independence referendum. In Canada, electoral reform has been the focus of their assemblies. In England, the granting of a citizens' assembly on climate change was seen as another victory for Extinction Rebellion.

For some citizens, however, a consultative process is just the start of restoring democracy. The *Guardian*'s John Harris and the *New York Times*' David Brooks have charted the resurfacing of grassroots community activism in the UK and USA. Harris points to a growing number of local and parish councils being run by independent groups who shun traditional political party allegiances. At a time of disillusionment with traditional party politics, it's not hard to see why this is happening. But books like

Flatpack Democracy (written by Peter Macfadyen, council leader of the town of Frome, Somerset) now serve as a toolkit for taking local control independently.

Similarly, Strive Together is a national network of over 70 community partnerships across the USA with the aim of ensuring equity in education for children, often living in deprived communities. Citizens, parents and professionals collaborate to track the progress of every child, from cradle to career, using masses of data to detect who is likely to fall through the cracks. Strive Together adopts the strengths-based approach we saw in Chapter Eleven, focusing upon the people and their strengths, rather than their deficiencies. Brooks described the approach thus: 'Exciting and potentially revolutionary. Trust is built and the social fabric is repaired when people form local relationships around shared tasks […] This is where our national renewal will come from.'

Free at last?

When Andrew Yang, entrepreneur and presidential candidate in the 2020 US election, announced his 'Freedom Dividend' policy in a televised debate, the other candidates couldn't suppress their laughter. Universal basic income (UBI) – the commitment to give citizens a fixed payment every month – isn't a new concept. Economist Henry George advocated for a 'citizen's dividend' in a speech in 1871. Martin Luther King Jr supported the idea, alongside many notable economists. It was Yang, however, who brought it into the spotlight, and giggles soon turned to endorsements as more candidates had to agree that it seemed like a good idea to ensure that people had an entitlement to an income in the wake of automation and the accompanying job losses.

It took the coronavirus, however, to convince the White House that reviving a post-virus economy would need to put cash directly into the hands of consumers. In March 2020, Yang was invited into the White House to discuss the logistics of making a form of UBI available during lockdown. In less than a year, giving people a guaranteed income, for them to use as they see fit, went from being a crackpot theory to received wisdom. Compared with the eye-watering and, frankly, unsustainable costs of some national job retention and rescue schemes created During and After Corona, UBI is a mere bagatelle.

Those who still resist the idea claim that there's no need for UBI, since every technological revolution creates as many new jobs as the old ones being eliminated. This revolution is different though because of machine learning (the ability for computers to learn as they receive more data). It really isn't science fiction to suggest that, in the near future, we will have robots that can make other robots, manage other robots and repair other robots. The previous revolutions have seen machines help people to be more productive, more creative. The coming wave turns that on its head, envisaging a future where the humans' role may simply be to assist the machine – if they have a role at all. Even at sparks & honey, where they have internally put the humans in charge of the machines, their reports[1] show that may not be a viable, long-term strategy.

If this sounds like a dystopian film script,[2] don't take my word for it. Martin Ford has been writing about technology-led unemployment for a long time. In *The Rise of the Robots*, he paints a depressing outlook:

> While human-machine collaboration jobs will certainly exist, they seem likely to be relatively few in number and often short-

---

1 See *AI Ethics & the Future of Humanity* for a fascinating, if disturbing, projection: www.sparksandhoney.com/reports-list/2018/10/5/ai-ethics.

2 In point of fact, Kurt Vonnegut's first novel, *Player Piano* (1952), took precisely this approach. Vonnegut himself described it as 'a novel about people and machines, and machines frequently got the best of it, as machines will'.

lived. In a great many cases they may also be unrewarding or even dehumanizing […] We are ultimately headed for a disruption that will demand a far more dramatic policy response.

For Ford (in common with many other people who really understand the technology involved in machine learning), part of that response *has* to be a universal basic income. If you believe – as I do – that there will be significant numbers of people who will experience prolonged joblessness, that there will simply not be enough human jobs to go around, we have a moral imperative to give those who miss out the dignity of a guaranteed income. If the coronavirus lockdowns have any silver linings, they have at least given us the time and space to consider what we do that feeds our spirit, that fulfils us. We have experienced a dry run of what happens when you break the coupling of remuneration and labour.

A case of mistaken identity

The UBI debate is often wrongly seen as an economic proposition. When our identity is wrapped around the job we do, however, how do we ensure that people find purpose and a sense of identity in their lives without 'a job'? The real power of the proposition Yang was making was this: UBI could give us the freedom to pursue a life that 'occupies' us, without the need for an occupation. Consider the stupidity of providing care home residents with a robot buddy, so they'll have *someone/something* to talk to in their loneliness. Their grandsons and grand-daughters have no time to visit because they're working three menial jobs on minimum wage. A UBI could restore family support, while giving young people the dignity of caring for others. One unexpected consequence of Covid-19 has been the rise in young people now wishing to be carers. The coming wave will disproportionately affect the under-35s. Youth unemployment is already higher among our young people than the rest of the working population. It's only going to get worse.

Imagine what progress we could make if we unleashed the cognitive surplus of our young people to tackle societal problems? Freed from the burden of having to scrape a living together, we could have an army of the kind of young social entrepreneurs we met in the previous chapter, collaborating and innovating together. Doesn't that sound more worthwhile than flipping burgers? As we've seen, the tools are out there to enable transnational task forces to ensure the power of us is driven by people-powered innovation, not self-approving administrations or corporations.

The future of work is just one example of the magnitude of challenges that will shape the next three or four decades. The After Corona world will bring as yet unforeseen consequences – but it will also present rich opportunities for us to be a better species than we were shaping up to be. The youth climate change army has already shown the kind of ingenuity, energy and organisational skills that put many of their elders to shame. As Greta Thunberg said in a speech in the Houses of Parliament in April 2019:

> Sometimes we just simply have to find a way. The moment we decide to fulfil something, we can do anything. And I'm sure that the moment we start behaving as if we were in an emergency, we can avoid climate and ecological catastrophe. Humans are very adaptable: we can still fix this.

A relentless optimism

Like Greta, author and environmentalist George Monbiot has often ploughed a lonely furrow in making politicians and the general public aware of the pressing need to change course. In his book *Out of the Wreckage: A New Politics for an Age of Crisis*, he somewhat surprisingly sings a song of hope. He details myriad initiatives and examples of 'participatory culture', indicators of a 'longing for belonging'. Participatory budgeting in Brazilian cities. Timebanking (a reciprocal work-trading system, where hours become currency) in Tokyo. Guerrilla gardening in Grimsby.

For Monbiot, our biggest failure has been our inability to find a new story to replace what he describes as the story of neoliberalism. Writing Before Corona, he rebuked the ideology of extreme individualism and competition that has left us feeling helpless and isolated:

> We struggle to recognise, let alone resolve, our common problems. This has frustrated our potential to do what humans do best: to see a threat to one as a threat to all; to find common ground in confronting our predicaments; and to unite to overcome them.

The solution, he argues, is a politics of belonging, where communities own and manage their own resources, and decision-making is restored to the smallest political units that are able to discharge it.

Reading those words After Corona, it's an even more persuasive argument, not least because, well, what's the alternative? If capitalism is designed around winners and losers, it's not a sustainable solution to simply see your responsibility to squeeze yourself into the winner's circle and let the losers fend for themselves. On each research visit I undertook, I read a different intellectual's response to the state we're in and how we emerge from the mess we've made. These included the already mentioned Monbiot, O'Brien and Friedman, but also Naomi Klein's *No Is Not Enough*, Malcolm Gladwell's *Talking to Strangers*, Valerie Hannon's *Thrive*, Barack Obama's *The Audacity of Hope* and Paul Mason's *PostCapitalism*. It was striking how so many of their conclusions ended up at the same destination: that we have no option but to reinvest in the power of ourselves. What I've tried to demonstrate in this book is that such reinvestment is well placed: the pandemic has graphically shown that our capacity to solve problems hasn't deserted us. Our desire for self-determination, mixed with our basic decency and a belief in helping others, makes us powerhouses of mass ingenuity. And that's just as well.

The urgent need for 'common' sense

The challenges we face, as a species, are not just daunting in magnitude but also in kind: putting the brakes on rising air and sea temperatures by 2030; feeding a global population that is set to hit 10 billion by 2050; losing 1 million species of animals and plants by 2050 through biodiversity loss; coping with mass international migration (estimates range from 500 million to 1 billion people) by 2050; 800 million jobs lost to automation by 2030; finding meaningful work for those automated out of a job – in the USA alone, it's likely to be 30% – by 2050; a burgeoning middle-class demand for *stuff* leading to raw materials extraction of 180 billion tonnes a year by 2050; 1% of people owning 40% of the planet's wealth by 2050. This is the world that is likely to face today's kindergarten children before they've completed their formal education.

To find solutions, they'll need to endure levels of sacrifice that my generation, frankly, refuses to contemplate. They'll need imaginative leaps that our education systems struggle to inculcate. Finding solutions, above all, will take an inordinate amount of 'common' sense – a desire to respectfully collaborate with people all over the world in the service of the common good. That, in a sense, is what my own search has been about: seeking reassurances that there are enough good people out there who can put aside cultural, racial and personal differences to make the world a better place.

At another turning point in history, Thomas Paine, the English-born philosopher and political theorist, inspired the American people to declare independence from mad King George of England. A key argument that Paine deployed was found in his pamphlet *Common Sense*. Reading it through the lens of the predicament we're in, a trio of phrases shine out: 'It is not in numbers, but in unity, that our great strength lies'; 'The cause of America is, in great measure, the cause of all mankind', and '*The time has found us*'. The power and poetry of his words are timeless – he could be writing of today's problems. The rise of nationalism has made it virtually impossible to reach international consensus and cohesive action. It took Covid-19 to make us realise the futility of that path. And our problems are not restricted to particular countries – they are global in nature and will require global responses. But it's the final phrase, 'The time has found us', that resonates the most. It's a line whose power is so great that it's been adopted by Breitbart to get Donald Trump into the White House, and also – by House Speaker Nancy Pelosi – to try to get him *out*.

I strongly believe that, in the urgency to fix these seemingly intractable problems, the time has indeed found *us*. Who are 'us'? We're the people whose stories I've told in this book. We're the CEOs who put purpose on the same footing as profit. We're the leaders and members of cooperatives who allow families and communities to become self-reliant and more in control of their lives. We're the lead patients who aren't waiting for governments and pharmaceutical companies to nurse their loved ones back to good health. We're the hackers and hobbyists with professional levels of expertise, happy to freely share our skills and inventions with others. We're the educators who selflessly give time, wisdom and love to the learners in their charge, so that they in turn can change the world. And, most of all, we're the young people, who, despite the appalling legacy they've been left, are insisting their voices be heard, their dreams taken seriously and who demonstrate their immense faith in each other through a collective determination to right the wrongs of their elders. Through the global pandemic, our species has been collectively tested like never before. Even bigger challenges lie in wait. But we now know that we have the power of us.

And that's enough.

*

Bringing the *Power of Us* to your organisation.

If you've been inspired by the organisations featured in this book, you might want to think how people-powered innovation can be grown in your organisation. We have a range of training webinars and workshops, for middle and senior leaders, that can help. For more information, go to: www.davidpriceobe.com/contact

A LETTER FROM DAVID

I want to say a huge thank you for choosing to read *The Power of Us*. If you did enjoy it and want to keep up to date with all my latest releases, just sign up at the following link. Your email address will never be shared and you can unsubscribe at any time.

www.thread-books.com/david-price

I wrote *The Power of Us* after a three-year journey around the world seeking out highly innovative organisations. It seemed to me that – even before the Covid-19 pandemic struck – we were going to have to find solutions to an unprecedented cluster of societal, economic, environmental and cultural problems, so I was curious to see how all kinds of organisations, from corporations to high schools, were responding to these challenges. What I didn't anticipate was how many of them cultivated *people-powered innovation,* creating porous *outside-in* environments where everyone – especially the users of products or services – played a part in figuring things out.

It was also noticeable that, during the three years of research, levels of public activism were rising sharply. Mass movements were not only springing up and spreading like wildfire, they were far more effective than such movements had been in the past.

So the '*Us*' became the driving force behind the book. How have we gone from sharing cat videos on social media to organising global protests? When did we stop passively consuming and start peer producing? Most importantly, what does it mean for how we organise ourselves going forward, and how can organisations harness the power of us?

Once the pandemic arrived, I had all the affirmation I needed that we, as a species, now demonstrate *mass ingenuity* at a speed and scale that was impossible just a few years ago. The mobilisation across the entire planet to shorten development timescales, to mass-produce protective equipment or build tracking apps, breached all the usual divisions of expert-novice, professional-amateur, producer-user, *simply because we had to*. At a time of global anxiety, it gave me great hope – and I hope it gives you hope, too.

In my 'other' job as speaker and advisor, I often get asked 'How do we make our people more innovative?' The organisations featured in this book demonstrate that we don't *need* to inflict or administer ingenuity upon people – we just need to nurture the mindset, operating system and culture that makes innovation an everyday occurrence. I really hope that the practical strategies I've put forward here can be adapted by you and the organisations you work with. Most of all, I hope we can build upon the *mass ingenuity* that is already evident in our young people. Because they'll have to fix enormous problems over the next couple of decades.

I hope you loved *The Power Of Us* and if you did I would be very grateful if you could write a review. I'd love to hear what you think, and it makes such a difference helping new readers to discover one of my books for the first time.

I love hearing from my readers – you can get in touch on my Facebook page, through Twitter, Goodreads or my website.

Thanks,
David

David-Price-Author-105246294587785

@davidpriceobe

davidpriceobe.com

www.amazon.co.uk/-/e/B00G726DBK

www.linkedin.com/in/davidpriceobe/

ACKNOWLEDGEMENTS

Between ourselves, it's a minor miracle this book was ever finished. During the course of its two-year gestation period, and then three-year research and writing phase, I had to face numerous health challenges, some of which caused me to abandon the project for months at a time. So my first thanks should go to my oncologist, David Bottomley at St James Hospital in Leeds, for keeping me alive for the past 11 years. You will never meet a more dedicated and open-minded professional.

During that horizon-scanning period I had cause to thank my son, Patrick, for doing some of the exploratory research. His input helped me work out the kind of book I *didn't* want to write, as much as the one I did.

I would never have even considered writing a book, let alone a series of them, had it not been for the encouragement of Sir Ken Robinson. To describe Ken as a mentor is wholly inadequate. He has helped shape my later life, when it was in danger of going off the rails, and I've treasured a great personal friendship for nearly 30 years, and love the bones of the man. The initial feedback I received from another much-respected friend and author, Mark Stevenson, made me completely rethink the book's opening, and his formative comments were invaluable. Given the importance of honest criticism from those who've been there, I also owe a debt of thanks to Valerie Hannon and Chris Harte – our joint workshops over the past two years have helped me explore these ideas and given reassurance that I wasn't alone in my convictions.

I'm fortunate to be able to combine writing with public speaking. This means that I can further try out fledgling ideas on unsuspecting audiences before converting them to the writing process. So I have to thank Maria Franzoni, the London Speaker Bureau and Raise the Bar for giving me ample opportunity to work out what I was trying to say.

Once I began to speak to inspirational leaders of organisations (and loose collectives), the shape of the book began to emerge, so I will be forever grateful to the inspirational people featured in this book. I'm not going to list them here again, but every interviewee gave me a clearer picture and a more positive mindset on our future prospects, *especially* the many young people I spoke to. In the darkest of times, you show us the way forward.

I looked for somewhere where I could shape the initial drafts in a scenic, yet solitary, location. An ex-student of mine, Sarah Randall, provided the perfect spot, in St Audrie's Bay in Somerset. Thank you, Sarah.

At the end of 2018, I got sick again, and we chose to move house – to a doer-upper – in a beautiful location on the edge of the Yorkshire Dales. During the following year, I learned how to write on a building site. Rob Wright, our builder, not only adjusted his schedule around my writing blocks and spurts – he also patiently listened while I tested my theories out on someone who was more interested in ordering breeze blocks than hearing about self-determination theory. Thank you, Rob. Books are transient, houses are permanent.

Once I had initial drafts worth reading, I called in tons of favours among the people I called my 'second readers': Vhairi Mackintosh, Adam Pain, Jamil Qureshi, Jamie Smith, Kyra Kellawan, Mark Stevenson, Maria Franzoni and Dan Fitzpatrick. If I have missed anyone off this list, I'm so sorry.

The book is punctuated with brilliant illustrations. I asked John Biggs to see if he could bring the chapters to life and he did so with flair and minimal direction in the midst of a pandemic. Thank you, John.

Writing a book is one thing, finding an audience quite another, so I can't end without thanking my literary agent, Charlie Viney, for giving me encouragement and advice just when I needed it most.

My final thanks must go to the two people who have done the most to make this book a reality. They're both Clares/Claires. My editor, Claire Bord, gently nudged me to completely restructure the manuscript, after four years, and gave me 14 days to do so. It was just the fuel-injection the book needed and transformed it. She worked around the lockdown clock, nipping and tucking, and I can't thank her enough.

And then there's my wife and always first reader, Clare. You haven't simply nursed me through successive books, you've also literally nursed me through critical episodes and life-threatening moments. I don't just owe you this book; I owe you my life.

Made in the USA
Middletown, DE
07 September 2020

18051870R00198